Signatures of Citizenship

Males	Females
...es Fisk	Jane Pleevant
...rge Young	Susan Fisk
... Robinson	Sarah Eastman
...mes Eastman	Mary Young
...rick Rooney	Ellen Rooney
...el Griffin	Cynthia Day
... Allen	Mary J. Day
... Griswold	
...nnan Wheeler	Eunice E. Abbi...
...inster	Sarah Allen
...nan Newbury	Parnel Allen
	Agnuss Denvent
...mason	Almyra Johnson
...chard Lowe	Lucy Griswold
...Bennett	Lucy Griswold
...et Bamford	Sarah Griswold
...in Bamford	
...ward Dale	Grace Newbury
	Eliza Newbury
	Maryann Kere

Signatures

of

PETITIONING, ANTISLAVERY, &
WOMEN'S POLITICAL IDENTITY
BY SUSAN ZAESKE
The University of North Carolina Press
Chapel Hill and London

Citizenship

The paper in this book meets the guidelines for permanence and durability of the Committee on Production Guidelines for Book Longevity of the Council on Library Resources.

Library of Congress Cataloging-in-Publication Data

Zaeske, Susan.

Signatures of citizenship : petitioning, antislavery, and women's political identity / by Susan Zaeske.

p. cm. — (Gender & American culture)

Includes bibliographical references and index.

ISBN 0-8078-2759-2 (cloth : alk. paper) —

ISBN 0-8078-5426-3 (pbk. : alk. paper)

1. Women in politics—United States—History.

2. Women abolitionists—United States—History.

3. Women social reformers—United States—

History.   4. Antislavery movements—United States—

History.   5. Women—United States—Social conditions.

6. Women political activists—United States—History.

I. Title.   II. Series.

HQ1236.5.U6Z34   2003

305.42'0973—dc21

2002008023

cloth   07 06 05 04 03   5 4 3 2 1

paper   07 06 05 04 03   5 4 3 2 1

For JULIE *and* KUMA

Douglass Jr.	Mrs. Fredk.
...n Sprague	Mrs. Nath...
...us Dorsey	Mrs. Juil...
...as H. Hunter	Mrs. Eliz...
... Moore	Mrs. Delph...
...H. Jones	Mrs. Sarah
...new G. Brown	
...ill Kelson	Mrs. Mary
...Brown	Harriett H.
...Louder	Caroline
...Sayles	Jane Lo...
...to Hill	Alice
...H. Shaw	Rozie
...sdale	Miss Le...
...yer	Miss Elizabeth
...Dunnington	

CONTENTS

ILLUSTRATIONS

ACKNOWLEDGMENTS

The idea for this book originated in two undergraduate courses I took during the same semester more than fifteen years ago at the University of Wisconsin. One was a women's history course taught by Gerda Lerner and the other was an American public address course taught by Stephen E. Lucas. Lerner enlightened me about the political activities of antislavery women, especially Sarah and Angelina Grimké, and Lucas acquainted me with the congressional debates over antislavery petitions, particularly the oratorical feats of Representative John Quincy Adams. Their inspiring lectures left me yearning to know more about the antislavery petition campaign, and when I visited the National Archives years later, I requested one of the dozens of trays of antislavery petitions. As I first held a petition, read its elaborate prayer, inspected the signatures inscribed by nineteenth-century women, and saw the inky fingerprints they left behind, I found myself in a state of fascination.

This fascination proved to be both a blessing and a curse. The petitions provided a treasure chest of thousands of pieces of primary evidence upon which to build a study, but finding this treasure chest also required analysis of thousands of pieces of primary evidence. It would have been nearly impossible to sustain research of this magnitude without financial support. I am grateful to the American Association of University Women for providing a fellowship that enabled me to complete my dissertation and to the Graduate School of the University of Wisconsin for providing a series of grants that allowed me to extend my research and significantly revise my manuscript. I also wish to thank Jane and Robert Fairman, who opened their home to me and served as most gracious hosts during my research visits to Washington, D.C.

Nor would I have been able to complete this project without the assistance of the Center for Legislative Research at the National Archives and Records Association. The task of gathering women's petitions was greatly facilitated by its *Our Mothers Before Us* project, which gleaned from the records of Congress thousands of documents submitted by women from

1787 to 1920. I am indebted to all the staff and volunteers who worked on the *Our Mothers* project, especially Lucinda Robb, Sarah Boyle, Carolyn Brucken, and Alysha Black. They have created an amazing resource that will no doubt fortify countless studies of the lives of American women. I should also like to thank Charles E. Schamel of the Center for Legislative Research for his assistance and advice throughout the course of my research as well as Katherine Snodgrass for her assistance in obtaining photographs of the petitions. I am particularly thankful that Nietzchka Keene lent her photographic talents at a moment of near crisis. In addition I wish to thank the staff of the State Historical Society of Wisconsin, especially that of the microforms room, for their tenacity and patience in helping me locate obscure materials. For their assistance in obtaining illustrations and permission to reproduce them I wish to acknowledge the Library of Congress, the Boston Public Library, the Massachusetts Historical Society, Boston Athenæum, and the Library Company of Philadelphia.

From its beginnings this book was inspired by the ideas of fellow scholars, and throughout its development it was sustained by the suggestions and encouragement of a wonderful community of colleagues and friends. For offering advice on my manuscript and engaging in what must have seemed like endless discussions about women's petitions, I wish to thank Jean B. Lee, Gregory Lampe, Andrew Hansen, Robert Asen, and David Bordwell. I am indebted to Seymour Drescher and Deborah Bingham Van Broekhoven for sharing their considerable expertise on antislavery petitioning and for commenting on portions of my manuscript. I thank Karlyn Kohrs Campbell for helping me see the petitions in a new light when she urged me to look more carefully at the signatures. Thank you to Lisa Tetrault, who for months not only lived with the petitions and their harried researcher but also served as a sounding board and an in-house historical consultant. Publication of this book would have been impossible without the groundbreaking scholarship of Gerda Lerner, from whose writing, teaching, and friendship I have learned so much about history and life itself. I owe a deep debt of gratitude to my dissertation adviser, colleague, and friend, Stephen E. Lucas, whose lofty standards prodded me to do better work than I ever imagined I could and who knew when he had given as much as he could.

It has been my good fortune to work with the University of North Carolina Press in publishing this book. I am indebted to my editor Kate Torrey, whose vision, patience, and unflagging confidence in my project substantially improved the manuscript and kept me afloat throughout the process. Ron Maner guided the manuscript into publication with expertise and kindness, and Stephanie Wenzel proved to be a most careful copyeditor. This work benefited from the generous suggestions of conscientious readers such as Ellen Du Bois, whom I thank for pushing me to clarify my ideas and recognize the significance of my research findings. Lori D. Ginzberg went well beyond the duties of a reader to invest an immense amount of time to provide several thorough, challenging, and supportive reviews. Words cannot express the depth of my appreciation for the scholarly advice and personal encouragement offered by my teacher, colleague, and dear friend, Jeanne Boydston. Throughout the revision process these women exemplified the highest ideals of interdisciplinary research and scholarly community, offering feedback that enhanced the complexity of analysis, readability of the prose, and confidence of the author. Despite their best efforts, shortcomings no doubt remain, and for these I claim full credit.

Dear friends expressed their confidence and support throughout the long process of researching, writing, and revising this book. For their faith in me and my work I wish to thank Mari Boor Tonn, Bonnie J. Dow, Amy Slagell, Katy Heyning, Judi Trampf, Joy P. Newmann, Kristin and Roger Lutz, Brenda and Erik Sande, and my parents, Rose and Ronald Zaeske. Finally, this book is dedicated to my beloved Kuma, who from the beginning of this project and almost to its completion, lay at my feet and made sure I was walked frequently. And most of all to Julie Holfeltz, who made many sacrifices, offered her unconditional love, and always believed it could be done.

Madison, Wisconsin
March 2002

Signatures of Citizenship

Sarah M. Grimké

Angelina E. Grimké

Eliza Philbrick

Fanny Bell

Sarah Celfe

Hepzibah Celfe

Chloe H. Whitney

Rebecca Gerry

Rebecca L. Gerry

Rosyra Jaquith   10

Ann A. Capen

Abigail Tolman

Mary J. R. Tolman

Elizabeth Whyte

Susan G. Whyte

A Touching, Ludicrous, Edifying History

Early in February 1834 Louisa, Maria, Abigail, Rosey, and Caroline Dickinson signed their names to a petition addressed to the Senate and House of Representatives of the United States. They were joined by Phebe Tinker, Alvira Means, and Comfort Harmon as well as scores of other Ohio women who together prayed Congress to abolish slavery in the District of Columbia. These westerners were among the first women in the United States to collectively petition Congress on a political issue. In so doing they defied the long-standing custom of females limiting their petitioning of Congress to individual prayers regarding personal grievances. During the coming years hundreds of thousands of women from throughout the North would join the petition campaign and risk association with the unpopular cause of immediate abolitionism. Maria Weston Chapman, a leader of the petitioning effort, recalled that when antislavery women began to petition Congress, many Americans—male and female alike— were not "wont to witness the appeals kindly." Time and again female petitioners were assailed for leaving their "proper" sphere of the home and abandoning benevolent charitable causes to engage in petitioning and political action in the public arena. Yet antislavery women persevered, leading Chapman to predict that "a history of their progress door to door, with the obstacles they encountered would be at once touching, ludicrous, and edifying."[1]

This book is a history of women antislavery petitioners' progress from door-to-door, of the obstacles they encountered, and of the important contributions that women's petitioning ultimately made to the success of the abolition movement. It is also a book about how by petitioning against slavery free women seized the radical potential of one of the few civil rights they were understood to possess—the right of petition—to assert substantial political authority. Indeed, the antislavery petition campaign marked one of the first instances in which large numbers of white and free black American women engaged in collective petitioning of Congress in an attempt to reshape public opinion and influence national policy. Enabling them to participate in national public dialogue over the controversial issue of slavery absent the right of suffrage, petitioning provided a conduit for women to assert a modified form of citizenship. Although at the beginning of their involvement in the campaign in 1835 women tended to disavow the political nature of their petitioning, by the 1840s they routinely asserted the right of women to make political demands of their representatives. This change in the rhetoric of female antislavery petitions and appeals, from a tone of humility to a tone of insistence, reflected an ongoing transformation of the political identity of signers from that of subjects to that of citizens. Having encouraged women's involvement in national politics, women's antislavery petitioning created an appetite for further political participation and more rights. After female abolitionists established the right of women to petition Congress collectively on political issues, countless women employed that right to lobby their representatives and agitate public opinion to promote causes such as temperance, antilynching, and ultimately, woman suffrage.

From 1831 to 1863 women publicly expressed their opinion about slavery by affixing approximately 3 million signatures to petitions aimed at Congress. The addition of women's names beginning in 1835 swelled to a flood what was previously a trickle of memorials submitted almost exclusively by men. Women's efforts enabled abolitionists to send enough petitions to Congress to provoke debate over the question of slavery, a feat petitioning by men alone had failed to accomplish. Sparking discussion of slavery proved to be a crucial victory for the abolitionist movement, for as William Freehling has observed, the debates prompted by antislavery petitions in the 1830s were "the Pearl Harbor of the slavery controversy." Deluged with petitions, in June 1836 the House of Representatives passed a rule immediately tabling all memorials on the subject of slavery. The rule proved a "godsend" to the struggling antislavery movement, for it linked the popular right of petition with the unpopular cause of immediate abolitionism. Petitioning was intended not only to pressure congressmen but also to rectify public opinion with regard to the sinfulness of slavery. By gathering signatures in family and female social networks as well as through soliciting door-to-door, women discussed the issue of slavery with people who would never go to hear an abolitionist lecturer and who could not read abolitionist tracts.[2]

Petitioning fit hand in glove with immediate abolitionists' strategy of moral suasion, which called for the use of moral appeals to awaken public sentiment to induce slaveholders to forsake human bondage. Although women's petitioning soon became highly controversial, at the outset the philosophy of moral suasion and the tool of petitioning seemed to offer an especially suitable means for women to participate in the abolition movement. Women could use the right of petition—a right that, unlike the ballot, they were generally understood to possess—to apply the force of their supposedly superior morality to reform public opinion with regard to the sin of slavery. Although petitioning was less direct than voting, in the 1830s at least, it was not necessarily considered less powerful. Petitioning was seen as a pure expression of individual moral conscience, as opposed to the vote, which was viewed as tainted with personal interest and party spirit. So central was petitioning to antebellum political culture that certain men, particularly radical reformers such as William Lloyd Garrison, eschewed voting in favor of petitioning as a tool to reform the morals of the republic. Although women did not have the luxury of forsaking the vote, they could use petitioning to join their male abolitionist colleagues in attempting to effect a moral transformation in public opinion.[3]

Central to comprehending the history of women's antislavery petitioning and its effect on women's political status is an understanding of the nature of the right of petition. At its core a petition is a request for redress of grievances sent from a subordinate (whether an individual or a group) to a superior (whether a ruler or a representative). As a genre of political communication, the petition is characterized by a humble tone and an acknowledgment of the superior status of the recipient. While the practice of petitioning began as an individual making a request of his or her ruler for redress of personal grievances, over time the meaning and function of petitioning changed drastically. By the advent of the Jacksonian era, men were frequently using organized mass petitioning to agitate public opinion in order to achieve their political goals. But even as a greater number of white men used collective petitioning, prior to 1829 the petitioning of white and black women remained limited for the most part to individual prayers regarding personal issues. A particular innovation of antislavery women was to defy on a mass scale the customary limitations on female petitioning and to justify the collective exercise of the right of petition by their sex.[4]

The supplicatory nature of the right of petition held radical potential for women, for natural law assumed that all subjects (and later all citizens) possessed the right of petition and that rulers (and later representatives) were obliged to receive and respond to petitions regardless of the subject of their prayer. Abolition women relied on the first assumption in order to claim and defend their right to petition amidst an environment in which their political status, like that of free blacks, was undergoing constant renegotiation. In fact, so labile was the political status of certain groups of inhabitants of the republic that state constitutional reform conventions of the 1820s and 1830s revoked free black men's voting rights, rights they had previously possessed and exercised. In 1837 the House of Representatives decided that slaves were not citizens and passed a resolution stating that they had no right of petition. For women, also a group whose political rights were vulnerable, petitioning amounted to an assertion that they possessed the right of petition and that they were citizens, though a type of citizen different from enfranchised men. By assuming the status of petitioners, women, though they lacked the vote, forced a hearing of their requests, for their representatives were obligated, in principle at least, to receive and respond to their grievances. Even when the House repeatedly passed gag rules that immediately tabled all antislavery petitions, through their continued petitioning, women kept alive the slavery question in public discourse. They added to congressional and general public debate, moreover, discussion of women's rights and the nature of female citizenship.[5]

This study seeks to contribute to an ongoing conversation about the role of women in U.S. political culture both by documenting women's impact on the public debate over slavery and by demonstrating how, by participating in that debate, women transformed their political identities. By exploring the rhetoric of female antislavery petitions, addresses calling women to petition, reactions to women's petitioning, and congressional responses to women's petitions, this book reconstructs debate over women's exercise of the one political right they could convincingly claim. By charting changes over time in the way women identified themselves in their petitions, the patterns of their signatures, and the arguments they employed in petitions as well as other discourse related to the campaign, this study excavates from rhetorical texts a history of transformations of individual women's political identities and formations of collective female subjectivities.[6]

Approaching the petitions and addresses with an eye to the reconstruction of female political subjectivity, I focus on a cultural process related to individuals' living experience and the ever-changing discursive resources available to them. This process involves discursive practices that facilitate not only development of an isolated individual identity but also "identity in relationship," or collective subjectivities. Yet as much as collective subjectivities function as categories of inclusion, they function also as rules of exclusion, particularly exclusion from political power along the lines of gender, race, class, and sexual preference. In other words, when requirements for inclusion in dominant subjectivities such as "citizen" differ from prevailing identities of certain groups such as women or free blacks, members of these groups are delegitimated from participation in the public sphere and denied political power.[7]

The dual nature of political subjectivities as paradigms of both inclusion and exclusion is readily apparent in the history of the Jacksonian period. The growth of party organizing and political participation during the mid- to late 1820s is widely accepted as a marker of a turning point in the nature of American democracy and the character of the political subject. Andrew Jackson's ascendancy coincided with the ongoing expansion of white manhood suffrage, mass literacy, proliferation of newspapers and magazines, and developments in transportation, all of which led to the politicization of the public. The "people" had come to exert greater power over their representatives not only through the vote but also through the pressure of public opinion. Yet although the rise of mass democracy enhanced the political power of white males, people of color and women continued to be excluded or were newly excluded from the rights of citizenship.[8]

Yet despite principles of exclusion and lack of access to popular means of participation such as public speaking, publishing in newspapers, and pamphleteering, women and people of color did find avenues to influence public debate. Mary Ryan has described the "circuitous routes" women traveled to enter public discourse in the nineteenth-century United States, such as "corrupted forms, like the cloying feminine symbols used in electoral campaigns" and deployment of "ladies" at political rallies as "badges of respectability." While I agree with Ryan that women were forced to seek alternative routes to the polis, I think we need not travel so far afield to find women in public during the antebellum period. By petitioning Congress, middle-class, northern, mostly white women insinuated themselves into public discussion through use of a highly traditional form of political communication. Rather than operating at the margins of the bourgeois pubic sphere, petitioning women inserted their opinions into central sites of public debate such as the U.S. Congress and newspapers circulated throughout the nation.[9]

The bulk of the research for this book was drawn from petitions sent to Congress, which are stored at the National Archives and maintained by the Center for Legislative Archives. It would have been nearly impossible to complete a study of this magnitude were it not for the existence of the *Our Mothers Before Us* project at the Outreach Branch of the Center for Legislative Archives, for which archivists systematically combed the records of every session of Congress to extract documents submitted by women. This study is based not only on extant petitions signed by women from the full gamut of their involvement in the abolition petition campaign (1831 to 1865) located by the *Our Mothers Before Us* project, but it also considers those signed by men or by men and women from 1819 to 1865 that remain uncataloged as well as oversized antislavery petitions that were not cataloged by the National Archives until 1995. It also draws on petitions employed in subsequent movements such as antilynching and woman suffrage, which have been identified by the *Our Mothers Before Us* project. To account for potential regional differences in the rhetoric of petitions, the forms used for close readings include those emanating from throughout New England, Pennsylvania, and New York as well as from the western frontier of Ohio and from both urban and rural communities.[10]

By offering a comprehensive study focused on women's petitioning of Congress, in no sense does this analysis gainsay the significance of antislavery petitioning directed at state legislatures. Indeed, thousands of women and men petitioned their legislatures at a time when state governmental bodies played a larger role in lawmaking than the federal government. It is certainly important to account for women's petitioning of state legislatures as a step in transforming female political identities, yet because of the enormous numbers of female antislavery petitions sent to Congress, accounting also for women's petitions to state legislatures is beyond the practical means of this study. I decided to focus tightly on women's congressional antislavery petitioning, moreover, because it marked a significant change in women's political activism and signaled the growth of an identity of national citizenship. While women's antislavery petitioning of Congress was coordinated at the state level and executed locally, it linked abolition women as a group to national institutions and leaders. In the process of seeking freedom for slaves from the federal government, female petitioners went from identifying themselves in their petitions as the "female inhabitants" or "ladies" of a given town during the 1830s to calling themselves "Women of America" in the later 1840s. Defining themselves as members of the national polity moved women closer to seeing themselves as national citizens entitled to the rights accorded by national citizenship.

This book proceeds chronologically in describing the fluidity in the meaning and function of the right of petition in Western political history, its adoption by antislavery women, and its use by women as an instrument to shape public opinion in social movements through the end of the nineteenth and well into the twentieth century. Chapter 1 places women's antislavery petitioning in the context of the changing function and meaning of the right of petition from its origins in the Magna Carta to its use in the mass politics of Jacksonian America. Long before abolitionists embraced petitioning in their campaign against slavery, other groups outside the domains of institutionalized government had exploited the subversive potential of the right of petition by using it as an entering wedge into various realms of political power. It was this radical potential of petitioning that antislavery women, denied the full rights of republican citizenship, seized in order to pressure their representatives by appealing to the power of public opinion, which propelled them into the midst of a major national political debate.

Chapter 2 identifies the multiple forces that led women to begin petitioning Congress to end slavery. It traces the transatlantic effects of abolitionism and demonstrates that the success of British women's antislavery petitioning played a large part in convincing American male antislavery leaders of the efficacy of encouraging women to petition. Before female antislavery societies took up the call to petition in 1834, they had concentrated their efforts on teaching free blacks, boycotting products of slave labor, and conversing with relatives and friends about the evils of slavery; they had generally refrained from petitioning, despite the fact that by 1833 antislavery men had embraced it as a major means of agitation. Chapter 3 demonstrates that during the first phase of female antislavery petitioning from 1831 to 1836, as women crossed into new terrain by petitioning their political representatives in hopes of influencing debate on a national issue, their petition forms employed a rhetoric of humility and disavowal. Rather than justifying exercise of the right of petition on the grounds of natural rights principles, women described their actions as motivated by Christian duty and as an extension of the religious speech act of prayer. Yet women's petitions were infused with republican and free labor rhetoric that in effect constructed a uniquely northern middle-class conception of citizenship, a conception that relied heavily on notions of virtue and elevated the moral power of women.

Chapter 4 argues that in addition to substantially increasing the appeal of abolitionism by linking the institution of slavery with the denial of northern civil rights, passage of the gag rule in June 1836 also had a significant impact on discourse about women's political rights. In four major addresses published during the summer of 1836, female antislavery leaders denounced the gag rule as an unjust law enacted by morally flawed men and instructed women to ignore the will of men who wished to suppress their pleas and to follow their own moral conscience with respect to the sin of slavery. The addresses directed women to ignore not only the will of slaveholding congressmen but also that of northern men who questioned the propriety of women petitioning Congress. Abolition women initiated further discussion of their rights and responsibilities as activists by taking the unprecedented step of meeting in convention and answering the gag rule by intensifying their petitioning. By doing so women gained important skills of political organizing and set in place a systematic petitioning plan, for which they adopted short petitions that excluded the expressions of humility and disassociation with politics characteristic of their previous petitions. Likewise, the addresses that issued from the convention advanced beyond those published in 1836 that claimed that women possessed a moral duty to petition to asserting that women were citizens and, as such, possessed a constitutional right to petition.

Chapter 5 maintains that for the hundreds of thousands of women who in 1837 lent their names to antislavery memorials, signing petitions marked a significant development in their political identities. By entering public dialogue on the issue of slavery, women transformed themselves from private individuals into public actors who operated independent of male guardians. Those women who circulated petitions, moreover, exercised a degree of political literacy by familiarizing themselves with antislavery arguments and employing them in face-to-face persuasive exchanges. Yet as more women than ever signed and circulated abolition petitions in 1837, northern defenders of male political dominance and traditional gender roles attempted to halt their progress. Such attacks succeeded only in pushing women abolitionists to develop stronger arguments about their right as citizens to petition, to take the unprecedented step of threatening to unseat congressmen who ignored them as constituents, and to link the right of petition with the right of suffrage.

Chapter 6 focuses on debates in Congress sparked by the influx of women's antislavery petitions from 1835 to 1839, which led to what was perhaps the first sustained discussion of the political rights of women in the history of the federal legislature. Slaveholding members as a well as a number of northern representatives conflated gendered norms of respectable behavior with constitutional rights, arguing that because it was improper for women to petition Congress, they had no right to petition Congress. Women, they argued, moreover, lacked basic qualifications for republican citizenship—they could neither reason logically nor act independently—therefore their petitions should not be seriously considered. Throughout the debates Representative John Quincy Adams responded to attacks on female antislavery petitions by exposing the confounding of acceptable gender conduct with the exercise of natural rights. There was no doubt that women possessed a constitutional right of petition, he argued, and exercise of that right should not be contingent on the character of petitioners. Not only did Adams attempt to safeguard women's right of petition, but he insisted that women were citizens and, notably, questioned whether women might not also possess the right to vote.

Chapter 7 argues that although female petitioning decreased appreciably after 1839 when abolitionists adopted a strategy of direct political action, those women who continued to petition embraced a more clearly political stance than they had in the past and identified themselves as national citizens. As they became involved in electoral politics and saw themselves as constituents to whom congressmen were accountable, their petitions instructed representatives about specific federal legislation such as the Fugitive Slave Law and the Kansas-Nebraska Bill in remarkably bold republican language. By the mid-1850s women's petitioning on the clearly political issue of slavery had become so acceptable that even one of the most outspoken critics of this practice during the 1830s, Catharine E. Beecher, signed a petition. Acceptance of the propriety of women exercising their right to petition on political issues, even an issue as political as amending the U.S. Constitution, was crucial to the success of 1860s petition campaigns, which were dominated by women, to win passage of the Thirteenth Amendment.

After 1865 the right of petition continued to function as a crucial and persistent means of influence employed by women determined to participate in politics despite the fact that neither the Constitution nor custom recognized their full rights as citizens. Women's antislavery petitioning not only contributed significantly to the abolitionist movement but also made the use of collective petitioning of Congress to push for legislation and arouse public opinion a more acceptable form of political activity for women. After female abolitionists set the precedent of mass petitioning of Congress, women took up this tool and began to work on a long list of reforms such as temperance, antilynching, and antipolygamy. Ultimately, mass petitioning provided a primary means through which women expanded their citizenship by securing the right to vote. Though she did not live to witness the enfranchisement of women in 1920, almost six decades earlier Susan B. Anthony had emphasized the importance of petitioning to women as political beings. "Women can neither take the ballot nor the bullet to settle" political questions of the day, she said. "Therefore, to us, the right to petition is one sacred right which we ought not to neglect."[11]

CHAPTER 1

The Unfortunate Word "Petition"

"The greatest difficulty seems to arise from the unfortunate word '*peti-tion*,'" complained antiabolitionist northern minister Calvin Colton in his 1840 pamphlet, *The Right of Petition.* "Nothing could exceed the confusion into which this single word has cast the whole nation." The particular con-fusion to which Colton referred was the river of antislavery petitions that had begun running into Congress in 1835. In 1836 the House had passed a temporary "gag" rule that immediately tabled all petitions on the sub-ject of slavery. Rather than sandbagging the flow of abolition petitions or quelling the discussion of slavery, the rule had the opposite effect. Pro-claiming that the gag proved that slaveholders were conspiring to under-mine the rights of free Americans, abolitionists redoubled their petition-ing efforts and won public sympathy for their cause. Renewal of the gag in each subsequent session of Congress sparked a highly charged national debate over the right of petition. When on January 28, 1840, the House enacted a permanent gag, public debate intensified, and Colton entered the fray with his pamphlet.[1]

Intending to chide the abolitionists for abusing a political privilege, Colton began by acknowledging petitioning as a time-honored right in the Anglo-American political tradition, but he emphasized instances in which it was curtailed when employed in a manner displeasing to rulers or representatives. After the right of petition became a law in England, Colton reminded, petitioners repugnant to the crown or Parliament were committed to prison. He concluded that petitioning had never been in-tended as a means to coerce the government but, rather, as an instrument of supplication through which individuals or groups might seek redress of personal grievances. "Not infrequently," Colton insisted, the abuse of the right of petition led to its suspension altogether. There was precedent for curtailing improper use of the right of petition, Colton asserted, and since abolitionists were employing the right in a manner that fell outside the proper historical definition of "petition," the imposition of the gag rule was both understandable and just.

Although Colton intended to chronicle the history of the petition as an instrument of humble supplication, the story he told hinted again and again at a rather different and more complex narrative. Colton wrote, for instance, that in the history of the United States "the popular and general mind" had changed the meaning of the First Amendment, which guaranteed the right of petition, "from its historical and true interpretations, to something else." What particularly disturbed Colton was that petitioning was being used "under the pretense of submission, for improper and unworthy purposes, while it clothes itself with the sanction of an apparent conformity to law." Thus he lamented, "This little word *petition* is, in this place, a most unfortunate one, and doing more mischief than can be told."[2]

Colton's admission that the meaning of the right of petition had changed in the minds and hands of the people from a form of submission to an instrument of mischief provides the basis for a history of the right of petition quite different from that presented in his pamphlet. In fact, long before women took up petitioning to influence national debate over slavery, other groups outside the domains of institutionalized government employed the right of petition as a wedge to enter realms of political power. These groups had seen what Colton refused to recognize: while, on one hand, the divine right of petition required use of supplicatory rhetoric due its antecedents in monarchical England, on the other hand, it was understood as carrying an incumbent obligation on the part of the receiver to read and respond to the grievance. Petitioning's ability to place demands on rulers or representatives, even while it obscured signers' motive of demand, gave the fundamental right of petition a deeply subversive potential. The radical potential of petitioning multiplied significantly when groups, rather than individuals (as in original practice), began to direct their grievances not only to governing bodies but also to the public. By the early nineteenth century in the United States, petitioning had emerged as a potent instrument through which minority political causes and people denied the full rights of republican citizenship could exert considerable pressure on their representatives by appealing to the power of public opinion.

Among those exerting such power were women. Female involvement in the petition campaign against slavery, which built upon previous though limited experiences of women petitioning collectively, constitutes an early instance of large numbers of women exercising their right of petition as a group to influence national policy making. Along with male abolitionists, women petitioners attempted to reshape public opinion, to pressure federal representatives, and to incite discussion of slavery both in Congress and among the public at large. Women's antislavery petitioning capitalized on the subversive potential of the right of petition to expand significantly the ability of women to participate in politics absent the right of suffrage and at the same time provided a means of asserting citizenship, albeit a modified form of citizenship compared with that claimed by propertied white males. By firmly seizing the right of petition and redefining it from a prayer for redress of private grievances to an instrument of collective public persuasion, women not only asserted their citizenship but also created a hunger for further participation in the political process and for more rights. After the right of women to petition Congress on political issues was established by female abolitionists, the petition was employed by countless women espousing causes such as temperance, antilynching, and antipolygamy. Ultimately, petitioning served as a primary means through which women agitated to win the vote.

*   *   *

Upon embracing petitioning as a means of political influence, antislavery women exploited the subversive potential of that right. As early as the thirteenth century both individuals and the developing institution of Parliament employed petitioning as a tool to erode the power of the monarchy. Although the Magna Carta made no direct mention of the right of petition, such a right was understood to derive from King John's promise that he would not deny or postpone justice to anyone. The twelfth clause of the Magna Carta, moreover, relieved knights and barons of the obligation to supply money to the king until he addressed outstanding grievances. During the late Middle Ages, written petitions, which had become the standard method to approach authorities, placed demands on rulers and tested their accountability to the people. While petitioners employed flattering adjectives such as "sage," "haut," and "puissant" to describe the sovereign they beseeched and referred to themselves as "humble," "*pover*," and "obeisant," through the very act of petitioning, subjects exerted some degree of power. The people's right of petition, after all, imposed a responsibility on the part of the ruler to hear their grievances and, whether it be positive or negative, give some response.[3]

By the early seventeenth century, political factions had begun to seize upon petitioning as a method of propaganda, and petitioners to Parliament assumed a more assertive tone. "Whereas, hitherto, petitions had in general been genuinely intended to bring a grievance to the notice of Parliament in some hope of a response in the shape of a redress," Colin Leys explains, beginning in the seventeenth century, a substantial number of petitions were "presented by political activists under no sort of illusion either that the grievance was unknown or that Parliament might reasonably be expected to respond by redressing it." During the English Civil War both men and women, especially Levelers, who sought to democratize the government, engaged in collective petitioning.[4]

The experience of Leveler women, who executed several well-organized petition campaigns between 1641 and 1655, illustrates the radical potential of petitioning as well as the reactions it could spark among those invested in protecting existing gendered political hierarchies. In the texts of petitions Leveler women justified their increased participation in the public sphere by emphasizing the shared origins of secular petitioning and religious praying. They urged representatives not to "withhold from us *our undoubted right of petitioning,* since God is ever willing and ready to receive the Petitions of all, making no difference of persons." They also claimed the right to have their petitions heard because the "ancient laws of England are not contrary to the will of God." Yet the Leveler women tempered assertions of their natural right to petition with assurances that they had no intention of subverting male political power. Women were "not acting out of any Self-conceit or Pride of Heart, as *seeking to equal ourselves with Men, either in Authority or Wisdom,*" promised a 1642 petition, but were merely "following herein the Example of the Men, which have gone . . . before us."[5]

The fact remained, nevertheless, that women were intruding into public deliberation in an unprecedented manner. Guardians of male political dominance were displeased. Parliament attempted to discourage the women by answering their 1649 petition, "The matter you petition about, is of an higher concernment than you understand, that the House gave an answer to your Husbands; and therefore that you are desired to go home, and look after your own business, and meddle in your huswifery." Likewise, a newspaper warned the women, "It is fitter for you to be washing your dishes, and meddle with the wheele and distaffe." Another predicted, "We shall have things brought to a fine passe, if women come to teach the Parliament how to make Lawes." And yet another declared, "It can never be a good world, when women meddle in States matters . . . and their Husbands are to blame, that they have no fitter employment for them." Questioning the rationality, femininity, morality, and social status of female supplicants, newspapers derided women petitioners as "oyster-wives," "dirty and tattered sluts," and "mealy-mouth'd mutton mongers wives." Attacks such as these demonstrate that the right of petition offered women a tool to expand their public influence, but when men recognized its potential for compromising male political dominance, they cast aspersions in hopes of checking burgeoning female activism.[6]

Despite efforts to discourage women from petitioning and to regulate the "tumultuous" use of petitioning by crowds who stormed Parliament, in 1669 the House of Commons restated that all commoners possessed an inherent right to petition and that the House was obligated to receive their petitions. By the eighteenth century petitioning had emerged as a well-protected right used most often to exert pressure on Parliament in matters of public policy. Leys notes that conditions during this era such as rapid economic change that led to working-class organization resulted in an unprecedented upsurge in the use of petitions as a political instrument. The widespread propagandistic use of petitioning during this period was noted by Dr. Samuel Johnson, who wrote, "This petitioning is a new mode of distressing government, and a mighty easy one."[7]

*   *   *

As in England, in America from the colonial to the Jacksonian period petitioning was transformed from a tool for airing individual grievances to an instrument for collective political action. Petitioning was the primary means through which citizens communicated with colonial assemblies, and information conveyed in petitions was particularly crucial in providing for needy inhabitants. Reflecting the fact that colonial assemblies functioned as quasi-judicial bodies, the petitions dealt primarily with local disputes, including alleged misbehavior of servants, regulation of tobacco packaging, and failure to pay wages. Responses to petitions often led to broader legislation, rendering petitioning a means by which individuals could shape the legislative agenda of colonial assemblies.[8]

Petitioning provided not only a means through which the people influenced colonial assemblies; it was also an instrument through which colonial bodies expressed grievances against England and, eventually, justified revolution. In eighteenth-century British constitutional law petitioning was understood as the appropriate means to seek redress for infringements upon rights, and failure by the king or Parliament to respond to repeated petitioning constituted acceptable grounds for revolution. Thus when colonists perceived various duties and taxes imposed by Britain as violating their constitutional rights, they turned to the petition as a means to demand redress and articulate their growing alienation from British rule. Ultimately, the failure of George III to fulfill his obligation to respond to his subjects' petitions provided a major justification for the colonists' revolution against England. Although not itself a petition, the Declaration of Independence drew much of its rhetorical and political power from its function as a history of failed petitions submitted by colonial bodies to the king in 1774 and 1775. "In every stage of these oppressions," the Declaration stated, "we have petitioned for redress in the most humble terms: our repeated petitions have been answered only by repeated injuries." In the face of this tyranny the colonists could justifiably declare themselves free and independent of Great Britain. In this important sense, as Garry Wills explains, the Declaration established itself in the direct line of those earlier petitions: "The Congress declared its independence in terms not basically at odds with its 'dutiful petitions'—in fact, as a logical culmination of them."[9]

Excluded from office holding, women were not among the signers of petitions to England that effected the Revolution. Yet in at least one case women elected petitioning as a means of political participation. In 1774 the women of Edenton, North Carolina, moved beyond boycotting tea to the more public action of forming a patriotic organization. Members of the organization composed a petition to the public in which they pledged to follow the colony's nonimportation resolves. Signed by fifty-one women, it was published in colonial and English newspapers. While the patriot women stressed that they petitioned out of duty to country and family, their tone was remarkably assertive. Their collective effort aimed at generating publicity for the patriot cause marked a significant departure from women's customary petitioning, constituted of private pleas for personal grievances.[10] It is not surprising, then, that the character of women who undertook this bold public act was called into question. Englishman Arthur Iredell wrote his relatives in North Carolina sardonically, "Is there a Female Congress at Edenton too?" He hoped not, "for we Englishmen are afraid of the Male Congress, but if the Ladies, who have ever, since the Amazonian Era, been esteemed the most formidable Enemies, if they, I say, should attack us, the most fatal consequences are dreaded." Undoubtedly Iredell's criticism was motivated in part by political differences, but the publicness of the women's petition rendered the signers vulnerable to gendered aspersions. The Edenton petition, after all, demonstrated that women were capable of political organization and that they possessed the right to enter public deliberation to declare their political allegiances and influence public opinion.[11]

Although after the Revolution most women petitioned for personal redress as they had previously, even in these more customary practices they employed petitions to articulate new political identities. In her analysis of divorce requests in Massachusetts from 1692 to 1786, Nancy Cott found that from 1775 to 1784, a period coinciding with the War for Independence, the number of divorce petitions sent to the legislature increased 61 percent compared with the decade before the Revolution. Cott argues that the correlation between the increased number of divorce petitions and the war might have been due to "a certain personal outlook" that accompanied the Revolution, "one that implied self-assertion and regard for the future, one that we might label more 'modern' than 'traditional.'" This greater self-assertion conveyed in petitions, Cott suggests, was fostered by republican claims to citizenship. As Linda Kerber explains, "The rhetoric of the Revolution, which emphasized the right to separate from dictatorial masters, implicitly offered an ideological validation for divorce, though few in power recognized it." Petitions for divorce provided women a means to assert this newly forged republican identity to their state representatives.[12]

In addition to petitioning for divorce, women suffering from the hardships of war were forced to petition state legislatures and Congress, resulting in a significant increase in female petitioning. In the Carolinas, for example, Cynthia Kierner has found that women sent 349 petitions to their state legislatures between 1776 and 1800, compared with only 32 in the entire preceding quarter-century. Kerber estimates that 5 percent of the petitions received by the Continental Congress emanated from women. The vast majority of women's petitions came from individuals, especially soldier's widows requesting pensions, while others sought compensation for war losses. Denied rights generally associated with full citizenship such as voting, office holding, and serving on juries, and discouraged by social conventions from standard forms of political expression such as public speaking and publishing broadsides, women recurred to petitioning, with its ambiguous public character, to seek relief from the hardships of war. "Petitioning afforded women a voice with which they could seek the aid and protection of public men while demonstrating their continued deference to male authority," explains Kierner. Conforming to rhetorical conventions, widows' petitions emphasized economic and emotional desperation. But, as Kerber notes, "many also testified to a strong belief that the widows had made real sacrifices to the state, and that the political system owed them something in return."[13]

During and after the Revolutionary War, then, women exploited the subversive potential of petitioning to participate in the patriot cause and to assert new political identities. That petitioning held the possibility for women to transform their political status in the new republic was evidenced in a letter from Abigail Adams to Mercy Otis Warren. Reacting to her husband's dismissal of her request to "Remember the ladies" in the writing of "the new Code of Laws," Adams suggested, "I think I will get you to join me in a petition to Congress." The idea was uttered half in jest and the proposal was never brought to fruition, but nonetheless Adams's statement illustrates that petitioning was a most logical means to urge the framers to revise "the Laws of England which [give] such unlimited power to the Husband to use his wife Ill."[14]

*   *   *

During the early national period petitioning provided poor and disenfranchised men a means to exert newly found political power and to assert enhanced political status. In 1786, for example, middling men from western Massachusetts engaged in mass petitioning against high land taxes. After their petitions were ignored, they united behind Daniel Shays in rebellion. In western Pennsylvania small farmers from the backcountry petitioned for repeal of an excise tax on whiskey enacted by Congress in 1791 in order to raise money to liquidate the national debt. The Whiskey Rebellion of 1794, in which farmers resisted the tax by attacking federal revenue officers who attempted to collect it, occurred after repeated petitioning failed to secure repeal. In Connecticut artisans expressed themselves collectively for the first time in the spring of 1792 with a petition to the general assembly against the state's system of taxation. In the course of their petitioning these men gradually transformed the language and tone of their petitions, replacing "flattery and fawning phrases" with "plain words and a direct assertiveness." These collective petitions reflected the notion that a democratized government should be responsive to the demands of the common people and that petitioning was an important mechanism to convey the peoples' opinions to their representatives.[15]

Tradeswomen's efforts to use petitioning to achieve economic reform were less common and less successful than those of their male counterparts. In 1788, for example, "sundry seamstresses" of Charleston, South Carolina, petitioned the general assembly complaining that they were out of work due to the importation of ready-made clothes. The seamstresses prayed that "a much larger duty be laid on the above articles, which will have a tendency to give employment to your petitioners and increase the revenue as they are bulky articles that cannot be easily smuggled." But unlike the petitions of male artisans and tradesmen who pleaded for economic reform, the women's petition was ignored. This neglect was politically possible, Kerber suggests, because the petition fell outside traditional categories of petitions sent by women, and it was ignored because there were no lobbyists to orchestrate presentation of the women's plea. The petition is significant, nonetheless, for the evidence it provides that tradeswomen, like men of their class, recognized the potential power of petitioning to influence their representatives and that for women of the new republic, the right of petition and reception was far from secure.[16]

Likewise, free blacks recognized the power of collective petitioning to pressure government, yet the impact of their petitioning was limited by their political status. In 1787 Prince Hall organized free blacks of Boston to petition the city for improvements in the education of black children. The petition was considered, but its prayer was denied. A year later Hall again took the lead in organizing a petition campaign aimed at halting the slave trade. The collective petition was presented to the Massachusetts General Court along with another appeal from the Yearly Meeting of New England Friends, which also asked for an end to the slave trade, and with yet another plea signed by all of Boston's clergy plus 100 other men. As a result of the combined outcry expressed in the petitions, the General Court enacted a law to prevent the slave trade and to grant relief to families of persons kidnapped from the commonwealth. Hall's second petition succeeded likely due to the great number of men demanding an end to the slave trade and, no doubt, because many of these men were white.[17]

Despite the growing use of petitioning and the new assertive language of petitions during the postrevolutionary era, the right of petition was not guaranteed to Americans by either the Articles of Confederation or the Constitution as drafted by Congress and ratified by the states. Yet the right of petition was included among proposed amendments to the Constitution. In August 1789 the House of Representatives debated a proposed amendment that stated that Congress shall make no law abridging "the right of the people peaceably to assemble and to petition the government for a redress of grievances." Although members debated whether the people might not also possess a right to instruct their representatives, the right of petition remained unquestioned. Approval of the First Amendment marked a turning point in the development of the right of petition, as for the first time it became part of written organic law. Thereafter debate over the right of petition would focus not on whether the people possessed such a right but, rather, as in the case of Colton's pamphlet, on the exact meaning and limits of that right.[18]

During the first decades of the federal Congress, white men employed the power of petitioning to influence public opinion and to pressure representatives on national issues such as contested election results, the national bank, land distribution, the abolition of dueling, government in the territories, the Alien and Sedition Acts, and the Jay Treaty. Yet when slaves petitioned Congress for emancipation, the inalienable nature of the newly guaranteed right of petition was questioned. In 1797 four manumitted slaves sent a petition explaining that each had been freed by his master but had been captured and sold back into slavery. The petitioners acknowledged that they possessed no right to vote but insisted on addressing Congress as "fellow-men" ruled by God. As soon as the petition was read, the House erupted into debate over whether it should be received. Southerners argued that the memorial should not be heard because it emanated from slaves, who had no right of petition. Representative William Smith of South Carolina claimed that acceptance of the petition would "tend to spread an alarm throughout the Southern States; it would act as an 'entering-wedge,' whose consequences could not be foreseen." In response Representative John Swanwick of Pennsylvania decried attempts to abrogate the right of petition: "If men were aggrieved, and conceive they have claim to attention," he argued, "petitioning was their sacred right, and that right should never suffer innovation." Swanwick's defense notwithstanding, the House voted 33-50 not to receive the petition.[19]

The House's refusal to hear the slaves' petition gains significance when viewed in light of the fact that throughout the 1790s Congress received and acted on petitions submitted by white abolition societies and Quaker organizations. Although proslavery southerners questioned the character of Quaker petitioners, many of whom were pacifists during the War for Independence, the right of these white men to petition, even on the sensitive subject of slavery, remained intact. Rather than refusing the petitions, as in the case of the slaves, Congress received, reported, debated, and voted on appeals from white men. Thus the House's refusal in 1797 to receive the slaves' petition signaled that despite its allegedly inalienable nature, the peoples' right of petition still could be abridged based on the status of petitioners and checked by Congress's right of reception. Like the rights of slaves and free blacks, whose status in the new republic was relatively undefined, the rights of women, including that of petition, remained open to negotiation.[20]

* * *

During the first decades of the nineteenth century a number of factors combined to increase the power of petitioning and render it a particularly useful tool for those who remained outside the formal political process. The spread of adult white manhood suffrage (twenty-one of the twenty-four states had some form of it by 1826) led to the decline of aristocratic politics and the rise of mass electioneering. The gentlemanly statesman who could rightfully expect deference from his constituents gave way to the professional politician who actively appealed to the mass electorate. This growing power of the public was nurtured by advances in transportation and communication, which "helped shrink the nation and enlarge the political community." Particularly important to the formation of the democratic public was the explosion in magazines and newspapers that occurred during these decades. Nationally circulated magazines appeared, including *Niles' Weekly Register,* founded in Baltimore in 1811; the *North American Review,* started in Boston in 1815; and *Godey's Lady's Book,* begun in 1830 and which attained the "extraordinary" circulation of 150,000 by the end of the decade. In the 1830s alone the number of newspapers rose from 800 to 1,400, and sales tripled.[21]

Contributing to the new emphasis on participatory democracy and the growing importance of public opinion, religious revivalists set aside older Calvinist notions of predestination to preach a modified doctrine of free will and active pursuit of salvation. The fiery preaching of revivalist ministers such as Charles Grandison Finney attracted hundreds of thousands of women and men to evangelical Protestantism. Most evangelicals believed that they were charged with a duty not only to cultivate personal morality but to employ their energies to safeguard the morality of the community and nation. As Richard J. Carwardine has observed, "Evangelicals offered an example of how the world might be changed through systematic public agitation" and "provided professional organizers and models for mobilizing public opinion." Petitioning in particular afforded evangelicals "a means of operating in an era of mass politics without being compromised by the corruption of new partisanship."[22]

Women motivated by the evangelical impulse to engage in benevolent activism such as providing relief for the poor, orphans, and the aged also seized petitioning as a means to accomplish their charitable work. After forming organizations and writing bylaws, one of the first major tasks women faced in starting a benevolent society was to compose a petition to the state legislature seeking incorporation. In 1812, for example, the white women of Petersburg, Virginia, formed the Female Orphan Asylum and petitioned the general assembly for legal incorporation. In addition to stating why they wished to incorporate, the women asked, in language that Suzanne Lebsock has characterized as "remarkably free of the deference that informed most petitions of the time," for the right to participate in litigation and the power to hold and convey property. Despite the fact that common law denied married women the right to hold property, the assembly granted almost every request of the petition, including the power to hold and manage the organization's funds. Petitions to incorporate associations such as the one from the women of Petersburg were common and aroused few questions of propriety. "In this age of wonders, when the liberal dare to devise liberal things," wrote Hannah Kinney, president of the Newark Female Charitable Society in 1816, "applications to legislators by females to become incorporate bodies are not novelties." Indeed, petitions for corporate charters were more often than not answered favorably when societies demonstrated that their goals fell under the category of traditional charity. After winning incorporation, female benevolent organizations often petitioned city and state councils for funds to provide relief to the "deserving" needy.[23]

Based on a posture of humility and influence available through personal contacts, these tactics resembled the deferential mode of politics of the eighteenth century and, according to Ann M. Boylan, "obscured the reality that organized women were involved in politics, primarily through the exercise of their right to petition their rulers." Charitable women, Boylan suggests, did not view petitioning as political because they were engaged in private efforts to influence powerful men rather than in attempts to seek collective power for women. The viability of these efforts was limited, however, to women who had access to powerful men, which effectively excluded societies of black women engaged in racial uplift as well as associations of white women from the working and growing middle classes.[24]

The evangelical impulse also gave rise to organizations aimed at reforming a variety of social ills by altering public opinion through pamphleteering, lecturing, and petitioning. The host of evils included intemperance, violation of the Sabbath, Indian removal, mistreatment of the mentally ill, and prostitution. Foremost among mass social reform movements sponsored by evangelical reformers was that of temperance, which recruited hundreds of thousands of members from throughout the nation in a campaign to promote abstinence. Although the temperance movement was dominated by male leaders, as early as 1818 women began to sign antialcohol petitions. By the 1820s large numbers of women in all regions of the country had joined male-run chapters of the American Temperance Society, organized their own female affiliates, and orchestrated petition campaigns. In 1834, for example, 500 women of Elizabethtown, New Jersey, signed a petition requesting that local officials control the proliferation of liquor shops. In 1837, 600 women in Wilmington, Delaware, mustered a similar petition. In 1838, 1,200 women in Portland, Maine, petitioned the state legislature seeking legal assistance for the temperance cause.[25]

In addition to playing a central role in the temperance movement, petitioning provided the basis of a campaign organized by evangelicals to halt removal of the Cherokee from their native land of Georgia. This campaign marked a significant event in the emergence of popular politics and the use of petitioning, for it constituted what Mary Hershberger has called "the deepest political movement the country had yet witnessed." The anti-removal campaign also signaled a turning point in the history of American women's political activism, for it inaugurated the practice of women from various states petitioning federal representatives to influence national legislation. By sending their petitions directly to Congress, women who opposed Cherokee removal advanced a step beyond benevolent ladies who limited their petitioning to local bodies and often employed a male intermediary. Women's petitioning against Cherokee removal, moreover, was part of a campaign involving people from many states in expressing and arousing collective opposition to a national policy, rather than an effort of personal influence limited to specific localities orchestrated by a small group of wealthy women. Opponents of removal transgressed the boundaries of acceptable female activism to participate in attempts to influence national policy, an activity generally understood to be reserved for men.[26]

The debate over Cherokee removal stemmed from a compact Georgia signed in 1802 with the federal government guaranteeing that if the state gave up its western land claims, the government would remove the Cherokee from Georgia as soon as peaceably possible. By 1829, when the cotton plantation system had expanded westward and coveted even more land, Georgia demanded that the federal government live up to its promise. Presidents James Monroe and John Quincy Adams had recognized Cherokee rights and had hoped to persuade the Indians to move peaceably. But Andrew Jackson, who had gained fame as an Indian fighter, did not acknowledge an independent Cherokee nation, and in his December 8, 1829, state-of-the-union address he ridiculed the Cherokees for having "pretensions" of erecting a sovereign state within Georgia. The president advised the Indians to emigrate beyond the Mississippi or to submit to the laws of Georgia. Jackson's partisans in Congress responded to his message by introducing the Removal Bill, which authorized the president to set aside lands west of the Mississippi that could be exchanged with the Indians for their eastern lands.[27]

A number of evangelical leaders viewed the Removal Bill as a national sin committed against a helpless people, and they organized efforts to arouse the "right-thinking populace" to influence their leaders.[28] Jeremiah Evarts, secretary of the American Board of Commissioners for Foreign Missions, an Indian missionary organization, wrote a series of articles published in the *National Intelligencer* between August 5 and December 19, 1829. Using the pseudonym William Penn, Evarts charged that if the United States committed the terrible sin of violating the Cherokees' rights, it would forfeit God's protection and blessings. Although he believed that Jackson and party leaders were about to defy God, Evarts maintained that the people of the United States — a Christian nation — had not strayed. He orchestrated a massive petition campaign that won signatures and covered congressmen's tables with petitions. Many women who engaged in benevolent work on behalf of the Cherokee were sympathetic to their plight and joined the antiremoval petition effort. During the summer of 1829 the well-known female educator and reformer Catharine E. Beecher attended a speech delivered by Evarts, who asked her to do what she could to avert the tragedy of Indian removal. Beecher returned to Hartford Female Seminary, of which she was the director, and called on her friends to discuss the removal issue. They decided that the best course of action was to initiate a petition campaign. So unprecedented was a national women's petition campaign that the Hartford women resolved to keep secret the identities of its organizers.[29]

Beecher composed a circular addressed to the "Benevolent Ladies of the United States," swore the printer to keep her identity as the author a secret, and sent the circular to persons on mailing lists of female benevolent organizations. After demonstrating the injustice of the removal policy, the circular urged that "energetic expression of the wishes and feelings of a Christian nation, addressed to the congress now assembling, and which is soon to decide [the Cherokee's] doom," was the best means to save the nation from taking sinful action. While calling on women to petition Congress, the circular also admitted the highly unusual nature of women engaging in collective petitioning of Congress on a matter of national policy. "It may be, that female petitioners can lawfully be heard, even by the highest rulers of our land," the circular said. But reflecting uncertainty about Congress's willingness to receive from women petitions relating to a federal policy decision, it also admitted, "It may be that this will be *forbidden.*" Women's petitions for the Cherokee were appropriate, it argued, because rather than "assuming any right to dictate the decisions of those who rule over them," the petitioners were merely supplicating "that we and our dearest friends may be saved from the awful curses denounced on all who oppress the poor and needy." Women may rightfully "*feel* for the distressed," it asserted, and "they may stretch out the supplicating hand for them, and by their prayers strive to avert the calamities that are impending over them."[30]

Thanks in no small part to the "Ladies Circular," hundreds of women from various regions signed petitions to Congress opposing removal of the Cherokee. Like petitions composed to win men's names, those aimed at women affirmed the rights of the Cherokee and threatened that God would seek revenge should those rights be abrogated. But because it was so unusual for females to collectively petition Congress, women's petitions devoted a great deal of space to defending such unusual behavior. Half of the text of the petition signed by sixty-three "ladies" of Steubenville, Ohio, was dedicated to justifying the act of women petitioning their federal representatives:

> Your memorialists would sincerely deprecate any presumptuous interference on the part of their own sex, with the ordinary political affairs of the country, as wholly unbecoming the character of American Females. Even in private life we may not presume to direct the general conduct, or control the acts of those who stand in the near and guardian relations of husbands and brothers, yet all admit that *there are times* when duty and affection call on us to *advise* and *persuade,* as well as to cheer or to console. And if we approach the public representatives of our husbands and brothers, only in the humble character of suppliants

in the cause of mercy and humanity, may we not hope that even the small voice of *female* sympathy will be heard?[31]

Reaction among antiremovalists to the women's petitioning campaign was mixed. Religious periodicals, on one hand, were chagrined by the women's overt political activity and urged them to follow the traditional route of exercising their influence over male relatives and friends. The *Christian Watchman*, for example, cautioned that because "God would preserve our Congress so pure and enlightened," there was no need for "all the females in the land [to organize] into 'societies' to get a question righteously decided." On the other hand, the *Watchman* repeatedly published the "Ladies Circular" without criticism, and other religious periodicals, such as the *Christian Advocate*, printed it on the front page with an implied endorsement. Widespread printing of the circular led to great speculation over its authorship, and Beecher, who jealously guarded her secret, was often asked who, in her opinion, the author might be. Eventually Beecher suffered a breakdown because of the anxieties of engaging in a political campaign while trying desperately to avoid publicity for fear of being accused of impropriety. "Not at all aware of the consequences of this additional excitement," Beecher wrote decades later in her reminiscences, "I suddenly found myself utterly prostrated and unable to perform any school duty without extreme pain and such confusion of thought as seemed like approaching insanity."[32]

Beecher's anxiety over the propriety of women's petitions was far from ill founded. When the petitions signed by women were debated in Congress, Jacksonian members fixed their responses on the sex of the signers. Women's petitions, they said, wasted the time of Congress, and for this they blamed antiremoval men who, they declared, failed to keep their women under control. Thomas Hart Benton, chairman of the Senate Committee on Indian Affairs, led the attack on the women petitioners with a sarcastic speech that mocked women for "acting in public meetings for the instruction of Congress on the subject of these Georgia Indians." Benton dramatized the female petitioners' alleged offense by threatening to "appear in the feminine [rather] than in the masculine gender" to march with the Cherokee. After demonstrating the supposed absurdity of their intrusion, Benton recommended that the petitioning "ladies" "not douse their bonnets, and tuck up their coats for such a race [the Cherokee], but sit down on the way side, and wait for the coming of the conquerors." The women petitioners, Benton's outburst insinuated, reversed proper gender roles by mistakenly giving women more power and casting aside chivalric males. In Benton's estimation at least, the women's petitions threatened to undermine political order.[33]

Although there was enough support to get a number of the petitions printed or referred to committees on Indian affairs for consideration, many, such as that of the Steubenville women, were laid on the table after they had been introduced. Nonetheless, the petition campaign prompted extensive debate in Congress on the Cherokee removal issue, beginning in February 1830 and intensifying in April and May. In the end Jacksonian forces won by a narrow margin, and the Removal Bill was signed by the president on May 28, 1830. Evarts then campaigned to get the bill repealed, sparking a new rash of petitions, but the effort was unsuccessful.[34]

Ultimately the campaign against Cherokee removal "ushered in a new age of popular politics." Radical activists such as William Lloyd Garrison, James Birney, and Arthur Tappan, who equated the tyranny of Indian removal with that of colonizing slaves, would transfer the strategy of petitioning Congress from their efforts on behalf of Indians to those on behalf of slaves. Likewise, a number of women involved in antiremoval efforts became leading female abolitionists. Lydia Maria Child, who early in 1829 published *The First Settlers of New-England: or, Conquest of the Pequods, Narragansets and Pokanokets,* which provided an extended argument against Cherokee removal, in 1833 began a long and illustrious career in abolitionism by writing *An Appeal in Favor of That Class of Americans Called Africans.* Angelina Grimké, who had expressed support for antiremovalists in her personal writings, became a fervent and active abolitionist. Harriet Beecher (Stowe), who worked enthusiastically on the Cherokee petition campaign, would go on to write her devastating attack on the institution of slavery, *Uncle Tom's Cabin.* Not only did similarities in the plights of the Cherokee and slaves as well as the ideologies of the two movements lead women from antiremoval to abolition, but the experience of petitioning "provided reform women with political skills valuable in subsequent antislavery and woman suffrage campaigns." Participation in the antiremoval petition campaign, Hershberger notes, allowed women to practice rhetorical skills such as writing persuasive appeals, educating members of their communities, and gathering signatures.[35]

* * *

Though Calvin Colton insisted that it was inappropriate to use petitioning to influence national policy, closer examination of the history of the use of the right of petition suggests otherwise. Colton held that in "proper" petitioning, one or more individuals approached their representatives "with an appeal to their kindness, or generosity, or sense of propriety and justice, or regard to public good, . . . *soliciting* the public authorities for these several objects, with submission to their judgment." Colton's criteria for the proper use of petitioning harkened back to early exercise of the right in monarchical England when it involved subjects humbly submitting requests to their rulers for assistance or judgment of a troublesome issue. Colton's definition of petitioning and his accompanying historical narrative obscured the fact that by the Jacksonian era petitioning had been transformed from an individual submissive act to a powerful instrument of mass democratic politics.[36]

That Colton aimed to delegitimize antislavery petitioning because he disagreed with abolitionists is all but certain. Yet his arguments reached beyond the slavery issue to fundamental notions of republican citizenship. Mass petitioning by men of all sorts, women, slaves, and free blacks, he warned, seriously endangered the foundations of republican government. "The people may well suspect those who, not content with the power of the franchise, seek to foist into its place the right of petition," he asserted. Those who persisted in petitioning rather than effecting their ends through exercise of the franchise, he feared, "would upheave the foundations of a throne, and of the temple of republican liberty, while bending and cringing at the footstool of the former, or lying prostrate as petitioners under the shade of the latter." He dismissed the right of petition as merely a negative right, whereas he praised the franchise as "a positive, great, and elemental power of the constitution." The abolitionists' strategy of mass petitioning bypassed the requirement of suffrage for political participation and created the opportunity for women and free blacks along with enfranchised men to influence debate over federal legislation. As Colton's protests reveal, women's antislavery petitioning posed a serious threat to the political status of those who possessed the power of the vote, namely propertied white males. Antislavery petitioning, then, figured centrally in the larger, ongoing, fluid struggle over defining and redefining antebellum American citizenship.[37]

"From whence comes the indifference manifested to the cause of the female slave?" demanded an essay printed in the Ladies' Department of the *Liberator* on May 5, 1832. "Have American women turned coldly away from her pleading voice, or are the fountains of benevolence sealed in their hearts to all those guilty of 'a skin not colored like their own?'" The article, published early in the formation of the organized white antislavery movement under the headline "Duty of Females," stated that women had a moral responsibility to act on behalf of abolitionism. The author, who signed with only the initials L. H., explained that slavery had "a claim on women; as sufferers in a common calamity, they must assist in its removal; as those involved in the commission of a deep crime, they must lift up their voices against it." Yet just how they were to act remained open to clarification. "The inquiry is often made, what can women do? Are not their voices weak, and their aid feeble? and would not any exertions they might make be considered obtrusive, and retard rather than accelerate the progress of freedom?" "True, the voice of woman should not be heard in public debates," L. H. acknowledged, recommending that instead of entering public deliberation, women should educate themselves about the subject of slavery so they might use their influence to direct family members and friends to the abolition cause. "Public opinion is the source of public action," the author averred, "and where is this opinion formed? In the shade of private life." Women, L. H. advised, should never allow slavery to be treated lightly in conversation, and they should use their voices to call into action "some more powerful and able advocate."[1]

L. H.'s recommendations echoed those of other antislavery leaders, male and female alike, who urged women to wield their influence over male relatives and friends, to teach free blacks, and to boycott products of slave labor. By and large, however, they did not encourage women to take direct action, such as public speaking or petitioning. Yet although by 1833 petitioning had emerged as the major tool through which male abolitionists pushed for an end to slavery, women were discouraged from this type

of public activism even by the antislavery press. As the abolition movement progressed, however, the proper role of women was constantly renegotiated, and by 1835 a number of forces led women to depart from custom and participate in public policy debate by mass collective petitioning
of Congress.

* * *

The groundwork for the abolitionists' systematic petition campaign of the
1830s that attracted women to the task of petitioning was laid before the
birth of the nation. Slaves themselves submitted the antislavery petitions,
which emphasized the contradiction between Revolutionary ideology and
the keeping of slaves. Petitioning by abolitionist organizations was begun
by Quakers, who were among the earliest whites to condemn slavery as a
sin. Philadelphia Quakers, for example, petitioned the Continental Congress in 1783 to end the slave trade only to be informed that under the
Articles of Confederation the central government had no power to regulate commerce. The Quakers had better luck in state legislatures, where
during the late 1780s their antislavery petitions led to passage of a number
of laws against the foreign slave trade.[2]

Three Quaker petitions submitted to the House in 1790 sparked heated
debate and forced Congress to specify the power of the federal government in the regulation of slavery, an issue largely ignored by the Constitution. The House report articulated what came to be known as the "federal
consensus," the position that only the states could abolish or regulate slavery within their jurisdictions. Approval of the report outlining the consensus created a new and significant barrier to persons hoping to fight domestic slavery at the federal level, for it forced abolitionists to limit their
petitioning to requests to end slavery and the slave trade in the District of
Columbia, which they maintained was clearly under the exclusive jurisdiction of Congress. Despite this setback, Quakers and other early abolitionists learned a valuable lesson: sending petitions to Congress stirred debate
about slavery. As the Pennsylvania Abolition Society reported, the petitions and the debates they sparked "served to disseminate our principles,
by exciting a commotion on the subject." Indeed, the Quaker petition of
1790 put into motion for the first time in the United States a strategy of
petitioning to spread the doctrine of abolition.[3]

About the same time that Americans started petitioning the Continental Congress, events were occurring in Great Britain that would profoundly affect future antislavery petitioning in the United States. Unlike

Americans, who sent a few petitions to Congress each year, as early as 1787 male British abolitionists petitioned en masse calling for an end to the slave trade. Petitioning allowed British abolitionists to draw on the power of the public rather than having to rely on private attempts to influence individual political leaders. By the 1830s the process of gathering signatures and presenting petitions demanding parliamentary action had developed into an elaborate ceremony, wherein the petitions symbolized a mobilized people and provided a tangible measure of public opinion. Yet if the antislavery constituency represented by the petitions was to be taken seriously, signers needed to be viewed as credible by members of Parliament and the public. Not surprisingly, antiabolitionists attempted to discredit abolition petitions by claiming that signers were juveniles, paupers, and criminals. As a result, abolitionists vigilantly monitored the circulation, signing, and submitting of petitions to Parliament to ensure the apparent credibility of signers. Women were excluded from signing for fear that the marks of these allegedly irrational creatures would undermine the integrity of abolition memorials.[4]

By the turn of the century, aided by massive petition campaigns that popularized the cause, abolitionism was burgeoning in England. In the United States, however, it remained intermittent, and the movement, which throughout the 1800s had made steady progress toward its goals, faced multiple setbacks. During the 1790s there was evidence to warrant abolitionists' optimistic belief that steady progress might continue and slavery eventually would become extinct. Prominent statesmen and clergy backed the abolitionist movement, and it even enjoyed support from slaveholders of the Upper South. Northern states set in motion both judicial and legislative mandates that eventually emancipated slaves, and during the 1780s and 1790s a growing number of slaves were manumitted in Maryland, Delaware, and especially Virginia. This progress was dealt a serious blow in 1787 with ratification of the federal Constitution, which failed to end slavery in the new nation. Although the Constitution permitted the federal government to end the African slave trade in 1808, not only did it fail to abolish slavery, but it affirmed the right of masters to recover runaway slaves. Most damaging, though, was the "three-fifths clause," which allowed slaves to be counted as three-fifths of a person for purposes of taxation and representation in the House. The clause, in effect, recognized slaves as individual property and created a strong incentive for perpetuating and extending slavery.[5]

Support for abolition was further weakened during the last decade of the eighteenth century by a number of bloody slave revolts throughout the world, which decreased tolerance for criticism of slaveholding. Americans learned of the massive 1791 slave uprising in St. Domingue from large numbers of French planters seeking refuge with their slaves in Virginia. The first major slave revolt in the United States occurred on August 30, 1800, when a Virginia slave named Gabriel assembled an army of at least 1,000 slaves to seize the Richmond arsenal. The effort was thwarted and the plotters were hanged, but the revolt greatly intensified fears of slave insurrection and further decreased tolerance for criticism of slavery. A final blow to abolitionism as it was practiced during the Revolutionary era occurred in 1793 with the invention of the cotton gin, which dramatically increased cotton production, which relied heavily on slave labor, and spread the plantation system throughout the lower South. What antislavery sentiment remained during the first two decades of the nineteenth century was embodied in the American Colonization Society, founded in 1816. Colonizationists advocated a plan of gradual emancipation by which masters would voluntarily free their slaves, who would be transported for "resettlement" in Liberia. Its chimeric humanitarianism combined with its gradualism won for the organization adherents from the upper echelons of American political society, including Thomas Jefferson and James Madison. Friends of colonization could be found among slaveholders as well as the evangelical clergy, who appreciated the idea of Christian missionary work in Africa. Ironically, James Birney and William Lloyd Garrison, who would become outspoken critics of the society, were colonizationists until the late 1820s.[6]

There was a burst of abolition petitioning in 1819 when the general mood of complacency toward slavery was interrupted by the sectional conflict over Missouri statehood. The question sparked particularly intense debate because at that time the Union was composed of twenty states—ten slave and ten free—and the proposed constitution of Missouri permitted slavery and barred the emigration of free blacks. Admission of Missouri as a slave state not only would have upset the balance of power in Congress, but because it would have created the first new state from Louisiana Purchase land, its status as slave or free carried considerable symbolic importance. Protests of northern congressmen were strengthened by an outpouring of petitions, such as those from Ohio emanating from a campaign organized by a Quaker, former Tennessee slaveholder Charles Osborn. Using his reform newspaper the *Philanthropist* to publicize the campaign, Osborn rallied Ohioans to hold public meetings in which they drew up petitions against admitting Missouri as a slave state. Petitioning efforts to halt the admission of Missouri were not confined to Ohio. On November 17, 1819, some 2,000 people gathered at a New York City hotel to denounce the idea of permitting slavery in new states and to draw up a petition. Similar petitions were sent from Pennsylvania, Connecticut, New Jersey, Delaware, and Vermont. In the end Congress reached a compromise whereby Missouri was admitted as a slave state, Maine was admitted as a free state, and slavery was excluded in the rest of the Louisiana Territory north of latitude 36°30'.[7]

Further groundwork for mass antislavery petitioning was laid in 1827 when Benjamin Lundy organized a campaign in Baltimore that asked Congress to pass a law providing that all children thereafter born to slaves in the District of Columbia be declared free at a certain age. After some wrangling, the House, by a large majority, negated printing of the petition and ordered it to lie on the table. Lundy was undeterred. In 1828 he launched a lecture tour through the North to encourage further antislavery petitioning. His message was not lost on a young reporter for the *Boston Courier* named William Lloyd Garrison, who subsequently urged Massachusetts to join other states in petitioning against slavery in the District. In October 1828 Garrison sent petition forms to Vermont postmasters, who paid nothing for their mail, requesting them to gather signatures and send the petitions to Congress.[8] Garrison and other opponents of slavery submitted enough petitions in 1828 to stir debate in Congress. Petitions for abolition in the District also flowed from citizens of Washington, D.C., itself as well as New York, Ohio, and Pennsylvania. Freemen, such as those in Adams County, Pennsylvania, lent their names to petitions, and the free black press praised the signature-gathering efforts of the predominantly white antislavery societies. "Nothing ever affords us more pleasure," wrote the Reverend Samuel Cornish, black abolitionist editor of *Freedom's Journal*, "than to find our friends active in the cause of oppressed humanity."[9]

The frequency of petitioning for African American civil rights increased significantly beginning in 1830 with the organization of the National Negro Convention. This movement was founded in response to abuses suffered by Cincinnati's free black population, which had expanded rapidly by the mid-1820s, spawning fierce competition for jobs between free blacks and immigrant (mostly German and Irish) workers. White Cincinnatians reacted by barring black children from the city's public schools and enforcing state "Black Codes," which had been largely ignored since their institution in 1807. The codes prohibited blacks from serving on juries, testifying against whites, or joining the militia and required them to post a $500 bond guaranteeing good behavior. The local African Methodist Episcopal church reacted by organizing a petition drive for repeal of the codes. White leaders responded with impunity, ordering the entire population of free blacks, some 2,200 people, to post the $500 surety bond in only thirty days or to leave town. Before the majority of the community had time to raise the money or flee, over the weekend of August 22, 1829, rioters set fire to the black tenement in the city's "Little Africa." Thousands were left homeless, and about 200 free blacks fled to Canada.[10]

The Cincinnati crisis spurred free blacks throughout the North to organize protests and to petition Congress for their civil rights. In direct response to events in Ohio, free black leaders organized the First National Negro Convention, held in Philadelphia September 20–24, 1830, which marked the beginning of a movement that would continue through 1861. The Third National Negro Convention, held June 4–13, 1832, in the wake of Nat Turner's rebellion, declared that free blacks must fight for their own rights but should do so through moral suasion alone. Many public demonstrations followed, and in Philadelphia, for example, large numbers gathered to send memorials to the Senate and House of Representatives asking for the repeal of legal restrictions against free blacks. In 1835 the convention recommended to free blacks "the propriety" of petitioning Congress and the state legislatures "to be admitted to the rights and privileges of American citizens, and that we be protected in the same." This call was sounded years earlier by Maria Stewart, a free black, who in 1833 entreated Boston's African Masons, "Let every man of color throughout the United States, who possesses the spirit and principles of a man, sign a petition to Congress to abolish slavery in the District of Columbia."[11]

Free blacks involved in the Negro Convention movement persuaded a number of key whites to oppose the Colonization Society, a crucial step in the emergence of immediate abolitionism and the growth of mass antislavery petitioning. Samuel Cornish and James Forten's 1827 essays attacking colonization as well as discussions with the free blacks led William Lloyd Garrison to reconsider his commitment to colonization. In 1832 Garrison published *Thoughts on African Colonization,* which accused the society of pledging not to interfere with slavery and of being grossly indifferent to the welfare of free blacks. Rather than colonization or gradual emancipation, Garrison advocated immediate abolition. "Immediatism" was defined more clearly by John Greenleaf Whittier in his pamphlet

Justice and Expediency, which explained that immediate abolition meant that the work of reforming dangerously mistaken public opinion must begin immediately. In doing this work immediately, he wrote, abolitionists must remember "that public opinion can overcome" the many obstacles in their way, and thus they should "seek to impress indelibly upon every human heart the true doctrines of the rights of man." The rhetorical strategy described by Whittier—moral suasion—presumed that slaveholders as well as Americans in general were at their core reasonable and virtuous. Once the evils of slavery were made apparent, it assumed, the public would pressure slaveholders, who, unwilling to withstand the pressure of public opinion, would emancipate their slaves. Petitioning fit well with the doctrine of moral suasion because it offered radical abolitionists a means to act immediately to seek emancipation by reshaping public opinion through mass moral appeals.[12]

In line with the tenets of moral suasion, in the first edition of the *Liberator,* published on January 1, 1831, Garrison urged readers to petition to rid the nation's capital of the "rotten plague" of slavery. He lamented the fact that hitherto "only a few straggling petitions, relative to this subject, have gone into Congress." They were too few, he concluded, "to denote much public anxiety, or to command a deferential notice." Garrison called on abolitionists to make a "vigorous and systematic" petitioning effort "from one end of the country to the other" to abolish slavery in the District of Columbia. A year later Garrison and eleven others formed the New England Anti-Slavery Society, pledging in its constitution, signed by seventy-two men (among whom about a quarter were free blacks), "to inform and correct public opinion" through a variety of methods, including petitioning. Early in 1832 the president and secretary of the society sent a petition to Congress for the immediate abolition of slavery in the District of Columbia, and in September the New Englanders prepared a petition for general circulation, which was published in the *Liberator.* Likewise, many other antislavery societies formed in New England and the West during the early 1830s incorporated pledges to petition in their founding documents.[13]

Petitioning was endorsed by abolitionist leaders at the national level in December 1833 at the founding convention of the American Anti-Slavery Society. Members resolved "to urge forward without delay" a petition to Congress for abolition in the District and named specific congressmen into whose hands the memorials should be entrusted. They also urged the president of the convention to write letters to members of Congress beseeching them to present petitions and to "fearlessly advocate" passage of abolition measures. The same issue of the *Liberator* that reported the new national organization's pledge to petition also reminded those already engaged in gathering signatures to send in their petitions. There would probably be 3,000 signatures on the memorial from Boston and vicinity, the paper reported, but it cautioned that the petitions undoubtedly would be referred to a committee of slaveholders and that "nothing favorable to the cause of freedom can be expected from those who traffic in human flesh."[14]

* * *

By the end of 1833, then, American antislavery men had embraced petitioning as a powerful weapon in the campaign for abolition of slavery. Based on a tradition of petitioning that antedated the founding of the nation, state, regional, and local societies of male abolitionists circulated petitions and sent thousands of signatures to Congress. Yet few of those signatures were women's.[15] In fact, judging from the records of Congress, only one antislavery petition sent to Congress before 1834 was signed by women. That petition was prompted in 1831 by Nat Turner's rebellion, in which fifty-one white Virginians were killed, which caused waves of fear and anxiety to sweep through the slaveholding South. So distressed by the uprising were white women of Fluvanna County, Virginia, that they petitioned the state assembly to end slavery so that when their menfolk were absent from home, women and children could be free of the fear of slave revolt.[16] Concern over the events in Virginia extended to the North, where Quaker preacher Lucretia Mott called together women of the Philadelphia Society of Friends to discuss "the propriety" of petitioning Congress. A committee of six women—Mary Earle, Mary Ann Jackson, Mary Sharpless, Alice Eliza Betts, and Leah Fell—was charged with coordinating the effort. The resulting petition stated that the women commiserated with "that portion of citizens of these United States, who are held in bondage." The women not only claimed to petition for the slave but stated that their "sympathies [were] also enlisted on behalf of the Slaveholder, on many of whom this evil is entailed, and who are involved in increased difficulties by the recent lamentable occurrences." The object of their petition was to pray Congress to abolish slavery in the District of Columbia, an act they believed would "have a happy influence on the Legislatures of the southern states."[17]

The Philadelphia women knew full well what they risked. "Your Memorialists are aware that at this juncture our attempts may be considered intrusive," they wrote, "but we approach you unarmed; our only banner is Peace." Ultimately the petition and its circulators won the signatures of 2,312 women. Upon sending the petition to Congress, the committee attached a letter that addressed the propriety of women petitioning on the explosive issue of slavery. In a humble, almost apologetic tone the women expressed confidence that congressmen would discern that "nothing less than a deep conviction of the necessity of the measure your petitioners would recommend, could have induced them to appear in this public manner." Although the petition from the Females of the State of Pennsylvania ultimately was tabled, it won the attention of male abolitionists. Printed in the *Liberator* of February 18, 1832, without comment, the women's petition was afforded a rather mixed, if not odd, commentary the following week: "If the spirit which actuates these fair ones of Philadelphia, should become general, the slaveholding states might well tremble for the fate of their institutions." But recognition of the potential power of female petitioning was followed by the ambiguous observation that if women entered politics in this way, citizens would have to "fill the House with such old bachelors as have shown themselves capable of resisting the formidable array of bright eyes and witching smiles."[18]

The Philadelphia women's petition proved at once unusual and representative of the relationship between antislavery women and petitioning before 1834. It was, on one hand, atypical because although petitioning had become a main feature in the activism of proliferating male antislavery societies, women sympathetic to the cause refrained from sending their names to Congress. The actions of the Quaker women defied the long-standing custom of women limiting their petitions to individual requests for personal grievances and marked the first instance of women petitioning collectively against slavery. By aiming to arouse discussion of ending slavery within the context of heightened fear of slave insurrection, the petitioners created the potential for disruption and disunion and, in so doing, risked being viewed by congressmen and members of their local communities as subversive. Yet, on the other hand, the response the petition provoked from the *Liberator* displayed abolitionists' typical ambivalent attitudes about the expansion of female activism in the movement. While the newspaper acknowledged that women's petitioning might have a marked effect, it denigrated the nature of this form of activism as mere flirtation. The risks evident in the rhetoric of the Philadelphia petition and the response it received from the *Liberator* amounted to two powerful restraints that deterred women from petitioning before 1834: the radical nature of immediate abolitionism and the radical departure from established norms of female petitioning.

The extremism of affiliating with abolitionists by signing a petition cannot be underestimated. To publicly declare oneself an abolitionist in the 1830s was to align with a small and despised minority. One placed oneself at the fringes of middle-class society and even risked the distinct possibility of violence against one's person. By raising an issue most Americans preferred to ignore, attacking a system that provided the basis of the national economy, questioning the very foundation of U.S. government, and advocating racial equality, immediate abolitionists professed to seek not just reform but massive restructuring of the social, economic, and political order. As such, abolitionists found themselves at the extreme end of the spectrum of antebellum reform movements. They not uncommonly incurred the disapproval, if not the wrath, of neighbors and even other reformers. Besides risking social rejection, persons who espoused immediate abolition also courted retributive violence. In 1835 alone, abolitionists endured thirty-seven mob attacks. In August of that year Lydia Maria Child reported that "very large sums" were being offered to anyone who would convey visiting British abolitionist George Thompson to the slave states. That same year Garrison fell victim to a mob that beset a meeting of the Boston Female Anti-Slavery Society. Rioters smashed through doors, captured Garrison, and dangled him from a window. The mob then fastened a rope around his waist and led him through the streets to city hall, where he was committed to a cell for disturbing the peace. Even the Yankee metropolis of New York was unsafe for abolitionists, for according to Child, $5,000 had been offered on the New York Stock Exchange for the head of leading antislavery philanthropist Arthur Tappan. The father of James Birney, a slaveholder turned abolitionist, warned that should he return to Kentucky, he would be murdered. Neither did antislavery literature escape the scorn of southerners. After learning that abolition materials were in the mail, a mob broke into the Charleston post office and made a bonfire of the sacks containing the offending literature. The flames illuminated the hanging effigies of Garrison and Tappan.[19]

While women were deterred from signing antislavery petitions for fear of disapproval and even violence from those hostile to the movement, their reticence was compounded by directives from within the movement about appropriate gender behavior. "You are called anew to the field of action," announced an appeal in the Ladies' Department of the *Liberator* in March 1832. "Some of you may plead the effeminacy of your sex, and some — mental inferiority; but oh! This is nothing else than mockery." The paper urged females to "firmly step in and fill our ranks" and instructed them to "arm your fathers and brothers with the patriotic feelings of liberty and equal rights." While the appeal called women "into the field of action," they were instructed to limit their efforts to indirectly influencing male relatives. There was no explicit call for women to petition, and the directive to sway fathers and brothers implied that women should confine their efforts well short of the halls of Congress. Likewise, "An Address to the Daughters of New England" published in the *Liberator* on March 3, 1832, commanded, "Think not because ye are women, that ye can take no part in the glorious cause of emancipation." "You have influence — exert it." Yet nowhere in the address did the author mention the idea of women petitioning.[20]

The absence of direct calls for women to petition was accompanied by articles and poems in antislavery newspapers during the late 1820s and early 1830s that praised women as silent creatures of sympathy and virtue. The sickroom, the *Liberator* described in 1831, was where one could behold woman at her "loveliest, most attractive point of view." There she moved with "noiseless step" and was "firm, without being harsh; tender, yet not weak; active, yet quiet; gentle, patient, uncomplaining, vigilant." *Freedom's Journal*, a free black newspaper, warned in 1827 that "a woman who would attempt to thunder with her tongue, would not find her eloquence to increase her domestic happiness." The next year the paper described the perfect wife as possessing a low, soft, musical voice "not formed to rule in public assemblies but to charm those who can distinguish a company from a crowd." The greatest advantage of such a voice, the *Journal* said, was that "you must come close to her to hear it." These writings reinforced the notion that the ideal woman was neither a public speaker nor a petitioner to Congress but, rather, a nursemaid and a silent helpmate.[21]

To portrayals of the sacrificing and silent female were added vivid warnings that the "fair sex" lacked the powers of deliberation and was ruled by the passions. "With reason somewhat weaker" than that of men, observed the *Liberator* in April 1831, women "have to contend with passions somewhat stronger." Prevailing notions about the danger of woman's suasive powers were evident in a poem published in the *Liberator* on January 15, 1831, titled "The Powers of Woman":

They charge! they charge! Oh! God, not *foe* to *foe*,
  But *friend* to *friend*—brother 'gainst brother's spear;
Knights to the self-same device bending low,
  Together rush—and meet in full career.
The shout of triumph—and the shriek of woe,
  The victor and the vanquish'd—all are here.
Why deck thee, man, with fratricidal spoils?
Gaze on the throne: he kneels—A WOMAN SMILES.

Strange wizard being! deem'd of weak estate,
  Yet with thy rod thou rulest sea and shore.
Man, scorner of fire—flood—wrestler with fate—
  Foil'd by thy magic charms—is man no more.
Sapp'd by thy love, or by thy withering hate,
  Palace and tower have groan'd and totter'd o'er.
Peasant and despot, all, enslav'd and free,
Have spurn'd thy name; and spurning, kneel'd to thee!

The poem concluded by reminding the reader that it was Cleopatra who caused the fall of Caesar and Eve who brought about the fall of man. Recapitulating the poem's theme, the closing line captured deep-seated fears about woman's suasive powers: "Woman! man's keenest scourge—man's kindest nurse; Thou art his blessing—yet thou art his curse!"[22]

Directives that women should remain silent and warnings about their propensity for deception were reinforced in antislavery newspapers by descriptions of the horrid fate that would befall outspoken women. In 1827, *Freedom's Journal* published the ironic tale of Tabitha Wilson, who according to the storyteller named Ned, was talented and beautiful but was "compelled to remain in a state of maidenhood." Why, asked Ned, was Tabitha deserted by beau after beau? "She had a tongue, that was indeed—a tongue." In one instance a man left Tabitha and married another girl "who took such particular care of that unruly member, the tongue, that all who saw her, regretted she used it so little." How did Tabitha cope with the loss of her lover? "She neither sighed, nor swooned, nor uttered hysterical laughs, . . . but her tongue went clickety, clack, click clack, until you would have sworn that the long-hidden doctrine of perpetual motion had been discovered, and that this honor was to Miss Tabitha Wilson, spinster, who had accidentally made the discovery, in the daily use and exercise of her tongue." Ned recounted that Tabitha's "faculty of tongue moving" increased with age until she "degenerated into a most venomous backbiting old maid" whom a jury eventually found guilty of slander. Ned concluded his tale with a stern warning:

> Young ladies, have you tongues? Beware how you conduct them. The tongue is a little thing to be sure, but a little axe will cut down a great tree. And a little tongue, in the mouth of a slanderous woman is sharper than a serpent's tooth. I speak this to you out of pure benevolence. I love you all, and I love to see you imparting smiles, 'mid the domestic hearth. It is your province. — You were made to soothe the toils, and cares of man's laborious life; to be his partner in affliction, his comforter in trouble, not the destroyer of his happiness and the ruin of his hopes.

The *Liberator* went so far as to remind readers that "women do not transgress the bounds of decorum so often as men; but when they do, they go [to] greater lengths. . . . Besides, a female by transgression forfeits her place in society forever; if once she falls, it is the fall of Lucifer." [23]

Given the negative attitudes, even among radical abolitionists, about women raising their voices in public debate, both black and white middle-class women eschewed petitioning in favor of other types of antislavery activism, especially boycotting the products of slave labor. As early as 1806 Alice Jackson Lewis of Chester County, Pennsylvania, urged members of the Philadelphia Friends Women's Yearly Meeting to avoid purchasing the products of slave labor. The American free produce movement was bolstered by widely circulated pamphlets published in 1824 and 1828 by British abolitionist Elizabeth Heyrick calling for boycotts of slave products. Women's boycotting efforts were further encouraged in 1826 when Elizabeth Margaret Chandler began writing a regular column in Lundy's *Genius of Universal Emancipation* in which she often sounded the free produce call. In 1829 two societies were organized to promote the use of free products: the Female Association for Promoting the Manufacture and Use of Free Cotton, formed in Philadelphia, and the Colored Female Free Produce Society of Pennsylvania, begun by the women of the Bethel African Methodist Episcopal Church. Between 1817 and 1862 some fifty-three free produce stores, at least five of which were run by women, were opened around the country. Boycotting slave-made goods was a favored activity among female abolitionists not only because it attacked the economic core of slavery but also, as Margaret Hope Bacon explains, because it was "one of the very few avenues open to women to express their opposition to slavery." [24]

Even when women formed antislavery societies during the early 1830s, they initially turned away from petitioning and confined their efforts to boycotting, fund raising, and educating free blacks. The Boston Female Anti-Slavery Society, organized in October 1833, pledged in its constitution to "aid and assist" the antislavery movement "as far as lies within our power." By this they meant disseminating antislavery propaganda and improving the "moral and intellectual character" of the community's free blacks. The society, composed of black and white women, met only four times a year and was initially "more a symbolic than a truly functional organization." It operated primarily as an auxiliary to the male-run Massachusetts Anti-Slavery Society by contributing funds and serving as audience members at the men's meetings. Likewise, members of the Ladies' New York City Anti-Slavery Society, organized in 1835, did not petition initially but focused their energies on the moral improvement of free blacks. The Philadelphia Female Anti-Slavery Society, on the other hand, was composed almost entirely of Quaker women, both black and white, who had developed a tradition of public speaking and social activism. While this group did begin some petitioning in 1834, their main goal before then was to assist in educating free blacks.[25]

Associations composed exclusively of African American women followed a similar course and did not petition during the 1820s and early 1830s. The earliest organizations of free black women were devoted to raising money to support churches, Masonic orders, and mutual aid societies formed by men in the 1780s and 1790s. When female benevolent organizations multiplied during the 1820s, African American women formed societies devoted to aiding those in need, to achieving intellectual improvement, and to accomplishing social change. Benevolent associations such as the Female Branch of Zion and the United Daughters of Conference, both of New York City, focused on aiding the sick, burying the dead, and supporting widows and orphans. Many African American women, particularly Philadelphians, also belonged to female literary societies. Although aimed partly at the self-improvement of their members, these societies also sought to benefit the entire race and to promote the cause of emancipation. Yet like most other female organizations, they did not petition Congress against slavery during the 1820s and early 1830s.[26]

Despite the fact that the antislavery press prescribed a role for women in the movement that stopped short of petitioning, by the mid-1830s a number of forces were at work that would weaken constraints against women's antislavery petitioning. The foundation for this shift had been laid in part by the 1830 campaign to block removal of the Cherokee from Georgia. During the mid-1830s, moreover, women were becoming increasingly involved in benevolent reform societies, which petitioned for incorporation and funding, and temperance women petitioned collectively to limit the approval of liquor licenses. Besides this experience petitioning local and state governments, the religious impulse behind immediate abolition provided women a rationale for expanding their antislavery activism to include petitioning Congress. Like many men who committed themselves to abolition, women commonly embraced the cause after undergoing dramatic conversion experiences fostered by evangelical revivals. Others located their duty to end slavery in the doctrines of Quakerism, Universalism, and Unitarianism. These commitments were intensified by widely held beliefs that women were more religious and more virtuous than men, which implied that women possessed a moral duty to reform the world. The ideology of female moral superiority expanded women's sense of their social duties and held radical possibilities for justifying their expanded activism. Women could convincingly rationalize broadening the scope of their abolition work on the particularly feminine grounds that because slaveowners repeatedly assaulted the virtue of female slaves and tore mothers from their children, it was especially women's duty to eradicate slavery from the Christian nation. Immediate abolitionists' philosophy of moral suasion, moreover, provided an opportunity for female reformers to attempt to influence federal policy, even though they lacked the vote, by reforming public sentiment.[27]

By 1834 a variety of factors, including the growing use of petitioning by female activists and the call of religious duty, enabled a number of antislavery women to expand their activism and join men in petitioning Congress. That year women sent a dozen petitions; in 1835 they sent nine, and in 1836 they amassed eighty-four.[28] The growing frequency of female antislavery petitioning was supported by three events during 1830–35 that led women to become more comfortable with the idea of petitioning Congress and convinced male abolition leaders of the benefits of enlisting women in petition drives. First was the campaign to end slavery in the British dominions, in which hundreds of thousands of British women signed petitions from 1830 to 1833. Though before 1830 British abolitionist leaders neither condoned nor encouraged women's petitioning against slavery, they eventually realized that women's signatures could substantially bolster petitioning campaigns. With the help of women, from 1831 to 1833 antislavery activists submitted 5,020 petitions to Parliament. The petitions presented in 1833 alone bore the signatures of 298,785 women, nearly a quarter of the total number of names. A large portion of the female signatures—187,157—were ascribed to a single petition circulated by the London Female Anti-Slavery Society for only ten days and without mention in the abolitionist press. The massive petition was presented to the House of Commons on May 14, 1833, the day the Emancipation Bill was introduced. Abolitionist George Stephen described it as a "huge featherbed of a petition, hauled into the House by four members amidst shouts of applause and laughter."[29]

Presentation of the female petitions to Parliament set the stage for American women to enter the ranks of petitioners. Garrison, who was on a mission to England on behalf of the New England Anti-Slavery Society, witnessed presentation of the national petition signed by some 187,000 women, which, he wrote, "excited considerable sensation and some merriment. . . . Cheers for the Ladies of Great Britain!" It is entirely probable that Garrison had in mind the success of British women's petitioning efforts when, after returning to the United States in September 1833, he issued a call for signatures and especially urged that "the ladies, too, and the free people of color, should unite in this good work." The petitioning feats of English women abolitionists were also cited in 1833 by Lydia Maria Child, an American novelist turned abolitionist, in her *Appeal in Favor of That Class of Americans Called Africans.* "*Sixty thousand* petitions have been addressed to the English parliament, a large number of them signed by women," Child claimed inaccurately. Though she admitted that it would be "useless and injudicious" to remonstrate for the abolition of slavery in the United States in general, Child proclaimed that with respect to slavery in the District of Columbia, "it is the duty of the citizens to petition year after year, until a reformation is effected."[30]

The potential for American women's petitioning was fostered also by reactions to the persecution of a Connecticut Quaker woman, Prudence Crandall, who with the help of the American Anti-Slavery Society had opened her school to free black girls. Outraged white residents of Canterbury, where the school was located, convinced the legislature to enact a law prohibiting education for out-of-state blacks. Despite the law Crandall continued to teach and was jailed three times, though her convictions were reversed. When town residents failed to close the school through legal means, they blocked Crandall's source of supplies, filled her well with manure, and finally, burned the school building. Although Crandall endured for almost a year, she eventually left town. The events in Canterbury angered abolitionists, and late in July 1833 the *Emancipator* published an *Appeal to the Females of the United States in Behalf of Miss Prudence Crandall*, which deplored the "elements of moral evil" that were "powerfully at work in the midst of us." To what "earthly influence" could the people look to save the country from "the most dismal scene," the writer asked, "but to the gentle yet firm remonstrances of WOMAN?" The appeal urged women to make their voices heard. *"Why should not the legislature of Connecticut ... be respectfully* MEMORIALIZED *by the females of every mountain glen, and hamlet in the United States, for the repeal of this most disgraceful enactment against* FEMALE *effort for* FEMALE *improvement?"* Although the outcry did little to secure Crandall's school to educate young black women, the events in Canterbury provided a rallying point for female abolitionists and set a precedent for petitioning on behalf of other women.[31]

Crandall's sacrifices inspired Scottish women to sponsor British abolitionist George Thompson's lecture tour in the United States, which succeeded in fueling American women's interest in antislavery and especially in petitioning. Beginning in August 1834, for fifteen months Thompson traveled throughout New England, where he lectured about abolitionism to huge crowds and persuaded women to form antislavery societies, many of which took up the work of petitioning. After he spoke to a group of women in Providence, Rhode Island, for instance, they formed a ladies' antislavery society, and 106 women signed its constitution. A year later, in their first annual report, the ladies were still praising Thompson: "When our friend and fellow-helper *George Thompson,* of England, came among us, and pled the rights of the poor, down-trodden slave, his pathos charmed us, and his eloquence riveted the eye and the mind of every hearer upon himself and his subject." In the autumn of 1836 the society agreed that petitioning Congress deserved their "hearty cooperation."[32]

By 1835 American abolitionists recognized the important role women could play in the petition campaign. Previous appeals to women, as we have seen, urged them to pray, to boycott the products of slave labor, and to employ female influence to convince male relatives of the evils of slavery. These calls, with few exceptions, stopped short of ordering women to influence public opinion directly on the subject of slavery. In 1835, however, abolitionist leaders began to exhort women to exercise their right of petition. The *New England Spectator* charged in March that "every man and woman in the northern states, who does not petition Congress to do something, and who does not pray for the extermination of slavery in the District of Columbia, is guilty of the sin of perpetuating slavery in the District of Columbia." In calling on abolitionists to petition that fall, the *Liberator* stated, "Let not our female friends forget that on them we rely for powerful and efficient aid in this work."[33]

An even stronger plea for women to embark on petitioning came from John M. Putnam, pastor of the Congregational Church in Dunbarton, New Hampshire, who on Christmas 1835 addressed the Female Anti-Slavery Society of Concord. "The united voice of females would immediately turn the scale of popular opinion from its present wrong bias, and place it on the side of truth and righteousness," he proclaimed. Abolition of slavery in the British dominions, the clergyman said, was won "in no small degree" thanks to the petitioning activities of women. When the petition containing 187,000 female signatures was presented, "the question was decided, that slavery must cease. It was said in Parliament, on the reception of this *weighty* petition, — 'It is now time for us to act, since the women have come thundering at our doors!'" Women "turned the scale" in England by petitioning, Putnam explained, because "ladies" possessed "the keys to truth and righteousness" as well as an "immense influence." Therefore, he told the Concord women, "a vast responsibility rests upon females, when any good cause is to be carried forward."[34]

*　*　*

As Putnam's entreaty demonstrates, by 1835 the limits of female antislavery activism were being significantly renegotiated. Emphasis on the importance of public opinion in Jacksonian political culture as well as the abolitionists' strategy of moral suasion had elevated petitioning to the top position in the antislavery movement's arsenal of propaganda. In the moral universe constructed within abolitionist rhetoric, both men and women were to be found guilty of the sin of slavery if they failed to employ all means at their disposal to bring about an end to human bondage. Deeply motivated by Christian commitment to stamp out the sin of slavery from the soul of the nation and recognizing the effectiveness of petitioning, many immediate abolitionists grew impatient with social prescriptions against women petitioning. While a few women began to petition Congress against slavery in 1834, it would be yet another year before female antislavery leaders articulated a full-fledged justification of this innovation in women's activism. Then women petitioners would "come thundering" at the doors of Congress.

During the winter of 1835 Hannah H. Smith of Glastenbury, New York, obtained a petition printed by an antislavery society in her state asking Congress to abolish slavery in the District of Columbia. After affixing her name, she convinced her relatives, Julia E. and Nancy L. Smith, to support the plea by signing their names. The petition then made its way to Pamela and Sarah Hale and then to Mrs. Joseph Wells and her circle of Lucy, Clarissa, Abigail, and Maria. By the time the petition had progressed through town, signatures had been added by clusters of women from various families such as the Collinses, the Hollisters, the Hales, and the Williamses. Elsewhere in the state the women of Marshfield were engaged in similar activities as 107 females scribbled their names on a printed petition form bearing the same words as the Glastenbury petition and sent it off to Representative John Quincy Adams.

During the winter of 1835 and the spring of 1836 the Smiths, the Hales, the Williamses, and other New York women lent their names to a form of petition that designated signers as "ladies" and depicted them "humbly" approaching congressmen. The message they sent Congress was expressed in a mere fifteen lines of print, nine of which were devoted to justifying the unusual behavior of women petitioning Congress on an issue of national policy. The lady petitioners acknowledged "that scenes of party and political strife are not the field to which a kind and wise Providence [had] assigned them." The women promised that they "would not appear thus publicly, in a way which, to some, may seem a departure from their place." They assured the congressmen that if the issue were "any matter of merely political interest," they would remain "silent." Nevertheless, they were petitioning Congress, they explained, not because it was proper for women to do so but because it was necessary. They were compelled to instruct congressmen, the petition disclosed, because "the weak and innocent are denied the protection of law" and "all the sacred ties of domestic life are sundered for the gratification of avarice." Knowing of these moral wrongs, the petitioners stated, "they cannot but regard it as their duty to supplicate for the oppressed those common rights of humanity."[1]

These 1835 petitions constitute examples of what can be viewed as the first of four major phases of women's antislavery petitioning. In this initial phase from 1831 to 1836, before passage of the gag rule, women used long forms, often a full page of single-spaced type. Many of these forms were written exclusively for women and employed deferential language to justify the propriety of women petitioning against slavery. In the second phase from 1837 to 1840, abolitionists adopted short, single-sentence forms that could be read quickly on the floor of the House before they were declared out of order. These short forms left no room for elaborate justifications of women's right to petition and, because they made little or no reference to the gender of the petitioners, were signed by both men and women. After the split of the American Anti-Slavery Society (AASS) in 1840 until passage of the Kansas-Nebraska Act in 1854, women's petitioning entered a third phase when control of the campaign shifted to the hands of Representative John Quincy Adams. After 1840 women's antislavery petitioning declined precipitously, though thousands of women continued to lend their names to memorials decrying the Fugitive Slave Law, the annexation of Texas, and the extension of slavery into the territories. By 1854, when women from throughout the expanding nation petitioned against passage of the Kansas-Nebraska Act, the language of their petitions had become much bolder than it had been during the initial phase in the early 1830s. The final surge of women's antislavery petitioning occurred from 1861 through 1865 when hundreds of thousands of women responded to appeals by the Woman's National Loyal League to sign petitions requesting emancipation of the slaves and passage of the Thirteenth Amendment.

During the first period of women's antislavery petitioning from 1831 to 1836, the rhetoric employed in petitions designed specifically to win female signatures attempted to cloak the political nature of signing and circulating memorials. As women crossed into new terrain by petitioning their political representatives in hopes of influencing debate on a national issue, their petitions employed a rhetoric not of newly found political authority but of humility and disavowal. Rather than invoking natural rights principles and demanding the right to petition, over and over again women described their actions as motivated by Christian duty and as an extension of the religious speech act of prayer. As products of the abolitionist crusade, moreover, many women's petitions were infused with republican and free labor rhetoric aimed at constructing a uniquely northern middle-class conception of citizenship, a conception that relied heavily on notions of virtue and thus elevated the power of woman.

* * *

Among the earliest female antislavery petitioning efforts was that of the self-titled ladies of New York who during the summer of 1834 attended mixed-race and mixed-sex antislavery meetings that inspired and organized the circulation of petitions. These women were especially courageous in soliciting signatures, for they defied criticism of the propriety of their behavior as well as threats of violence. When on July 8, 1834, about 50 free blacks of both sexes met with about 100 whites to discuss abolition, the rabidly antiabolitionist *Morning Courier and New York Enquirer* lamented that "white women were, we are sorry to say, among the latter." The editor warned "the colored people of this city" against attending another antislavery meeting scheduled that evening: "No one who saw the temper which pervaded last night, can doubt, that if the blacks continue to allow themselves to be made the tools of a few blind zealots, the consequences to them will be most serious." As predicted, and probably because the *Courier* fanned the flames of prejudice, riots erupted that night. The mob attempted to vandalize the dry goods store of Arthur Tappan, president of the AASS, but was thwarted by a watchman. Unable to lay their hands on Tappan, the crowd turned its anger on free blacks. The African Church on Center Street and the adjoining home of its minister were vandalized as were homes in the free black neighborhood of Five Points. The mob even attacked the Mutual Relief Society Hall on Orange Street, and one black man was robbed of $192, four watches, and several other articles. Despite violence aimed at free blacks in retribution for antislavery activities and the accompanying threat against whites associated with abolitionism, the New York women persisted in circulating an antislavery petition and won 800 signatures.[2]

That same year elsewhere in the northern states, significant numbers of women began to circulate abolition petitions. Early in 1834, 218 women of Jamaica, Massachusetts, and vicinity asked Congress to enact laws to prevent the slave trade in the District of Columbia and to educate the District's black children. Months later women in neighboring Boston instructed Congress "to declare every person coming into the District free." Also in 1834 members of the Philadelphia Female Anti-Slavery Society began circulating petitions asking Congress to abolish slavery, and a year later the organization formalized plans for circulating petitions for abolition of slavery in the District of Columbia and federal territories. On the frontier of Ohio on February 18, 1834, Mary Ladd joined Henry Ladd, Hannah Harrison joined Miles Harrison, and Eliza Coe joined Lot B. Coe in signing an antislavery petition sent to Congress. About five months later Chloe Richmond shepherded another abolition petition through the women's circles of Harrisville, Ohio.[3]

By the spring of 1836 antislavery petitions were circulating in New York, Connecticut, Maine, New Hampshire, Vermont, Rhode Island, Pennsylvania, New Jersey, Massachusetts, and Ohio. Unlike British abolitionists who employed handwritten petitions, a method that implied spontaneous requests from individual citizens, in the United States officers of both male and female antislavery societies wrote and then usually printed petitions in newspapers and on handbills. British abolitionist Harriet Martineau credited Maria Weston Chapman, a leader in the Boston Female Anti-Slavery Society, with drawing up a form of petition circulated widely throughout Massachusetts as well as other New England states. Chapman's petition, which Martineau deemed "a fair specimen of the multitudes of petitions from women which have been piled up under the tables of Congress," decried the sinfulness of slavery and asked Congress not only to abolish slavery in the District of Columbia but also "to declare every human being free who sets foot upon its soil." It concluded with a pledge to present the same petition to Congress every year, "that it may at least be a 'memorial of us,' that in the holy cause of Human Freedom 'we have done what we could.'"[4]

Although thousands of women signed antislavery petitions from 1834 to 1836, and although hundreds of separate petitions were circulated, many appeals said exactly the same thing. Sometimes several petitions of the same form were circulated throughout a county and then returned to a petition committee whose members glued the lists of signatures together and topped them with one copy of the form. Other times signed copies of the same form of petition were sewn together with red string. Commonly a single form of petition circulated throughout a state and even through all northern states. For example, the message that the slave trade constituted piracy was sent to Congress in 1836 on identical petitions signed by Patience Chandler in Ohio and Susan Roe in New York.[5]

Published forms enabled abolitionists not only to circulate large numbers of petitions but also to take advantage of typographical techniques such as bold print and capital letters to call attention to the most important elements of their petition. Lest there be any question as to the nature of the document presented to potential signers or congressmen, the forms often were headed by the word "PETITION" in large, thick letters. Set apart from the text by white space and printed usually in italics or large, upper-case letters came the address: "TO THE HONORABLE THE SENATE AND HOUSE OF REPRESENTATIVES OF THE UNITED STATES OF AMERICA." Also set off from the text and often italicized were a line or two indicating the origin of the petition, such as, "*The petition of the undersigned Ladies of the County of Orange respectfully sheweth.*" Because forms were printed for mass circulation and were used in many different towns and several different states, the printer left blanks for those who circulated the petition to write in the city from whence it originated (for example, "The petition of the undersigned Ladies of _____ humbly sheweth").

Many of the petition forms circulated from 1834 to 1836 immediately indicated whether the petitions emanated from men or women. Petitions printed for women's signatures represented subscribers as "Ladies," "Females," and "Women," while those printed for men's signatures denoted the signers as "Citizens," "Electors," and "Voters." When women could not obtain a petition crafted specifically for their sex, they employed standard petitions that represented the signers as "citizens." But from 1834 to 1836 at least, women understood that it would be controversial to describe themselves as citizens, so they commonly scratched out the label "citizen" and replaced it with "women" or "ladies." When women signed petitions with men, it could no longer be asserted that the memorial came from citizens. Faced with this situation, canvassers sought a term to represent the status of the signers. Because it was too awkward to write something like "citizens and their female relatives and neighbors," the petitioners settled for "inhabitants" or "residents" of a certain town.

These labels encoded the perceived political status of potential signers, their authority to instruct elected representatives, and their expectations about how heavily their requests would be weighed. The distinct contrast between labels male and female petitioners applied to themselves is telling. Male abolition petitioners, most of whom were white and enfranchised, asserted their status as voters, electors, and citizens. Female petitioners, however, avoided naming their relationship to the state in the same way as men by consciously rejecting the label citizen. Instead the majority of women presented themselves and expected to be heard as ladies, females, and female citizens. What these differences in naming make clear is that antislavery petitioners understood women to possess a form of citizenship distinct from that of men—a citizenship modified by femaleness.

The hierarchy of gender status in the republic conveyed by the titles subscribers gave to themselves was reinforced by the manner in which the petitions were signed. Throughout the 1830s antislavery petitioners took great pains to maintain strict separation between the signatures of male and female signers. Typeset forms often labeled the left column MALES and the right column FEMALES. Even when the titles were absent and even when canvassers glued several sheets to the bottom of the petition, men signed in the left column, while women signed in the right. This practice might be accounted for as a logical ramification of the ideology of separate spheres; women's signatures were not intermingled with men's because they would be a record of improper sexual mixing. Such behavior would have been construed as promiscuous, and the indecorous petition would have been ejected from Congress.

That explanation is inadequate, however, in light of the fact that a number of forms contain three columns of signatures. In such cases the third column is reserved for minors, and there the names of boys and girls are mixed indiscriminately. Abolitionists separated the names of men from those of women and minors, we may conclude, because they believed that men's signatures—the marks of full, voting citizens—carried greater weight in the eyes of their democratic representatives than those of women, girls, and males too young to vote. We can also conclude that abolitionists thought that adult females were distinct from children. Indeed, on some petitions the columns were labeled LEGAL VOTERS and LADIES. Because the rule of maintaining the separation was almost never violated and instructions to keep men's signatures distinct were often repeated, it appears that men expected that their requests would be heard in stronger tones than would the pleas of women. Apparently women recognized that they approached their representatives wielding a power different from that of men.[6]

The purpose of male and female antislavery petitions from 1831 to 1836 was nevertheless the same: to convince congressmen to agree with the request that slavery and the slave trade be ended. Short of provoking Congress to pass an emancipation measure, abolitionists hoped that a constant stream of petitions would stir debate over slavery that would be reported in newspapers and influence public opinion. To meet either of these goals, abolitionists recognized that they must limit the requests of their petitions to the District of Columbia because in 1789 Congress had decided that it possessed no control over slavery in the individual states. Petitions that touched on the regulation of slavery in the states were rejected immediately on the grounds that they were unconstitutional. In response antislavery activists narrowed the focus of their petition campaign to the District, knowing that most representatives recognized the absolute authority of the states but agreed that Congress was charged with legislating for the District. The ladies of New York, for instance, stated in their 1835 petition, "We understand that this District is under the sole jurisdiction of the National Government, who are fully authorized to mold, according to their own will, the provisions of its legislation." The women also made clear that their intention was not to bid Congress to transcend the constitutional limits of its powers. "It is to the exercise of no doubtful, or contested prerogative that we would move you. With the sovereignty of state rights we ask you not to intermeddle."[7]

In addition to Congress, antislavery petitions were aimed at another important audience: potential signers. After all, the canvasser's first task was to convince women to sign petitions. Failure to justify female petitioning to members of the public among whom petitions were circulated would result undoubtedly in women rejecting entreaties to sign for fear that their reputations would be compromised. Convincing women to sign was no small task because besides the campaign against Cherokee removal, no precedent existed for women's collective petitioning of Congress. While women's organizations such as the New York Female Benevolent Society, which sought the charitable goal of building a state-funded asylum for "wandering women," carried out their petitioning relatively unhampered, the petitioning of antislavery women differed from that of women's charitable societies. Petitions from charitable societies were almost always limited to seeking money for the poor from local governing bodies. Female antislavery petitions, by contrast, addressed distant male representatives with the goal of instructing them how to deal with the national controversy over slavery. While petitions of benevolent groups encoded an act of humbly requesting or begging a favor from legislators, those from female abolitionists inscribed the action of telling male representatives what to do.[8]

Besides this implicit assertion of political power, women's antislavery petitions were liable to criticism as a result of the cause they advanced. Immediate abolitionism was at the radical or "ultraist" extreme of antebellum reform movements. Motivated by religious zeal, male and female abolitionists alike sought to dismantle the institution of slavery and to effect a moral reconstruction of society. Many other women were involved in less drastic reform efforts, such as tract societies, which sought self-improvement or "perfectionism," while still others, almost exclusively the wealthy, undertook the traditional female work of charity, or "benevolence." These women drew little criticism for their efforts. Indeed, they were typically praised for meeting their womanly obligations by aiding the needy. Lori D. Ginzberg explains that the goals of ultraist women, among them abolitionists, "provided sufficient excuse for attacks by those who in other settings supported female organizing but who suddenly took a stand against women's public activity." In other words, women who signed anti-slavery petitions risked repudiation not only from those who desired to limit women's influence but also from those who wanted to arrest the growth of abolitionism.[9]

These rhetorical constraints necessitated that petitions be written in a manner that potential signers would find so appropriate that they would be comfortable conveying the expressed sentiments to their representatives in the exact words of the petition. Because no one person took credit for writing the petition, by ascribing her name, each signer assumed responsibility for its content. In this way each petition implied a multiple authorship because even though the petition was written by a single person, once it was signed by others, it became authorized as a message from dozens, if not hundreds or thousands, of individual women. A major rhetorical challenge for the authors of petitions, therefore, was to create within the petitions the ethos of those most likely to sign, so that signers could feel confident that the petitions embodied their personal ideas and language.

Far from intruding on the scene of politics, petitions depicted women as assuming a humble stance and politely seeking the attention of representatives rather than making political demands on male authorities. The tone of the petition submitted by the 800 women of New York, for example, was extremely complaisant. "That while we would not obtrude on your honorable body, the expression of our opinions on questions of mere pecuniary expediency or political economy," they said, "yet we conceive that there are occasions when the voice of female remonstrance and entreaty may properly be heard in the councils of great nation." The petitioners, who approached as ladies rather than citizens or voters, described themselves as "wives and daughters of American citizens," constituents who were a step removed from full citizenship. Drawing on the biblical story of Esther, the petitioners reminded their leaders that through-out history "female entreaties . . . have prevailed, even in the counsels of absolute monarchs, whose decrees 'from India to Ethiopia' have been sup-posed changeless as the laws of the Medes and Persians." The antislavery women said that they were compelled to address their leaders because they feared that the country had been dishonored and would be punished by God. They petitioned not from self-interest, the signers claimed, but for those who could not petition for themselves. Recognizing in every en-slaved woman a sister, said the New Yorkers, "[we] plead for her as we would plead for ourselves, our mothers, and our daughters. We plead for our suffering and abused sex."[10]

Perhaps the most deferential of all female antislavery petition forms was the "Fathers and Rulers of Our Country" form, which cultivated for its signers a stance of humility and supplication commensurate with the degree to which it was considered acceptable for women to attempt to in-struct their legislators. This form was signed by women from almost every northern state and was the most popular of all petition forms employed by abolitionists before 1837. Interestingly, authorship of this form has been attributed to Theodore Weld by the editors of his correspondence, who cite as evidence for this attribution the existence of a printed copy of the Fathers and Rulers form at the bottom of which was scribbled in Weld's handwriting, "T.D.W. 1834." Yet in January 1836 the *Emancipator*, the offi-cial organ of the AASS, attributed authorship of the Fathers and Rulers form to "a woman from North Carolina who was residing in Putnam, Ohio." Five months later the form was attached to the appeal published by the Female Anti-Slavery Society of Muskingham County, which met in Putnam. Although we cannot know for sure whether the petition was written by the North Carolina woman or by Weld, its rhetoric offers clues about what sort of claims and tone abolitionists believed would appeal to potential female signers.[11]

Unlike petitions signed exclusively by men, which were addressed "To the Honorable Senate and House," the Fathers and Rulers form replaced that appellation with "To the Fathers and Rulers of our Country." Such phrasing elevated the recipients from political representatives to even more powerful figures and diminished the petitioners from constituents to dependents. The text of the petition continued in this supplicatory vein, stating in its first line, "Suffer us, we pray you, with the sympathies which we are constrained to feel as wives, as mothers, and as daughters, to plead with you in behalf of a long oppressed and deeply injured class of native

To the Honourable Senate and House of Representatives of the United States, in Congress assembled, *Boston*

THE petition of the undersigned, ~~citizens~~ *Ladies* of *Massachusetts*, respectfully represents—That they consider the toleration of Slavery in the District of Columbia, as inconsistent with justice, humanity, and Christianity.

Your petitioners will not dwell upon the rights of six thousand fellow men, whom the laws of the United States, retain in abject servitude, or the physical, moral, and political evils which spring directly from Slavery. But, in addition to these reasons for the interference of Congress, the Domestic Slave Trade, of which this District is the seat, is an enormous abuse which calls loudly for redress. The District of Columbia is a great market to which human flesh and blood are almost daily sent for sale, from the neighbouring States, and there sold again to supply the markets of the more remote South. Your petitioners need not call to your recollection, the cruelties which accompany this traffic, the fetters which bind the Slaves, the whips with which they are driven, the auctions at which they are sold. These are sights often before your eyes. Public and private prisons in the District are crowded with the wretched subjects of this trade. Besides this, the permission of this traffic often leads to the enslaving of free men, who are sometimes kidnapped by violence, and sometimes sold under the laws which Congress permits.

The laws in relation to people of colour, which have been passed by the city of Washington, and suffered by Congress, are inhuman and disgraceful to a civilized community.

Your petitioners, therefore, pray, that Congress will, without delay, pass a statute to abolish, immediately, Slavery in the District of Columbia; to declare every person coming into the District free; to annul all the regulations and ordinances of any municipal corporation there, which make any distinction of right between persons of different colours; and to provide for the education of all coloured children in the District.

[signatures]

Women signers crossed out the word "citizens" in the address and inserted the term "ladies" on this form of petition circulated in Massachusetts during 1834 and presented to Congress in February 1835. (Courtesy of the National Archives)

To the Hon., the House of Representatives,
        and Senate of the United States:

We, the undersigned, citizens of *The Town of Lockport Niagara Co.* in the State of New York, believing that SLAVERY as it exists in America, is a heinous sin against God, and a flagrant violation of the rights of man, inconsistent with Christianity, with our Declaration of Independence, and with our Republican Institutions, impeding the march of liberal principles abroad; and detrimental to the interests and *subversive of the liberties of the labouring population of our republic*, at home; a reproach to us in the eyes of the world, and a national crime, exposing us to the judgements of Heaven, a fruitful source of sectional jealousy, perpetually tending to discord and disunion; a constant and increasing source of danger, which threatens every hour to involve us in a contest in which 'the Almighty has no attributes which could take sides with us,'—Do solemnly and importunely petition and implore your Honourable bodies, to take all measures within the scope of your constitutional powers, for the abatement and removal of this great evil.—By immediately abolishing Slavery and the Slave Trade in the District of Columbia and Territories subject to the jurisdiction of Congress, by prohibiting the internal and coasting Slave Trade between the several States and by taking effectual measures to prevent the exportation of Slaves from the United States and its territories to Texas, or the dominions of any foreign power.

Adults.

Minors	Males	Females
Nelson Titus	James Fisk	Jane Stewart
David Hall	George Young	Susan Fisk
John Galloway	John Robinson	Sarah Ear...
John Gill	James Cartwal	Mary Young
William Robertson	Patrick Rooney	Ellen Rooney
William S. Farnell	Isaac Griffin	Cynthia Day
Eliza Howe	King Allen	Mary J. Day
Joseph Howe	Jere Griswold	Eunice E. Abbot
Hiram Allen	Lyman Wheeler	Sarah Allen
Mary M. Abbot	Harry Kinsley	Parnel Allen
David Drain	Leonard Newbury	Agness Denvent
Daniel Skinner	James Mann	Almyra Johnson
Mary Drain	Richard Lowe	Lucy Griswold
D. S. Pratt	Short Kinney	Lucy Griswold
Henry Richardson	Daniel Bamford	Sarah Griswold
John Nickerson	Adam Bamford	Grace Newbury
Smith Raynolds	Richard Dale	Eliza Wherbury
Ephraim Tompson	Columbus Torr	Maryann Hare
		Ann Mann

Throughout the 1830s petition signers kept their signatures in separate columns based on their political status. While the names of minors of both sexes were combined, those of adult white males and females were separated because the signatures of electors were understood to carry greater weight with their representatives. (Courtesy of the National Archives)

PETITION OF LADIES, RESIDENT IN THE STATE OF OHIO.

Fathers, and Rulers of our Country:---

CONSTRAINED not only by our sympathy with the suffering, but also by a true regard for the honor and welfare of our beloved country, we beg leave to lay before you, this, our humble Memorial, in behalf of that oppressed and deeply injured class of native Americans, who reside within the limits of your exclusive jurisdiction. We should poorly estimate the virtues which ought ever to distinguish your honorable body, could we anticipate any other than a favorable hearing, when our appeal is to men, to philanthropists, to patriots, to the legislators and guardians of a christian people. We should be less than women, if the nameless wrongs of which the slaves of our sex, are made the defenceless victims, did not fill us with horror, and constrain us, in earnestness and agony of spirit, to pray for their deliverance. By day and by night, their woes and injuries rise up before us, throwing shades of mournful contrast over all the joys of domestic life, and filling our hearts with sadness, at the recollection of those whose hearths are desolate.

Nor do we forget, in the contemplation of their other sufferings, the intellectual and moral degration to which they are doomed! how the soul formed for companionship with Angels, is despoiled and brutified and consigned to ignorance, pollution and ruin.

Surely then, as the Representatives of a people, professedly Christian, you will bear with us, when we say with Jefferson, "we tremble for our country, when we remember that God is just, and that his justice cannot sleep forever;" and, when—in obedience to a divine command, "we *remember* those who are in bonds as bound with them." Impelled by these sentiments, we solemnly purpose, the grace of God assisting, to importune High Heaven with prayer, and our National Legislature with appeals, until this christian people abjure, forever, a traffic in the souls of men, and the groans of the oppressed no longer ascend to God from the dust where now they welter.

We do not ask your honorable body to transcend your Constitutional powers, by legislating on the subject of slavery within the boundaries of the slave-holding states—but we do conjure you, to abolish slavery in the District of Columbia, where you exercise "exclusive legislation." In the name of humanity, justice, equal rights, and impartial law, our country's weal, her honor, and her cherished hopes, we earnestly implore for this our humble petition, your favorable regard. If, both in Christian and Heathen lands, Kings have revoked their edicts at the intercession of woman, and Tyrants have relented when she appeared a suppliant for mercy, surely we may hope that the legislators of a free, enlightened and christian people, will not regard our prayer as "abominable, malicious and unrighteous," when the only boon we crave, is the deliverance of the fettered and the down trodden from the bondage under which they groan.

And as in duty bound, your petitioners will ever pray.

Eliza Ann McConnel
Rebecca Robison
Martha Bigger
Pamelia Woodruff
Eliza Bigger
Margret Parks
Nancy Wilson

Charlotte Patton
Jane Patton
Margret Robison
Sarah Bosserman
Margret McConnel
Martha Jane Long
Nancy Long
Martha Jane Powers

The Fathers and Rulers of Our Country form reigned as the most common antislavery petition used by women from 1834 until 1837. Although its authorship has been attributed to Theodore Weld, the Emancipator *printed the form in January 1836 and ascribed its authorship to a woman from North Carolina who was residing in Putnam, Ohio.*
(Courtesy of the National Archives)

Americans." Rather than directly stating why they approached their representatives, the petitioners begged and prayed to be heard. The signers implied that they were not even worthy of claiming their own thoughts but that they had been "constrained to feel" those thoughts by some unidentified outside force. After fawning, they switched to flattering: "We should poorly estimate the virtues which ought ever to distinguish your honorable body could we anticipate any other than a favorable hearing when our appeal is to men, to philanthropists, to patriots, to the legislators and guardians of a Christian people."[12]

This prayerful, supplicatory stance reflected the women's religious motivation for taking action against slavery. But it also functioned rhetorically to obfuscate the nature of their petitioning, which was public, political, and considered inappropriate for women, by aligning it with praying, which was private, religious, and regarded as entirely appropriate for females. These sentiments were evident in many of the petition forms circulated by women from 1834 to 1836, but nowhere were they more apparent than in the Fathers and Rulers form, which read like a public prayer and described signers as engaging in the speech act of praying. In its opening the petition employed and elaborated on the verb "to pray" twice in short compass. After listing numerous wrongs perpetrated against the slave, the Fathers and Rulers form restated that the petitioners were importuning "high Heaven with prayer, and our national legislatures with appeals," until "this christian people abjure forever a traffic in the souls of men." The petition also followed the standard form of prayer by offering a salutation, recognizing the power and goodness of those solicited, stating requests, and concluding with a reiteration of the supplicant's commitment to the request (such as "amen," which in essence means "be it really so," or in the case of the Fathers and Rulers petition, "And as in duty bound your petitioners will ever pray"). The prayerful petition was appended to *An Address to Females in the State of Ohio,* published by the Female Anti-Slavery Society of Muskingham County, in which Corresponding Secretary Maria A. Sturges wrote, "Let every petition, as it goes forth on its silent embassy, . . . be baptized with prayer, and commended with weeping and supplication to Him in whose hands are the hearts of all men, that he would turn the channel of their sympathies from the oppressor to the oppressed."[13]

Aligning the act of petitioning with Christian duty in the texts of petitions was a particularly fitting rhetorical strategy, considering the audience from whom signatures were solicited. While women likely felt hesitant about instructing their representatives on a matter of national policy, undoubtedly they felt more comfortable engaging in the act of praying. Prayer was not only acceptable behavior for women, but it was considered to be the duty of Woman, who was believed to be inherently more religious than Man. Women reformers, abolitionists among them, often prayed and sang hymns at their regular meetings, in addition to holding special "concerts of prayer." These practices, Julie Roy Jeffrey has noted, "showed not only the belief in the sacred nature of the antislavery cause but how easily women might fall into the familiar patterns of the prayer meeting." Likewise, Deborah Bingham Van Broekhoven has commented on the similarities between the rituals of signing one's name to a church membership roll, an earthly recognition that God had written names in "the lamb's book of life," and letting one's "name be enrolled" on the constitution of a female antislavery society to indicate formal membership.[14]

This is not to suggest that female antislavery petitioners employed religious discursive rituals only, or even primarily, as rhetorical strategies to downplay their increasingly political behavior. There is no evidence to cast doubt on the claims of women signers that they were motivated by moral commitment and Christian duty. In fact, it is unlikely that they viewed religious duty as distinctly separate from political action. The virtually seamless blending of Christian conviction with antislavery activism is illustrated by the words of Catherine Birney when she recalled that prayer was at first woman's "only idea of aid in the great cause" of abolition. She wrote that men universally granted during the 1830s that prayer was woman's "special privilege" and encouraged woman to pray as long as she limited her supplications to "private prayer—prayer in her own closet—with no auditor but the God to whom she appealed." Before long, though, antislavery women sought to intensify their efforts and began to "make their prayers public in the form of petitions to legislatures and to Congress." It was then, remembered Birney, that the "reprobations began."[15]

In hopes of escaping such reprobations, in their antislavery petitions women exhibited extreme deference to elected male authorities, a complaisance absent from those composed for and most often signed by men. Petitions aimed at winning men's signatures identified signers as citizens and spent no time justifying the propriety of men petitioning their legislators. The tone of men's petitions, moreover, was declaratory rather than hedging. In a petition submitted to Congress in 1834, for example, Massachusetts men made no apology or explanation for their petitioning. They launched immediately into arguments and declarations that slavery was wrong and should be abolished because it violated laws, and they sternly reminded legislators that Congress possessed jurisdiction over the District. "By the plain words of the Constitution," the petition stated, "the remedy for these evils, by abolishing slavery, is placed in the power of Congress. No other body can, constitutionally, legislate on the subject." Whereas women's petitions often supported claims by alluding to Bible verses, men's petitions were more likely to cite laws and especially the Constitution. Overall the tone of men's petitions was legalistic, confident, and insistent rather than, like women's, religious, tentative, and hedging.[16]

The noticeably humble stance of women petitioners compared with that of men reflected in part the petition authors' understanding, which they assumed would be shared by potential signers, that women possessed political status separate from men. Rather than instructing their representatives because it was an exercise of their natural rights or privileges of citizenship, both of which were unclear and unstable, in this first stage with few exceptions women indicated that they petitioned in order to fulfill their Christian duty. An 1834 petition calling for abolition of slavery in the District of Columbia signed by women from Harrisville, Ohio, made it clear that they were doing so "as Christians wishing to act in conformity to the precepts of our Lord." Even though it was unusual for women to petition about an issue such as slavery, the form stated, women could "no longer keep silent," and though they were aware that they were violating notions of respectable female behavior, they expected to be protected by "Him that has numbered the very hairs on our heads." A petition circulated throughout Vermont during 1835 and signed by women proclaimed that as Christians they mourned toleration of slavery and deprecated a system that so clearly violated the "pure and benignant precepts of our Holy Lawgiver." An 1836 petition signed by females of Winthrop, Maine, stressed upholding Christian principles as a motivation for petitioning: "We believe the time has fully come when this Christian nation should wipe the foul blot of slavery from our national character." Time and again in this fashion petitions designed to win female signatures called on women as Christians to overturn slavery and invoked Christian duty as a justification for lending their names to the cause. These arguments served a dual function. On one hand, they emphasized that petitioning against slavery was an action motivated by Christian duty rather than political gain. On the other hand, these arguments implied that should a woman refuse to sign, she was neither upholding her religious duty nor acting like a respectable, pious woman.[17]

Women also professed to petition in order to fulfill obligations based on their connection with other members of their sex, with female slaves. A petition circulated during the fall of 1835 in Massachusetts and New Hampshire emphasized that "your petitioners believe it to be their duty to urge upon your serious consideration the perpetual wrongs of women and children, whose husbands and fathers are deprived of all legal power to protect them." The women explained that they could not remain silent "while thousands of their sex are condemned to helpless degradation, and even denied the privilege of making known their sufferings." "History would blush for American women," the petitioners predicted, "if, under such circumstances, they ever allowed their voice of expostulation and entreaty to cease throughout the land." Signers from Washington County, Vermont, explained: "As females, we deeply sympathize with the disgraced and afflicted of our sex, and feel constrained by every sentiment of humanity to plead for scourged and heart-crushed woman, whose anticipations of domestic happiness are often ruthlessly blighted by the hand of insatiable avarice, and her dearest ties in life forever severed, while her benighted soul is excluded from a participation in the consoling hopes and sustaining promises of eternal life, and her solitary progress to the tomb unenlivened by one gleam of holy joy."[18]

It is not surprising to find in the petitions an emphasis on the similarities between free and slave women. During the 1830s the woman-and-sister appeal permeated a host of antislavery literature directed at women. In its verbal form the woman-and-sister motif stressed that because free and slave women belonged to the same sex, they shared common concerns, such as children, family, domesticity, religion, and sexual vulnerability. These shared relations were conveyed in phrases such as "slaves of our sex," "am I not a woman and a sister," and "we are in bonds bound with them" (Hebrews 13:3). In its pictorial form the woman-and-sister motif usually featured a kneeling slave woman who covered her bare breasts with raised arms, clasped her hands, and cast her gaze toward heaven while praying for emancipation. In some depictions the bowing slave woman looked up to an elevated white woman draped in robes and glowing with the light of saving grace.

The woman-and-sister image originated with British antislavery women, who reproduced it in their reports and appeals starting in 1826. In May 1830 Elizabeth Margaret Chandler, who edited the Women's Repository in the *Genius of Universal Emancipation*, an antislavery newspaper published by Benjamin Lundy, mentioned receiving from Englishwomen "a seal, bearing the device of a female kneeling slave, and the very appropriate motto 'Am I Not a Woman and a Sister?'" In that same issue Chandler, inspired by the image, printed a poem she had composed titled "Kneeling Slave," in which she contrasted the lady's pleasant life with the slave's miserable existence and demanded that the reader work to bridge that gap. By 1832 Garrison had adopted the woman-and-sister image to head the Ladies' Department of the *Liberator*, and the next year Child selected a version of the image as the frontispiece for her *Appeal in Favor of That Class of Americans Called Africans*. Thereafter, as Jean Fagan Yellin has noted, American antislavery women "individually and informally, as well as collectively and officially" adopted the image and the motto as their own. They reproduced it in words, in drawings, in needlework, on stationery, and in their petitions.[19]

The woman-and-sister theme was especially valuable for getting women to empathize with the plight of slaves even though for most northerners slavery was a mere abstraction. Chandler explained the abolitionists' rhetorical strategy in an article called "Mental Metempsychosis." Drawing on the concept of metempsychosis, which is the soul's passage at death into another body, Chandler urged readers to move beyond a mere intellectual response to feel the same cruelties that were inflicted on slave women. Readers, Chandler insisted, should imagine themselves to be slaves in fetters, "its wearing weight upon their wrists, as they are driven off like cattle to the market, and the successive strokes of the keen thong fall[ing] upon their shoulders till the flesh rises to long welts beneath it, and the spouting blood follows every blow." The woman-and-sister image aimed to make vivid the horrors visited on female slaves and to arouse such emotion that action would be inevitable.[20]

Descriptions of the horrors of slavery in women's petitions dwelled on the particular afflictions suffered by slave women. Over and over again, petitions lamented that female slaves were "degraded," "brutified," "the victims of insatiable avarice," "wronged," and "denied of male relatives to offer them protection." The ladies of Dousa, New Hampshire, for instance, mourned, "The universal tendency of this system is degradation of the female character; for it unavoidably places a large class entirely out of the protection of law or public opinion. . . . Your petitioners believe it to be their duty to urge upon your serious consideration the perpetual wrongs of women and children, whose husbands and fathers are deprived of all legal power to protect them. They cannot be silent while thousands of their sex are condemned to helpless degradation, and even denied the privilege of making known their sufferings." These images emphasized the sexual and spiritual vulnerability of the slave woman and implied that slavery was not only the purchase of labor, but also of flesh and soul. The concern of white women over the harsh and indelicate treatment of slave women, at least one critic has concluded, "redefined [slave women's] suffering as feminine, and hence endowed with all the moral value generally attributed to nineteenth-century American womanhood."[21]

For northern women who read the petitions and contemplated adding their names, such language conveyed the notion that slavery gave men unrestrained power over women and that slaveholding men were using their unchecked power in the most evil way. Even though northern middle-class women were far removed geographically from slavery, the image of a man lording villainous power over a sexually vulnerable woman would easily evoke a visceral reaction. A good deal of the literature of antebellum female moral reformers (those involved not in charitable and benevolent work but, rather, in more radical causes) warned that men of all sorts were lustful and licentious and at all times sought to ruin the virtue of women. Ginzberg emphasizes that "one cannot exaggerate the hostility toward men" in female moral reformers' journals, constitutions, and especially discussions of poverty and prostitution. "Lust appeared to be a disease that had infected the entire male population," she writes. Prompted by class shifts and economic anxieties during the early to mid-1830s, many radical female reformers harbored intense hostility toward men. Moral reformers argued that women possessed little control over their material wealth and that they were completely dependent on men for their economic well-being. When men failed to do their job, reform literature professed, women were abandoned to become the victims of seduction and vice. The narrative of women being completely at the mercy of men and becoming the victims of men's inherent licentiousness was echoed by the woman-and-sister theme. By focusing on the ruthless behavior of the slave master toward the defenseless slave woman, the petitions could provoke northern middle-class women to feel the same anger toward the slaveholder that they felt toward the men whom they perceived as controlling their lives through economic power. Yet while the motif enhanced the persuasiveness of antislavery petitions for an audience of northern free white women, it obscured the vast differences between the sexual vulnerability of female slaves and free white women, especially those of the middle class.[22]

Emphasizing the connection between enslaved African American women and free white women not only provided a means to articulate anxieties about sexual vulnerability that could be appreciated by free white women, but it also provided a crucial rationale justifying white women's petitioning. The petitions repeatedly stressed that a major reason northern women were obligated to petition for their slave sisters was that slave women could not petition themselves, nor could slave men seek redress for their wives and daughters. Female petitioners from Ohio deemed it "not only our privilege but our duty" to come before Congress "to open our mouths for the dumb" to plead the cause of "the poor and those that have none to help them." Vermont women declared, "We plead for the enslaved, the smitten, the oppressed!" Vina Wendell, along with 358 other ladies of Massachusetts, complied with the statement that it was her duty as a woman to urge upon congressmen the sufferings of women and children "whose husbands and fathers are deprived of all legal power to protect them." These arguments implied a narrative of the helpless slave and the valiant liberator, which reinforced the idealized moral superiority of white women by demonstrating that they were acting in a benevolent manner befitting their gender and class.[23]

Although the emphasis on concern for enslaved women implied a shared identity based on sex, women's petitions enacted a significant power differential between free women (most of whom were white) and female slaves. As long as the female slave could not petition for herself, the petitions insisted, free women were obligated to petition for them. In this way the rhetoric of female moral duty combined with a certain notion of stewardship was appropriated by free women to elevate themselves from dependents to representatives of those who lacked the autonomy to speak for themselves. By adopting the mantle of public representative of female slaves, abolitionist women in essence reappropriated the political power arrangements between white men and all women. Similar to the rationale that endowed white men with the political power to represent the interests of their dependents—wives, daughters, and sisters—the petitions claimed that free women were qualified to represent the interests of female slaves, who, they claimed, depended on them. In so doing the petitions constructed identities for antislavery women and slave women that intersected along the line of gender but diverged along the line of race. The discursive act of identification, in other words, amounted not only to appropriation but to exploitation. Ironically, the petitions' radical aim of expanding female abolitionists' access relied on the conservative rhetoric of woman's moral superiority. Even more ironic, perhaps, is that despite the fact that petitions served an ultraist movement that professed to seek the overturn of the dominant social, economic, and political structures, the petitions invoked a deeply conservative political vision of indirect representation in an era of growing democracy that privileged a language of direct representation.[24]

Positioning themselves to represent slaves was but one element of the rhetoric of women's antislavery petitions that elevated the political power of white and free black women. That small minority of northern women and men who were abolitionists during the 1830s appropriated the issue of slavery to construct a concept of American nationhood built on revised notions of republicanism. Abolitionist rhetoric, as Daniel J. McInerney has demonstrated, insisted on the virtues of an economy built on free labor and critiqued the slave labor system as not only harmful to the republic but defying the principles of the American Revolution. The most common manifestation of the rhetoric of antislavery republicanism in the female forms was the warning that slavery was ruining the nation's character and that the American people would be punished by God. "As daughters of America, we blush for the tarnished fame of our beloved country," proclaimed a petition signed by the Females of Washington County, Vermont, in 1836. "We lament her waning glory, and we entreat that you, as patriots, will erase this stain from her dishonored character." The popular women's petition attached to the *Address of the Female Anti-Slavery Society of Philadelphia* declared that slavery was "inconsistent with our declaration that 'equal liberty is the birth-right of all,'" and thus the signers urged abolition in the District. A petition from the female inhabitants of South Reading, Massachusetts, decried,

> That the Congress of the United States—the Representatives of a free, republican and Christian people—in the nineteenth century, and at a period when the nations of the earth are modifying their institutions in favor of the rights and liberties of mankind, should deliberately, and of their own free will and pleasure, declare in the presence of the whole world, their consent to and approval of the extension of the evils of slavery in our land, and of the perpetual and everlasting bondage and degradation of any portion of the human family, would be a blot on our

national character that could never be effaced, and a sin which would invoke the judgments of Heaven.

The Ladies of Dousa, New Hampshire, and of Massachusetts argued in 1836 that they considered the toleration of slavery in the District of Columbia as shamefully inconsistent with the principles promulgated in the Declaration of Independence.[25]

At the root of these apprehensions about the health of the republic was a fear and conviction that the institution of slavery threatened the northern free labor system. Slavery should be abolished in the District of Columbia, argued a popular petition signed by women and men alike, because it was "oppressive to the honest free laborer, and tends to make labor disreputable as well as unprofitable." The same petition, which was circulated in Vermont, Ohio, and New York, claimed that immediate abolition was practicable because "it will not annihilate the laborers nor their labor, but will merely make it necessary for the employers to pay fair wages." Men and women of Lockport, New York, ascribed their names to a petition that demanded abolition in Washington, D.C., and the western territories and argued that slavery was "detrimental to the interests and *subversive of the liberties of the labouring population of our republic.*"[26]

Statements about the superiority of free labor in antislavery petitions encapsulated characterizations of virtue and vice familiar to many northern women through their reading of popular novels. During the 1830s Catharine Sedgwick, Sarah Hale, Eliza Follen, and others published novels that boasted that free labor was the fairest system because it allowed all people to rise through hard work. Characterizing northern women as industrious and conscientious while depicting elite southern women as slothful and selfish, these novels functioned as powerful proof of the moral superiority of free labor over slavery. By demonstrating that only the northern free labor system recognized individual independence and natural rights, the novels argued that the North, not the South, preserved the ideals of the American Revolution.[27]

Female antislavery petitions that featured the idealized moral superiority of woman strengthened abolitionists' claim to the virtues that constituted the founders' vision of the republic. Assertions of Christian and womanly duty to speak out against slavery aided abolitionists in condemning slaveholders as morally unqualified to call themselves true republicans and heirs to the legacy of the American Revolution. Slaveholders were, according to abolitionist rhetoric, unfit to be American citizens. In essence, then, antislavery women joined men in decrying wealth, especially wealth gained from slave labor, as a warrant for political power. The radical potential of women embracing in their petitions the rhetoric of antislavery republicanism lay in the fact that northern women could claim the virtues cultivated by free labor and could thus position themselves over elite southerners and especially slaveholding congressmen. As true republicans under the cosmology created by abolitionist republicanism, free laboring women possessed a stronger claim to U.S. citizenship than even the wealthiest, most powerful slaveholding senator. Moreover, it was the duty of the free laboring woman as a citizen to exercise her right of petition in order to safeguard the republic.

It would not be long before the assertion that duties were grounded in the responsibilities of citizenship led to the argument that duties implied rights. Recognizing their roles as moral caretakers and emboldened with republican duty, the women of Harrisville, Ohio, on June 13, 1834, put into circulation an exceptionally bold petition. Bathseba Brown, Susan Hicklen, and others approached their leaders not only as wives, mothers, sisters, and daughters who valued the endearments of domestic life but as "good citizens desiring the prosperity of our nation." Deeply affected by the "degrading and unprecedented sufferings . . . [of] our brethren of the African race," the petitioners urged abolition in the District. But they asked for much more:

> And believing that the wisdom and calm reflection that should influence the deliberation of those who give laws to nations will be capable of presenting to your minds the incalculable advantages of having your legislative halls surrounded by a pure moral atmosphere; . . . your memorialists further petition for the immediate enfranchisement of every human being that shall tread this soil; that since righteousness alone exalteth a nation, ours may no longer suffer the additional abasement of the foulest stains in the catalogue of our crimes.[28]

Fourteen years before the Seneca Falls Woman's Rights convention where the wisdom of seeking woman suffrage was debated, Ohio women petitioned Congress for universal suffrage. The petition, signed by more than thirty-five females, implied that suffrage should be extended especially to women because they were needed to cleanse the nation of the "foulest of stains"—slavery. Although based on essentialized notions of superior female morality rather than natural rights principles, the petition considerably disrupts the widely accepted chronology of American women's struggle for suffrage. Its existence provides evidence that neither the 1848 Seneca Falls convention nor state constitutional conventions held a few years earlier were the first instances in which women appealed to legislators for enfranchisement. Indeed, the 1834 petition adds yet another piece to what Jacob Katz Cogan and Lori D. Ginzberg have called the "newly emerging puzzle of women's past political and intellectual lives." It demonstrates that even as far back as the early 1830s some women rejected the tenets of separate spheres and "dared suggest that only the vote would guarantee them the influence due adult Americans."[29]

*   *   *

The petition of Hannah H. Smith, Sarah Hale, and other ladies of Glastenbury, along with that signed by the ladies of Marshfield, arrived in Washington, D.C., for consideration during the first session of the Twenty-fourth Congress, which convened on December 7, 1835. Besides the New York women's handiwork, Congress received 174 other antislavery petitions; 84—almost half—were from women, a ninefold increase in female petitions over the preceding session. The pleas had been signed by 34,000 people, 15,000 of whom were women. Faced with more abolition memorials than ever before, Senator John C. Calhoun complained that the petitions came not as in the past, "singly and far apart, from the quiet routine of the Society of Friends or the obscure vanity of some philanthropist club," but "from soured and agitated communities."[30]

The general disposition in Congress toward abolitionists and their petitions was anything but friendly. Like many Americans, members of Congress were fuming over the "incendiary" literature abolitionists had been sending South through the federal mails. With the bloody scenes of Nat Turner's rebellion emblazoned in their minds, southerners and northerners alike blamed Arthur Tappan and William Lloyd Garrison for inciting Turner and his followers to revolt against their masters. Antiabolitionist sentiment ran so deep that one northern representative, Samuel Beardsley, a Jacksonian Democrat, had been elected to Congress in large part because of his fight to keep antislavery societies from holding their state convention in Utica, New York. Animosity toward abolitionists was compounded by the fact that 1836 was an election year, and northern Democrats who hoped to elect New Yorker Martin Van Buren to the presidency wished to dodge discussion of slavery for fear such talk would upset southern Democrats and voters.[31]

On December 16, 1835, a little more than a week into the congressional session, Representative John Fairfield of Maine, the first state called upon for petitions, presented a memorial signed by 172 females praying for the abolition of slavery and the slave trade in the District of Columbia. He then moved that it be referred to the Committee on the District of Columbia, which had become the routine way to dispose of antislavery petitions with almost no chance that they would reappear for discussion. Before the motion could be debated, however, John Cramer, a Democrat from Van Buren's home state of New York, moved that the women's petition be laid on the table. A companion petition, sent by 172 male citizens of Maine, met a similar fate, though this time it was Fairfield himself who, after presenting the petition, moved that it be tabled.[32]

Despite the fact that the mood of the House toward abolition petitions was made clear by its treatment of the Maine memorials, two days later Representative William Jackson of Massachusetts presented a petition from sundry inhabitants of the town of Wrentham against slavery in the District of Columbia and asked that it be referred to a select committee. South Carolina's representative James Henry Hammond, fed up with what he perceived as the constant insult he and his section suffered from the petitions, in a motion unprecedented in the annals of Congress asked that the petition not be received. Hammond explained that he was gratified by the resounding rejection of the abolition petitions two days earlier, and he hoped that the large majority for tabling would convince all members of the impropriety of presenting abolition petitions. Judging from Jackson's motion, however, Hammond deduced that was not the case. Consequently the South Carolinian asked the House to "put a more decided seal of reprobation on them, by peremptorily rejecting" the petition at hand.[33]

After Hammond was seated, Representative John Patton of Virginia moved for reconsideration of a petition that earlier had been presented to the House and referred to the Committee on the District of Columbia. He did so because he believed that the only way to get rid of the petitions was to deal once and for all with the question they raised. "Mr. Speaker," said Patton, "it is necessary that this House should be apprized and fully impressed with the necessity of quieting the anxiety, the agitation, and the alarm for the institutions of the country, which are abroad in the land, and that as the means, perhaps the only means, of doing so, it should meet those questions directly, and dispose of them decisively and permanently." At this point Representative John Quincy Adams rose to give the first of many speeches on the issue of antislavery petitions. Adams said that he hoped the motion to reconsider would not prevail for the same reason Patton hoped it would. "It appears to me," Adams stated, "that the only way of getting this question from the view of the House and of the nation, is to dispose of all petitions on the same subject in the same way." To accomplish this, Adams urged that the House follow the twofold method it had been using for years: first, refer the petitions to a committee that would report on them and, second, unanimously accept the committee's report. Then Adams issued a dire warning to the House about the consequences that would follow if it decided to discuss the issue of slavery. He predicted that speeches by representatives on the evils of slavery would be turned into incendiary pamphlets that would be printed for the entire country to read.[34]

The controversy over the treatment of petitions raged for months and pushed aside all other business of the House. The situation became so severe that in February 1836 the House appointed a special committee headed by Representative Henry L. Pinckney of South Carolina, who, like Adams, was a son of one of the framers of the Constitution, to study the petitions and report to the body as a whole. From that day until Pinckney's committee reported, all abolition petitions were referred to it. On May 18 Pinckney presented the report, which proposed three resolutions aimed at silencing the abolition petitioners. These resolutions were debated by the House for more than a week before members agreed to vote on each separately. On May 25 the House approved by a vote of 182-9 the first resolution, which held that Congress possessed no constitutional power to interfere with slavery in any of the states. The next day the second resolution, stating that Congress ought not to interfere with slavery in the District of Columbia, was approved by a vote of 142-45. Then the vote was taken on the third resolution, which read, "*Resolved*, That all petitions, memorials, resolutions, propositions or papers, relating in any way, or to any extent whatever, to the subject of slavery, or the abolition of slavery, shall, without being either printed or referred, be laid upon the table, and that no further action whatever shall be had thereon." This resolution would come to be known as the gag rule. When Adams was called to vote, he rose and exclaimed, "I hold the resolution to be a direct violation of the constitution of the United States, the rules of this House, and the rights of my constituents." Calls of order rang out from all parts of the hall as Adams took his seat. The resolution was adopted by a vote of 117-68. For the rest of the first session of the Twenty-fourth Congress, which lasted until July 4, 1836, abolition petitions were tabled upon presentation.[35]

After passage of the gag rule, abolitionists faced a strategic decision. Should they cease to petition? After all, was not petitioning a waste of time, since Congress tabled the memorials without considering the requests? Quite to the contrary James G. Birney, a repentant Kentucky slaveholder, recommended that "every effort ought to be made to get up petitions for the abolition of slavery in the District of Columbia." Birney believed that petitioning would be a forceful, persuasive strategy because southern congressmen treated antislavery petitions with such "rabid contempt" that the people would see clearly that slaveholders would protect their peculiar institution at any cost, even by trampling northerners' rights. Petitioning, Birney stressed, "would give us a great means of moving people." In order to stimulate even greater petitioning activities, antislavery societies published addresses appealing to abolitionists to circulate petitions despite the affront in Congress. It was at this time that female antislavery societies joined the petition drive in earnest. In fact, passage of the gag rule inspired women abolitionists to produce a major outpouring of discourse aimed at encouraging female activism and articulating in greater detail an emerging ideology of female citizenship.[36]

CHAPTER 4

A Firebrand in Our Hands

Passage of the gag rule incensed abolitionists. As soon as a copy of the report that proposed and justified the gag rule reached Boston, it was splashed over the pages of the *Liberator*. The Pinckney report, editorialized Garrison, was "weakness itself." Early in July 1836 the executive committee of the American Anti-Slavery Society (AASS) published *An Appeal to the People of the United States* in hopes of attracting to the antislavery cause Americans who were unsympathetic to abolitionism but who cherished the First Amendment. "Let no one think for a moment that because he is not an abolitionist, his liberties are not and will not be invaded," the *Appeal* warned. Angered by what they perceived as a bald abrogation of their constitutional rights, abolitionists denounced Pinckney as "foolish and infatuated" to suppose that his report would induce them to cease agitating the slavery issue. Instead they pledged that the rule "shall be a 'firebrand' in our hands to light anew the flame of human sympathy and public indignation."[1]

Garrison and the AASS were not alone in seizing the "firebrand" of the gag rule to ignite public indignation. Passage of the first gag rule also inspired female abolitionists during the summer of 1836 to issue calls for intensified petitioning and to denounce slaveholders for conspiring to trammel northerners' civil rights. In four major printed addresses female abolitionists elaborated at length on their justifications for petitioning, situating this form of political influence in a broad discussion of women's proper role in antislavery activism. Although representatives passed the gag rule to silence abolition petitioners, instead the rule functioned as a catalyst for female antislavery leaders, who in their addresses constructed the Pinckney resolution as an immoral law enacted by morally flawed men. The addresses repeatedly instructed women to ignore the will of men who wished to suppress their pleas and to follow their own moral conscience with respect to the sin of slavery. The implications of these appeals were radical, for they urged women to trust their own judgment and to abandon millennia of customs and law requiring women to submit to the desires of men.

The 1836 addresses persuaded more women to lend their names to the cause, which contributed significantly to the success of the campaign that in December of that year deluged Congress with abolition petitions. Aggravated congressmen reacted by instituting a second gag rule, refusing to receive a petition from slaves, and questioning the right of free blacks to petition. In response female abolitionists, determined to multiply the number of names submitted to Congress and concerned about the security of their right of petition, took the unprecedented step of meeting in convention. At their convention, which marked the beginning of the second phase of female antislavery petitioning, women practiced important skills of political organizing, such as running meetings, forming networks, debating resolutions, and writing circulars. The convention also provided an opportunity for women to debate what constituted their appropriate role in the antislavery cause and to formulate justifications of their expanding activism. These justifications were articulated in published resolutions and addresses that, unlike the 1836 appeals, advanced beyond claiming that women possessed a moral duty to petition to asserting that women were citizens and, as such, possessed a constitutional right to petition. Antislavery women also asserted a bolder, more straightforwardly political identity in the new petitions they adopted at the convention. These petitions were much shorter than those circulated in the first phase of female involvement and left no space for women to excuse their petitioning as motivated by female duty. Not only did women cease offering elaborate justifications for their petitioning, but they more frequently signed the same forms that men signed.

* * *

Though the Pinckney gag was intended to deter antislavery petitioning, it inspired an outpouring of discourse in which female abolitionists encouraged women to follow God's will to eradicate the sin of slavery and called on them to defy political representatives who wished to quell the petitions. Women's alleged moral purity freed them from political motivations that corrupted congressmen, the 1836 addresses argued, urging them to ignore the dictates of men who opposed their petitioning and to follow their own consciences to instruct representatives to abolish the evil of slavery. While the addresses extended moral appeals to inspire women to increase their antislavery activism, they also bemoaned denial of northerners' civil rights, which eventually led to particular defenses of women's right of petition based on constitutional arguments. Among the addresses was that of the Boston Female Anti-Slavery Society, published in July 1836 and likely written by Maria Weston Chapman, that lamented that with passage of the gag rule, "we may not know whether the men we call our representatives are truly such." Approval of the Pinckney resolution, it decried, made the whole nation "feel the Slave-holder's scourge." It nonetheless urged, "Let us petition;—petition, till, even for our importunity, we cannot be denied. Let us know no rest till we have done our utmost to convince the mind, and to obtain the testimony of every woman, in every town, in every county of our Commonwealth, against the horrible Slave-traffic." A month earlier Maria A. Sturges, corresponding secretary of the Female Anti-Slavery Society of Muskingham County, Ohio, and coordinator of women's antislavery petitioning in her state, had published *An Address to Females in the State of Ohio*, which was circulated as a handbill throughout Ohio, reprinted in the *Philanthropist* and the *Emancipator*, and sent to New England female antislavery societies. In August, Angelina Grimké published her *Appeal to the Christian Women of the South*, which was sold as a pamphlet in both the United States and England. In mid-October there appeared *An Address of the Female Anti-Slavery Society of Philadelphia to the Women of Pennsylvania with the Form of a Petition to the Congress of the U. States*, signed by the organization's president, Esther Moore, and its secretary, Rebecca Buffum. In addition to advancing arguments about slavery and the importance of petitioning, the addresses sought to accomplish the practical tasks of distributing petition forms (the Ohio appeal, for example, included the Fathers and Rulers of Our Country form) and providing directions for their circulation.[2]

Passage of the gag rule presented an added constraint to female petitioning efforts, for it compounded general negative attitudes toward women's collective petitioning with congressmen's formal disapproval of abolition petitions. In response the appeals repeatedly urged women to ignore the will of men who attempted to thwart their petitioning. "Women are not excused from obedience to the Apostolic injunction, '*Remember them that are in bonds as bound with them*,'" preached the Ohio *Address*, bidding women to "labor with untiring vigor" for the slave because the Bible promised that on the day of revelation, "not our sons only, but our daughters shall prophesy." If women were to share in the blessings of the coming of the Lord, the *Address* reminded, "surely it must be our duty, as well as privilege, to be auxiliaries in accelerating it." Grimké invited women to ignore man's laws and man's opinions and to take as their sole source of guidance the word of God as they interpreted it. Women should not follow the lead of men if they believe male direction to be immoral, she advised. In fact, they should resist the will of men to satisfy the will of God even if it meant sacrificing their lives just as biblical women such as Miriam, Huldah, Anna, Deborah, and Esther had "stood up in all the dignity and strength of moral courage to be the leaders of the people, and to bear a faithful testimony for the truth whenever the providence of God has called them to do so."[3]

Furthermore, the addresses emphasized that given the sectional and partisan nature of debates over slavery and the gag rule, because of their alleged moral purity, women were uniquely qualified to petition for an end to the moral evil of slavery. Women, stated the Ohio *Address*, were particularly suited to send antislavery petitions to Congress because they remained "untrammeled by party politics, and unbiased by the love of gain," while men, on the other hand, were "ready to prostrate themselves before the swift running car of this mighty Juggernaut which slavery hath set up." The *Address to the Women of Massachusetts* claimed that it was especially incumbent upon women to counteract the "hatred of [God's] character and laws" that was "intrenched in *men's* business and bosoms." "As *wives* and *mothers,* as *sisters* and *daughters,* we are deeply responsible for the influence we have on the human race. We are bound to exert it; we are bound to urge men to cease to do evil, and learn to do well." Women's petitions would be "irresistible," assured Grimké, "for there is something in the heart of man which *will bend under moral suasion.*" Even if only six signatures could be obtained on a petition, she urged women to "send up that petition, and be not in the least discouraged by the scoffs and jeers of the heartless, or the resolution of the house to lay it on the table." Women should persevere because they could introduce the subject of abolition "in the best possible manner, as a matter of *morals* and *religion,* not of expediency and politics."[4]

Perhaps most significantly, the addresses warned that slaveholders were conspiring to destroy northerners' civil rights and included women's right of petition among those guaranteed by the Constitution. The Boston Female Anti-Slavery Society's appeal deplored that because of the gag rule, "the whole nation is being made to feel the Slave-holders's scourge" and that the "Slave-system" caused the "institutions of the free" to break down, and thus the lives of those who avowed the principles of the Declaration of Independence were threatened. The Ohio address cited the gag rule as evidence that northern members of Congress were plotting with slave-holders and were willing "to appease the blood-stained god of southern slavery." By advancing these arguments, the women's addresses contributed to propagation of what Russell Nye has called the "great slave power conspiracy theme," which, after taking root in abolitionist discourse in the 1830s, became a primary weapon in the abolitionist rhetorical arsenal during the 1850s. Gradually abolitionists—women and men—began to claim, as would Abraham Lincoln some years later, that the Union could not exist half-slave and half-free. Although Nye credits only male abolitionists with perpetuating the conspiracy theme, decades before Lincoln would speak nearly the same words, the Boston women's address warned, "Weak and wicked is the idea, that union in oppression is possible. Every nation that attempts it, 'God beholds, and drives asunder.'"[5]

Not only did the appeals advance the slave power conspiracy theme, but in the course of decrying destruction of northerners' civil liberties, the Philadelphia address advanced beyond claiming that women possessed a moral duty to petition to asserting that women were citizens endowed with a constitutional right of petition. "Will you say that woman's duties lie within the hallowed precincts of home, not in the field of controversy, or the halls of Congress?" the Philadelphia address asked readers. Employing arguments used to deny women access to public debate, the address accused congressmen of corrupting the deliberative process by letting "loose the storms of passion . . . instead of listening to the voice of woman's entreaty for the rescue" of the slave. Congressmen, the Philadelphians complained, "would fain rob her of the right of petition, and the privileges of a citizen, in order to close her lips for ever in behalf of her outraged sisters." In the course of calling women to petition, again and again the Philadelphia address asserted in no uncertain terms that women were citizens and must fulfill the duties incumbent upon citizens. This was no time for women to "keep silence," no time "for *woman* to shrink from her duty as a citizen of the United States,—as a member of the great human family." "As Northern citizens *we* are bound, dear sisters, to put forth all *our* energies in this mighty work. Yes, although we are *women, we* are still citizens, and it is to *us,* that the captive wives and mothers, sisters and daughters of the South have a peculiar right to look for help in this day of approaching emancipation."[6]

* * *

Inspired by appeals published by women during the summer of 1836 after passage of the gag rule, during the fall northerners sent to Congress more antislavery petitions than ever before. When the second session of the Twenty-fourth Congress convened on December 5, 1836, congressmen found that despite the Pinckney report and resolution of the last session, the petition issue had not gone to sleep. So "conspicuous" were the "sedative properties" of the gag rule, John Quincy Adams remarked facetiously in his diary, that in the new session of Congress "it multiplied fivefold the antislavery petitions." When the first abolition petition was presented on December 26, the Speaker of the House, Tennessee slaveholder and future president James K. Polk, decided that the rules and resolutions of the last session, including the gag rule, had expired. That meant that abolition petitions were no longer tabled immediately upon presentation; the floodgates were opened, and antislavery memorials washed into the House. As in the preceding session, debates over how to dispose of the abolition petitions dragged on. Much time was spent dealing with the petitions, and other business of the House ground to a halt. Finally, on January 18, Representative Albert G. Hawes of Kentucky moved for adoption of a resolution with the same wording as the previous gag rule. After no debate the resolution was adopted by a vote of 129-69.[7]

Passage of the resolution, however, did not keep Adams and others from presenting abolition petitions. On February 6, for example, Caleb Cushing of Massachusetts presented a petition signed by 3,824 ladies of the city of Lowell and the towns of Amesbury, Andover, Haverhill, Newburyport, Reading, and Salisbury. He also presented petitions signed by women from twenty-seven towns in New Hampshire. All were received and, under the Hawes resolution, laid on the table. The effect was "electrical" when time after time a few members to whom the memorials had been entrusted rose to state the content of the petitions. "If a nest of rattlesnakes were suddenly let loose among them," reported a Capitol observer during the first days of 1837, "the members could manifest but little more 'agitation'—except perhaps, that they retain their seats a *little* better. . . . The Southern hotspurs are almost ready to dance with very rage at the attack, as they called it, upon their peculiar domestic institutions."[8]

But the greatest commotion was caused by Adams, who on February 6 presented a petition from nine free black women of Fredericksburg, Virginia, and inquired of the Speaker whether it would be acceptable to present a second petition signed by twenty-two persons purporting to be slaves. Polk referred the question to the House, igniting a fiery debate over whether slaves possessed the right of petition. Immediately after the inquiry about the alleged slave petition, "the torrid zone was in commotion," Adams recalled. He heard "half-subdued calls of '*Expel him, expel him*'" from various parts of the chamber. One southern member declared that should any representative "disgrace the government under which he lived" by presenting a petition from slaves for their emancipation, the House should order the petition "committed to the flames." The man who presented such a petition, pronounced another, also should be consigned to the combustion. Invectives such as these were restated as formal resolutions condemning Adams's behavior and denying adamantly that slaves possessed the right of petition. One such resolution offered to the chamber by Representative Bynum of North Carolina stated "that any attempt to present any petition or memorial, from any slave or slaves, negro or free negroes, from any part of the Union, is a contempt of the House, calculated to embroil it in strife and confusion, incompatible with the dignity of the body; and any member guilty of the same justly subjects himself to the censure of the House." Bynum's resolution expressed slaveholders' distaste for petitions from slaves and free blacks, but it did not explicitly deny slaves the right of petition. That task was left to Representative John M. Patton of Virginia:

> *Resolved,* That the right of petition does not belong to the slaves of this Union, and that no petition from them can be presented to this House, without derogating from the rights of slaveholding states, and endangering the integrity of the Union.
>
> *Resolved,* That any member who shall hereafter present any such petition to the House, ought to be considered regardless of the feelings of the House, the rights of the South, and an enemy of the Union.

Patton's resolution went beyond claiming that it was improper for slaves to petition and stated clearly that slaves had no right of petition. While the precedent for denying slaves the right of petition had been set in 1797, Patton's resolution also indicted the goodwill and patriotism of representatives who would present slave petitions, thus censoring members' right of free speech. In the end the House debated a resolution brought forth by Representative Charles Jared Ingersoll of Pennsylvania that proclaimed that the body could not receive the slave petition "without disregarding its own dignity, the rights of a large class of the citizens of the South and West, and the Constitution of the United States."[9]

Adams responded systematically to each averment. Rather than disregarding the dignity of the House, Adams argued, receiving the petition would maintain its dignity. Most Americans would view a refusal to hear a petition, said Adams, as "beneath the dignity of the General Legislative Assembly of a nation, founding its existence upon natural and inalienable rights of man." The petition did not encroach on the rights of southern and western citizens because although it was purportedly from slaves, it prayed for the preservation of slavery, and likely came from slaveholders. Adams's revelation incensed southern members, who saw themselves as the butt of a parliamentary practical joke.

In the course of his response to the claim that the Constitution denied slaves the right of petition, Adams argued that the Constitution "expressly forbids Congress from abridging, even by *law*, the right of petition, and which, not by the remotest implication, limits that right to freemen." He urged congressmen and their constituents to read the Constitution, where they would find that "in a compact formed for securing to the people of the Union the blessing of liberty," in respect to decency there is no use of the word "slave." Instead, every allusion to slaves employed the word "persons," and according to Adams these persons were recognized as members of the community and as human beings who possessed rights. "Their right to be represented in Congress is admitted," he maintained, "even in the provision which curtails it by two fifths, and transfers the remainder to their masters."[10]

After lengthy debate the House adopted by wide margins Ingersoll's and another resolution denying slaves the right of petition. Passage of these resolutions constituted an important chapter in the continuing negotiation of the meaning of the right of petition and the meaning of U.S. citizenship. The event demonstrated that when it came to controversial issues such as slavery, Congress was capable of denying the right of petition outright to certain classes of the nation's inhabitants, namely slaves. Debate over whether slaves possessed the right of petition raised other fundamental questions: Is the right of petition linked to citizenship? Are slaves citizens? Is a person denied the right of petition a citizen? The decision to deny slaves the right of petition, moreover, left open the possibility that because of the questionable citizenship status of women, their right of petition was vulnerable to similar incursion. After all, Bynum's resolution called for any attempt to present a petition from "a negro or free negroes" to be ruled in contempt of the House. As Adams warned, the deprivation of the right of petition in the case of slaves "yields a principle that may be applied in numberless others, till the whole right of petition

shall, . . . be numbered among the *spoils of victory*—the exclusive possession of the dominant party of the day." Because women's political status
remained unclear, their right of petition could easily be challenged (and as
we shall see, it was). This debate over slaves' and free blacks' right of petition supports Jan Lewis's observation that during the first three-quarters
of the nineteenth century, "women's membership in civil society would
be defined in relationship to that of free blacks." She notes in particular
that "the understanding of women's civil rights emerged most clearly in
discussions about attempts to limit the civil rights of free blacks."[11]

*   *   *

Outright denial of slaves' right of petition combined with passage of a second gag rule outraged abolitionists, especially abolitionist women, thousands of whom had circulated and signed the petitions that were tabled.
Abuses hurled by southern congressmen against the petitioners and
disrespectful treatment of the venerable Adams did little to discourage
antislavery women from petitioning. Instead they sought to streamline
petitioning into a more effective operation. Female abolition leaders
recognized that the haphazard approach of leaving petitioning to local
antislavery societies would not suffice. One problem with allowing local
societies to run the campaign was that often volunteers started gathering
signatures too late for petitions to reach congressmen before the dead-
line for presentation. In some cases, moreover, congressmen alleged that
the petitions bore false signatures, an accusation abolitionists could not
refute without a systematic plan for checking the names. A further weakness was that the memorials circulated by local societies were drawn up by
individuals who often lacked the rhetorical acumen necessary to compose
petitions befitting presentation to Congress. Instead, petitions written by
local male and female antislavery societies often employed harsh language
to which more than one congressman took offense. In addition, rather
than strategically selecting a sympathetic representative to present the
petitions, local volunteers sent hundreds of legitimate petitions to their
own congressmen, many of whom were hostile to abolition and refused
to introduce the memorials. As a result, hours of grueling work spent persuading people to sign petitions were completely wasted.[12]

In response to events in Congress and to rectify problems with the
signature-gathering process, leaders of several New England female abolition societies suggested the idea of coordinating petitioning to the next
session of Congress. On August 4, 1836, Maria Weston Chapman, cor-

responding secretary of the Boston Female Anti-Slavery Society, sent a letter to Mary Grew, her counterpart in the Philadelphia Female Anti-Slavery Society, proposing formation of "a general executive committee" to systematize the work of petitioning. Grew replied that the Philadelphia society found the idea "expedient and desirable" but noted that some members of her society "would much prefer a recognition of female members and delegates in the American Society." The Boston women responded by suggesting that a national female convention be organized in May 1837 at the same time and in the same city as the meeting of the AASS. The Philadelphia organization then sent a letter to female antislavery societies throughout Pennsylvania and another missive to Methodist women inviting them to participate in the convention.[13]

Likely these invitations were greeted with surprise because during the 1830s the notion of women meeting in convention to debate and to pass resolutions was highly unusual. Women commonly gathered in parlors and churches to participate in sewing circles, literary organizations, and charitable societies, but seldom had American women from several states assembled to discuss a controversial public issue such as the abolition of slavery. In fact, the 1837 female antislavery convention likely was the first public political meeting of American women and, as Dorothy Sterling has noted, "the first interracial gathering of any consequence."[14]

The dearth of women's conventions at a time when such gatherings had become an effective means for influencing public opinion can be explained by the abundance of warnings against females holding such meetings. Newspapers and ladies' magazines published satirical accounts of women meeting in fictitious conventions to discuss trifling issues such as fashion and the availability of husbands. In 1812 an article in Philadelphia's *Lady's Miscellany,* for example, portrayed women as collectively petitioning the legislature against efforts "to deprive them of the indefeasible right of dress." Articles such as these published during the early national period, Rosemarie Zagarri explains, were meant to stifle women's growing political aspirations by implying that women were foolish and could not possibly deliberate. During the Jacksonian era even radical male reformers, including abolitionists, curtailed full female participation in conventions. When, for example, sixty-four men gathered in Philadelphia during the first week of December 1833 to found the AASS, four women observed the proceedings. Of these four women—Lucretia Mott, Lydia White, Esther Moore, and Sidney Anne Lewis—only Mott spoke, and she did so during only one meeting. Mott's oratorical outburst was so unusual that a male delegate recalled, "I had never before heard a woman speak at a public meeting." Male abolitionists expressed appreciation for Mott's contributions; but none of them recognized the women as full delegates, and no woman was invited to sign the organization's founding document, the Declaration of Sentiments.[15]

Nevertheless, female antislavery leaders were familiar enough with the process of holding conventions that they followed the accepted practice of publicizing their meeting by issuing a circular. The convention circular, likely written by Chapman, was published in March 1837 by antislavery newspapers such as the *Liberator,* the *Emancipator,* and the *Friend of Man.* Like the circular issued before the founding convention of the AASS, a major goal of the women's call was to attract a large number of participants, which would appear to reflect public opinion in the free states. But unlike the AASS's call, the women's announcement needed to overcome both the unpopularity of abolitionism and the taboo against females attending conventions. Rather than protest too much by directly addressing the issue of propriety, the call portrayed meeting in convention as a common and acceptable thing for women to do. "We believe there will be hundreds, if not thousands of the women of New England, whose gushing sympathies will impel them to attend this convention, to join the glorious company of faithful women who will be there assembled," the circular proclaimed.[16]

The major argument of the circular was that because women in particular suffered the effects of slavery, women were especially responsible to work for emancipation. Chapman's rhetorical strategy was to appeal to the self-interest of her readers by demonstrating for her primary audience of northern white women that they were affected by slavery both as mothers and as women. She appealed to women as "mothers of New England," asking if they could passively "send your sons abroad in the world, exposed to the scorching fires of temptation enkindled by slavery, while you are doing nothing to quench the flame." Every year, Chapman warned, young men born and bred in the North visited the South, where they were "soon swallowed in the whirlpool, in which they sink to rise no more." Nor, she warned, were the "blighting influences" of slavery confined to the South. Every summer slaveholders came North to evangelize their proslavery ideals: "They call evil good, and bitter they call sweet. . . . They put light for darkness, and darkness for light, and accustom their northern friends to do the same." Women had to put aside their fears of impropriety in order to save the nation, Chapman claimed, because if they "sleep over the iniquities of slavery for another generation, . . . they will leave their children exposed to God's severest judgments."[17]

In addition to appealing to her readers as mothers and moral individuals, Chapman emphasized the horrid effects slavery wreaked on women as a group. Slavery, she charged, held "more than a million of our sisters" in an unholy institution where they were unable to find "protectors who can perform the duties of a husband." Thus slave women were left "down in a state of universal prostitution" and faced "punishment of death, if they presume to protect themselves." This argument, which was employed often by women abolitionists in their petitions to Congress, drove slaveholders apoplectic with anger. It violated southern gentlemen's implicit agreement that sexual relations with slaves were acceptable as long as they remained unmentioned in polite company. It insulted the honor of slaveholding men, their wives, and their legal children. As such, it appealed to northerners' sense of moral superiority over southerners.[18]

To bolster the circular's call for a convention, the *National Enquirer* defended the unusual event by emphasizing that the antislavery movement needed woman's moral power. The editors ridiculed anyone who would balk at the idea of a female convention. New modes of proceeding were necessary at this time, they proclaimed, because abolitionists sought to remove a "stupendous mountain of evil" so as to accomplish an important reformation. The convention of women was necessary for the abolition movement because "every avenue, hitherto open, has been studiously barricaded. Other means are requisite to bring our artillery to bear upon the Bastille of despotism." The *Enquirer* was especially desirous of selecting a new site on which to "erect the lever of moral power" for the "overthrow and annihilation" of slavery. "Let no genuine Female Philanthropist hold back, from a timid apprehension of exceeding the limits of propriety, of deviating from the acknowledged principles of female duty, or of transgressing the legitimate privileges and immunities of her sex," the newspaper exhorted. Indeed, the editors concluded, "We look forward with the pleasing expectation, that a mighty convocation of female piety, philanthropy, and talent will be witnessed."[19]

On Tuesday, May 9, 1837, 71 delegates gathered in the Third Free Church at the corner of Houston and Thompson Streets for the First Anti-Slavery Convention of American Women. In addition to the delegates, the convention was populated by 103 corresponding members, who attended in an unofficial capacity and were allowed to vote. The largest representations came from Massachusetts and Pennsylvania, both of which sent

22 delegates. New York sent 19; Rhode Island, 3; New Hampshire and Ohio, 2 each; and New Jersey, 1. Membership of the convention was 94 percent white, and the makeup of corresponding members was 84 percent white. Among the African American women attending were Maria Stewart, who was living in New York, as well as Philadelphians Sarah Mapps Douglass and Grace Douglass. Mary S. Parker was elected president of the convention due in large part to the fact that she was president of the influential Boston Female Anti-Slavery Society, which had achieved singular success in its petitioning efforts. The convention chose six vice-presidents: Mott (Philadelphia), Grace Douglass (Philadelphia), Lydia Maria Child (Boston), Abby Ann Cox (New York), Sarah Grimké (representing South Carolina), and Ann C. Smith (New York). Four secretaries were also selected: Mary Grew (Philadelphia), Angelina Grimké (representing South Carolina), Sarah Pugh (Philadelphia), and Anne Warren Weston (Boston). Women who had gained leadership skills and confidence in local antislavery societies refused Theodore Weld's offer to help them run the first national female convention, telling him that they had "found that they had *minds* of their own and could transact their business *without* his direction."[20]

"Petitions to Congress," the convention resolved, "constitute the one central point to which we must bend our strongest efforts." The women set as their main goal "to collect a million signatures on petitions calling on Congress to abolish slavery in the District of Columbia and in Florida." The convention discussed a systematic plan for circulating petitions to achieve this goal. Child proposed establishing three Central Committees with whom abolition workers could correspond. These committees were to be anchored in the major urban centers and included Grew, Pugh, Sarah Mapps Douglass in Philadelphia; Rebecca Spring, Juliana A. Tappan, and Anna Blackwell in New York City; and Chapman, Henrietta Sargent, and Catharine Sullivan in Boston. State antislavery offices were to appoint one woman in each county who would in turn name one woman in each town in her county to whom the Central Committee could send blank petitions. Cities were to be divided into districts, and antislavery women were directed to "visit every house and present every female over sixteen years of age, a petition for her signature." Rather than sending the petitions from cities and towns directly to congressmen, as had been the practice, they were now to be forwarded to the county coordinator, who would check the signatures. From there the petitions were to go to the state committees, where they would be counted, recorded, and sent to

Congress. After the petition plan was discussed and agreed on, "the Free States were called in rotation, and from most of them pledges were given by their daughters rising to the call, and promising their exertions in this cause."[21]

The fact that the women adopted a detailed plan of petitioning at their May 1837 convention has been overlooked by historians who attribute invention of the petition strategy to AASS men who met at the same time and in the same city. Not only did women precede men in organizing their petitioning, but it is likely that the AASS derived its national campaign strategy from the method instituted by the women. It was only after the conventions had adjourned and after the women's plan had been published that Weld, John G. Whittier, and Henry Stanton went about the task of organizing the AASS petition campaign. Their plan, developed for the most part by Stanton, was remarkably similar to the one implemented by the women's convention. Indeed, it is plausible that Stanton used the women's plan as a model, for by the time he was charged with developing a petition scheme for the AASS, Stanton was familiar with the Boston women's system of collecting signatures. In November 1836 he had reported to the Rhode Island Anti-Slavery Society convention that "the ladies of Boston had districted the whole state [of Massachusetts] with reference to the circulation of petitions" and had succeeded in gathering twice as many names as their male counterparts.[22]

Along with instituting a petitioning strategy for the free states, much of the 1837 female antislavery convention was devoted to discussing whether it was proper for women to partake in various forms of antislavery activism such as petitioning. The discussion was long overdue because women had been attacked by the clergy and others for petitioning and otherwise stepping outside their proper sphere to do the work of abolition. Because convention participants varied in class, race, and regional and religious backgrounds, they far from agreed on what constituted acceptable boundaries of female activism. At the vanguard was Angelina Grimké, who, like Mott and the other Philadelphia delegates, was comfortable with females exerting themselves on behalf of moral causes, due perhaps to her association with Quakerism. Grimké offered a resolution stating that certain rights and duties were "common to all moral beings" and that the time had come "for woman to move in that sphere which Providence has assigned her, and no longer remain satisfied in the circumscribed limits with which corrupt custom and a perverted application of the Scripture have encircled her." It was the duty of woman, the resolution maintained, "to plead the cause of the oppressed in our land, and to do all that she can by her voice, and her pen, and her purse, and the influence of her example, to overthrow the horrible system of American slavery."[23]

But Grimké's assertion of women's natural rights and the claim that scripture had been "perverted" was too strong for some delegates. According to the convention minutes, her resolution touched off an "animated and interesting debate." After several amendments were offered, the resolution was adopted without changes, though as the proceedings noted, "*not unanimously.*" Twelve women were in such deep disagreement with Grimké's resolution, which in essence redrew the proper sphere of female activism, that they voted against its adoption and asked that their names be recorded in the minutes as disapproving parts of the resolution. Ten of the twelve negative votes came from New York City women who were Presbyterians and Methodists, denominations that tended to be less radical than their Quaker and Unitarian counterparts in Philadelphia and Boston. Later in the convention, in the interest of unity Child tried to resuscitate discussion of the province of woman by moving that Grimké's resolution be reconsidered, but the motion was defeated. Then Cox and Spring, both from New York, attempted to make peace by offering a resolution couched in the acceptable terms of motherhood. Cox stated, "There is no class of women to whom the anti-slavery cause makes so direct and powerful an appeal as to *mothers.*" Cox encouraged mothers to "lift up their hearts to God on behalf of the captive," not only because they could sympathize with the slave mother's condition, but also to guard their own children from evils of slavery and prejudice. Cox's resolution was approved unanimously. The unhampered passage of Cox's resolution based on the duties of motherhood as opposed to the troubled journey of Grimké's resolution based on the notion that women and men possessed common rights and duties demonstrated that many antislavery women did not view rights as grounded in individuals but as deriving from their collective status as women.[24]

Undaunted, Grimké presented another resolution stating that "the right of petition is natural and inalienable, derived immediately from God, and guaranteed by the Constitution of the United States." Grimké's resolution was a condemnation of the House's passage some three months earlier of measures that denied slaves the right of petition. In an attempt to establish the rights of both abolitionists and women to petition, the resolution further stated that the delegates regarded every effort by Congress to abridge the sacred right of petition, whether exercised by a man or a woman, the slave or the free, "as a high-handed usurpation of power, and an attempt to strike a death-blow at the freedom of the people." This resolution was approved unanimously, indicating perhaps that antislavery women perceived a link between the civil rights of slaves and free blacks and those of free women.[25]

More questions about the propriety of expanding female activism were raised in New York newspapers not long after the convention adjourned. William Stone, a staunch colonizationist and editor of the *New York Commercial Advertiser,* published a report of the convention under the headline "Billingsgate Abuse" and dubbed the meeting an "Amazonian farce" attended by "a monstrous *regiment* of women" who were "petticoat philanthropists." Questioning the femininity of those who attended the convention, he referred to them as "female brethren" and accused them of being deluded by "the charming" George Thompson, the British abolitionist who had recently concluded a speaking tour of the northern states. "The spinster has thrown aside her distaff—the blooming beauty her guitar—the matron her darning needle—the sweet novelist her crow-quill," wrote Stone. He continued to rant: "The young mother has left her baby to nestle alone in the cradle—and the kitchen maid her pots and frying-pans—to discuss the weighty matters of state—to decide upon intricate questions of international polity—and weigh, with avoirdupois exactness, the balance of power." Stone also ridiculed the convention's "oratoresses" and the "rich rivers of rhetoric which flowed through the broad aisle."[26]

Soon after it adjourned, the convention of antislavery women issued *An Appeal to the Women of the Nominally Free States,* which urged northern women to work against slavery in several ways, especially by petitioning. The *Appeal* was drafted by Angelina Grimké before the convention and, according to the convention minutes, a committee of Grimké, Lydia Maria Child, Grace Douglass, and Abby Kelley was appointed to edit the document. The poem that appeared on the title page was written by Sarah Forten, and the section of the *Appeal* that discussed race prejudice was based in part on information supplied by Grace Douglass's daughter, Sarah Mapps Douglass.[27]

The pamphlet enumerated the ways in which the peculiar institution violated political, moral, and religious principles held dear by all people regardless of sex. Slavery, it stated, robbed "MAN" of his humanity, of his "inalienable right to liberty," of the fruits of his labor, and of the ability to protect himself. But slaves were not the only victims, it argued, for so, too, were northerners. Slavery outlawed "every Northerner who openly avows our Declaration of Independence," destroyed northerners' ability to communicate through the mail, threatened with assassination any congressman who dared speak about it, and trampled "the right of petition when exercised by free men and free women." To stamp out the institution that had denied slaves access to the Bible, creating "A NATION OF HEATHEN IN OUR VERY MIDST," the *Appeal* urged women to read about slavery and join abolition societies. By gaining information about slavery, it explained, "you will prepare the way for circulation of numerous petitions, both to ecclesiastical and civil authorities of the nation." The *Appeal* urged that "*every woman, of every denomination,* whatever may be her color and creed, *ought to sign* a petition to Congress for the abolition of slavery and the slave trade in the district of Columbia—slavery in Florida—and the inter-state slave traffic."[28]

In the course of calling women to participate in the petition campaign, the *Appeal to the Women of the Nominally Free States* sounded arguments that were much bolder than those employed in the 1836 addresses. Rather than attempting to distance women's antislavery activism from politics, the *Appeal* readily acknowledged political aspects of women's activities and shirked the notion that women possessed no duties beyond the parlor and the nursery. Asserting that "every citizen should feel an intense interest in the political concerns of the country," it demanded that women be recognized as citizens. "Are we aliens because we are women? Are we bereft of citizenship because we are the *mothers, wives,* and *daughters* of a mighty people? Have *women* no country—no interest staked in public weal—no liabilities in common peril—no partnership in a nation's guilt and shame?" Instead of attempting to move slavery into the home, where it would seem proper for woman to attack it, the *Appeal* attempted to lay a republican path on which women, whom it characterized as citizens of the republic, could walk a route of expanded political participation.[29]

The convention's *Appeal,* moreover, went beyond emphasizing the duties incumbent upon women as members of the female sex to stress their responsibilities based "on the broad ground of human rights and human responsibilities." "All moral beings have essentially the same rights and duties, whether they be male or female," it proclaimed. Instead of arguing that it was appropriate for woman to petition because she was more moral than man, the *Appeal* declared that women should be allowed to petition because they were equal to men and possessed the same rights. In making this demand, the *Appeal* moved beyond a critique of male social dominance based on alleged masculine moral inferiority to the claim that men were denying women their natural rights. "The denial of our duty to act is a bold denial of our right to act; and if we have no right to act, then may we well be termed 'the white slaves of the North'—for, like our brethren in bonds, we must seal our lips in silence and despair." In this passage the *Appeal* deconstructed the attacks leveled against women petitioners by explaining that questioning the propriety of female petitioning ("denial of our duty to act") in effect entailed a denial of women's constitutional right to freedom of speech. Because their right of petition had been abrogated and they were denied the right to vote, the *Appeal* contended, women were no better off than slaves when it came to the exercise of political rights. Although this argument obscured the significant material differences between the lives of slaves and those of the predominantly white, middle-class antislavery women, by articulating the denial of women's natural rights and placing it in perspective, the *Appeal* made a major contribution to nineteenth-century feminist thought.[30]

* * *

The convention's *Appeal* directed women to petition because slavery violated the principles of Christianity and natural rights, but it made no mention of the issue of Texas annexation. Yet during 1837 abolitionists had elevated the Texas question, along with the gag rule controversy, to the forefront of their case against slavery. Abolitionists devoted their attention to the issue of Texas after Benjamin Lundy published a series of essays and a widely circulated pamphlet titled *The War in Texas*, which argued that the drive for Texan independence was part of the ongoing conspiracy to expand the slave power. Lundy demonstrated that the Texans were rebelling not because they had been oppressed by the Mexican government but because they wanted to break away from Mexico, whose constitution prohibited slavery. Not only would an independent Texas perpetuate slavery in the West, Lundy argued, but it would likely spawn six to eight new slave states. This shift in the balance of power between the sections, according to Lundy, threatened to dissolve the Union. Lundy's interpretation of the events in Texas and his predictions about the future of the Union were accepted by Adams, who encouraged Lundy to circulate his arguments as widely as possible to rouse public sentiment against annexing Texas.[31]

Because none of the pamphlets published by the women's convention discussed the important issue of Texas annexation, immediately after the convention the Boston Female Anti-Slavery Society issued *An Address to the Women of New England*. It was signed by Parker, who was president of both the society and the convention. In addition to being printed in the *Liberator*, the *Address* was published on letter sheets to which were attached petitions opposing the annexation of Texas. Like Lundy's pamphlet, the *Address to the Women of New England* claimed that if slaveholders succeeded in their plot to annex Texas, the freedom and the very lives of northerners would be endangered. But why, asked the Boston entreaty, should women care about Texas? Because, it answered, if Texas were annexed to the Union, "our husbands and our sons should be drafted from our household-floors, to encounter the storm of fire and blood that will sweep along the south-western border." The Union would be dissolved, "brother should battle against brother and friend against friend," and the slaves would take advantage of the crisis and "rise to the shedding of blood on every southern threshold!" The Boston women warned that "the unutterable destruction that sooner or later awaits our country, unless slavery is abolished, is as certain as that God judges and punishes nations, in this world, according to evil deeds." In light of the destruction sure to follow from annexation of Texas, women were asked to petition Congress against this policy. "Let every woman into whose hands this page falls, INSTANTLY (for the work must be done before the extra September session) prepare four rolls of paper, and attach one to each of the annexed forms of petition; and with pen and ink-horn in hand, and armed with affectionate but unconquerable determination, go from door to door 'among her own people,' that every one of them may have an opportunity of affixing her name to these four memorials."[32]

Like the *Appeal to the Women of the Nominally Free States*, which more directly asserted that women possessed the right of petition than previous female antislavery publications had, the Boston Female Anti-Slavery Society *Address* directed women to take action on a specific issue that was undoubtedly political. Women must petition against annexation, the Boston *Address* explained, so northern representatives would know the true wishes of their constituents. More explicitly than ever before, this address described female petitioning as advising representatives on a political matter, rather than as "praying" to the "guardians of our nation" to do what was right. Furthermore, the *Address* insisted that women were not just the "mothers, wives, daughters and sisters" of male constituents but that women themselves were, in fact, the constituents of northern congressmen—that they were full citizens. "Remember that the *representation of our country is based on the numbers of population, irrespective of sex*," the

Boston women prompted. Here was a novel argument for women's rights that harkened back to the rhetoric of the American Revolution, to abolitionist critiques of the three-fifths clause, and to Adams's defense of the right of slaves to petition. When calculating population in order to determine how many representatives each congressional district would be awarded, the *Address* observed, a female was counted as a full person. If the Constitution acknowledged women as worthy of being counted to determine representation in Congress, the *Address* claimed, then surely they possessed the right to make their opinions known to their representatives.[33]

* * *

Appealing to women to continue petitioning was but one of the means of persuasion set in motion at the 1837 convention. Another important task accomplished as a result of the meeting was the introduction of new petition forms. In the first phase of women's antislavery petitioning from 1831 to 1836, local antislavery societies had relied on long, printed petition forms that ran about a page in length and emphasized that slavery was sinful. But when male and female abolitionists implemented strategies discussed at the 1837 conventions, they cast aside the petition forms that they had been using for several years. During this second major phase of women's antislavery petitioning, no longer were the lengthy forms with their protracted explications of the evils of slavery, their sentimental statements about woman's duty to petition, and their detailed descriptions of slave auctions within sight of the nation's Capitol able to meet the demands of the situation in Congress. Passage of the gag rule necessitated a change in strategy. After no small amount of contemplation, petition campaign coordinators realized that the gag did not prevent Adams and his cohorts in the House from stating the title of a petition. To get their message across before cries of "Order!" rang out from all sides, abolitionists did away with the long petitions and composed short forms that in the same breath announced the title and the prayer of the petition.[34]

The switch to short forms not only affected presentation of the petitions in Congress but also marked a major change in the way women went about petitioning. More and more women signed the same forms as men, though they kept their names in separate columns, and short petitions allowed no room for veiling the political requests of women or for elaborate discussions of the propriety of female petitioning. The language of humility, ever present in women's petitions submitted during the early 1830s,

Lucretia Mott, who helped organize Philadelphia Quaker women in 1831 to send the first collective female antislavery petition to Congress, played a leading role in the 1837 female antislavery convention. (Courtesy of the Massachusetts Historical Society)

Maria Weston Chapman, a leader in the Boston Female Anti-Slavery Society, wrote petition forms and public addresses and led implementation of a systematic plan of petitioning. (Reprinted with permission of the Boston Public Library/Rare Books Department — Courtesy of the Trustees)

PETITIONS! PETITIONS!! PETITIONS!!!

Reader! Examine the following petitions, and if you wish to *live* in a country where the people *enjoy* *the right of* petition, then EXERCISE that right in such a manner as to prevent it from being taken away.—And ask your neighbors to join with you in this work. *Cut the petitions apart,* and paste them on separate *half sheets* of white paper, for signatures. Then sign your own name, and go among your neighbors for their names. The petitions respecting TEXAS, should be in Washington by the first of September. For further directions, see the first page.

1. *To the Senate and House of Representatives of the United States:*
   The undersigned,   of   in the State of
                                    Respectfully pray your honorable body immediately to abolish SLAVERY and the SLAVETRADE in the DISTRICT OF COLUMBIA,

2. *To the Senate and House of Representatives of the United States:*
   The undersigned   of
                    in the State of   Respectfully pray your
   honorable body, immediately to abolish SLAVERY and the SLAVETRADE in those TERRITORIES of the United States where they exist.

3. *To the Senate and House of Representatives of the United States:*
   The undersigned,   of
                    in the State of   Respectfully pray your honorable body, so to exercise the Constitutional power vested in you to "regulate COMMERCE AMONG THE SEVERAL STATES," as entirely to prohibit the Domestic Slave Trade.

4. *To the Senate and House of Representatives of the United States:*
   The undersigned,   of
                    in the State of   Respectfully pray your
   honorable body, not to admit any NEW STATE to this Union, whose Constitution tolerates DOMESTIC SLAVERY.

5. *To the Senate and House of Representatives of the United States:*
   The undersigned,   of
                    in the State of   Respectfully pray your honorable body
   promptly to reject all proposals for the annexation of TEXAS to this Union, from whatever source they may come for the following, among other reasons:
   1. Although the independence of Texas has been recognised by this government, yet, it has not been acknowledged by Mexico, and is now forcibly resisted by that power:—therefore its annexation to the Union, might involve this nation in a war with Mexico. Against any measure tending to such a result, we remonstrate.
   2. While we do not claim for Congress the power to *abolish* slavery in the several states, we are opposed to its *further extension* by that body, and hence are decidedly hostile to the annexation of Texas to the Union, with a Constitution which expressly sanctions slavery, and encourages the slavetrade between that country and the United States.
   3. Texas has a territory of sufficient extent to make six large states. It being the avowed intention to continue it a slaveholding country, its annexation to the Union will give predominant power, in our national councils, to the slaveholding interest, and will reduce to complete subjection, *the interests of the free states,* and especially the interests of their FREE LABOR, which is the foundation of their wealth and prosperity. Such a result would probably lead to a DISSOLUTION of the UNION,—an event we sincerely deprecate.

In 1837 abolitionists switched to short forms, which allowed John Quincy Adams and other sympathetic representatives to shout out the statement of the petition before being silenced by calls for order. Short form petitions were often printed in reform newspapers, from which they were cut out and pasted on sheets of paper to be circulated for signatures.

To the Honorable the House of Representatives of the United States.

The undersigned *women* of *Brookline* in the Commonwealth of Massachusetts, have learned with astonishment and alarm, that your honorable body did, on the 21st of December last, adopt a resolution in the words following, to wit:

'Resolved, That all memorials, petitions, and papers, touching the abolition of slavery, or the buying, selling, or transfer of slaves in any State, territory, or district of the United States, shall be laid on the table, without ~~reading, or reference, or printing, and that no further action whatever shall be had thereon.~~ *being debated printed read or referred & that no further action whatever shall be had thereon.*

Your memorialists 'consider this resolution a violation of the Constitution of the United States—of the right of the people of the United States to petition—and of the right of their Representatives to freedom of speech as members of your honorable body:' They further regard it as an assumption of authority, at once dangerous and destructive to the fundamental principles of republican government, to the rights of minorities, to the sovereignty of the People, and TO THE UNION OF THESE UNITED STATES: They therefore present this their solemn and earnest remonstrance against said resolution, and respectfully ask your honorable body to IMMEDIATELY RESCIND IT.

Sarah M. Grimké

Angelina E. Grimké

Eliza Philbrick

Fanny Bell

Sarah Celfe

Hepzibah Celfe

Chloe H. Whitney

Rebecca Gerry

Rebecca S. Gerry

Rosyra Jaqueth   10

Ann K. Ogan

Abigail Tolman

Mary J. R. Tolman

Elizabeth Whyte

Susan G. Whyte

Ellen S. Whyte

Sarah M. Grimké and Angelina E. Grimké joined the women of Brookline, Massachusetts, in signing this short petition protesting passage of the gag rule. The sisters' 1837 New England lecture tour won many signatures to petitions like this one. (Courtesy of the National Archives) began to disappear. Gone was the elaborate type; gone was the palaverous prose. The typical short form cut directly to the chase:

To the Senate and House of Representatives of the United States:
    The undersigned, _____ of _____ in the State of _____ Respectfully pray your honorable body immediately to abolish SLAVERY and the SLAVE TRADE in the DISTRICT OF COLUMBIA.[35]

Plain and simple, most of the short petitions rarely exceeded five lines. Some were longer, usually about ten lines, but rarely did they reach the length of petitions circulated in previous years.

Not only could antislavery congressmen state the short form request quickly, but up to twelve different requests could easily be printed on a single handbill. Canvassers—women and men alike—were supplied with forms and instructions printed in New York by the national office of the AASS and reproduced in abolitionist periodicals. Immediately after the May convention the AASS published a large edition of a petitioning circular, which provided eleven petition forms. Six of the forms were addressed to Congress; five, to state legislatures. The first petition related to slavery in the District of Columbia, an issue that "is now a test question. As it shall be decided, so will be the fate of liberty in this nation." The second petition, which involved slavery in the territories, was described in much the same manner as the first. For the third petition, regarding the interstate slave trade, the circular provided petitioners with an argument: "Congress has declared the traffic in men on the high seas and on the coast of Africa, *piracy*. Is it less practical in *America?*" The fourth petition addressed the admission of Florida to the Union as a slave state. On this issue the circular urged adherents to "be ready in season, so that we may not be taken by surprise, as in the case of Arkansas."[36]

The last two petition forms addressed the most important issue for abolitionists in 1837: the admission of Texas. The petition drive to halt Texas annexation not only laid the groundwork for the political organization of abolitionists in general, but it pushed women closer to overt political activity. By signing petitions for repeal of the gag rule and against annexation of Texas, women joined men in voicing their opinions to Congress on issues of national policy. Moreover, the short petition forms did not provide space for women to divorce their activism from politics and to insist that their goals were purely benevolent. From 1837 on, women expressed their requests in petitions by using the same language and by assuming the same stance as male petitioners. Prominent black abolitionist women

Margaretta and Sarah Forten and Sarah and Grace Douglass signed a petition that assumed this new bold attitude. Lucretia Mott, Mary Grew, and 222 other women of Philadelphia joined the others in affixing their names to a petition that read,

> To the House of Representatives of the United States:
>
> The memorial of the subscribers, citizens of Philadelphia, respectfully represents: That we have perceived, with deep regret, that a resolution has passed your distinguished body, virtually denying to all the inhabitants of the free States the right of petition, and consequently abridging the freedom of speech. As such an act is obviously contrary to the constitution of our country, we do respectfully protest against it, and ask for its immediate reconsideration and repeal.

This petition is noteworthy both for what it said and for what it did not say. It said that the female signers were willing to affix their names to a petition that claimed to emanate from "citizens." In previous years the vast majority of women had scratched out the word "citizens" on printed petitions and replaced it with "inhabitants" or "residents." By using the appellation "citizens," women claimed for themselves a new status in the young republic. Unlike most female petitions sent between 1831 and 1836, this one did not describe women as approaching their representatives deferentially, nor did it insist that women were motivated by a unique female morality.[37]

These changes came about partly because of the lack of space on standardized short form petitions and also because of changes in attitudes about women petitioning. When given the opportunity for elaboration, women expressed in their petitions a new, bolder stance. Nowhere is this more evident than in the petition of women against the admission of Texas to the Union circulated among the women of Ohio. Even though it was much shorter than the Fathers and Rulers and other long petition forms, this entreaty was about three times as long as the short forms and offered ample space for the petitioners to develop a rationale for approaching their representatives and for explaining their objections to annexation. Whereas in 1836 the women of Ohio had addressed their legislators as the "Fathers and Rulers of Our Country," in 1837–38 their display of deference had vanished, and they addressed their petition "To the honorable, the Senate and House of representatives of the United States." Absent also were characterizations of the humility of female petitioners. No longer did they "pray" with "sympathies" they were "constrained to feel as wives, mothers, and daughters." Instead they said in the first line of the petition, "Women have one inalienable mode of representing what might be for their own interests or for the interests of mankind, namely, supplication." Unlike the Fathers and Rulers form, which began by stating that the signers would not dare to "obtrude" on the business of Congress unless the issue was pressing, in the antiannexation petition the women of Ohio opened by forthrightly stating that petitioning was women's "inalienable mode" of communicating their sentiments to their representatives. No longer did they describe their petitioning as motivated by some outside force. No longer did they identify themselves as adjuncts of male citizens.[38]

Furthermore, when stating grievances against the policy of annexation, the women's antiannexation petition did not mention Christianity or the suffering female slave. Unlike the sentimental expressions of the evils of slavery common in the long form petitions, the later Ohio form was almost legalistic. It stated, "One prominent reason amongst others, why we deprecate its [Texas's] annexation, is, its constitution expressly sanctions slavery, and encourages the slave trade between [Texas] and the United States. When most governments in the civilized world, where slavery has been instituted, are taking measures for its abrogation, we humbly pray that our Republican Legislators will not be found legislating for its extension, and augmenting the horrors of its traffic." The petition grounded rejection of the Texas annexation on constitutional law and republicanism rather than on benevolence or female duty. Indeed, the word "duty" was used only once in the petition, when the signers stated that they considered it their "imperative duty" to entreat Congress to reject the proposal for annexing Texas. But even here the duty was not that of wives, mothers, sisters, or even Christians, but of republican citizens.[39]

In addition to altering the petitions strategically, coordinators of the campaign recognized that volunteers needed specific directions on how to circulate and submit petitions. To this end they printed circulars in which a number of short petitions were accompanied by explicit instructions directing volunteers when to begin petitioning, how to petition, and when the completed petitions were to be submitted. The volunteers were encouraged to start gathering signatures immediately and not to confine their efforts to abolitionists. "All who hate slavery, and love the cause of mercy, and would preserve our free institutions, should put their names to them, without regard to their view of abolitionism. It should be a movement of THE PEOPLE." This consideration, the circular stated, should be "emphatically urged." Volunteers were instructed to circulate all the petition forms at the same time because this method would be most economical and because individuals willing to sign one petition would be likely to sign them all. Yet the petitions were to be separated in case those called on were willing to sign some but not others. The circular also asked readers to make sure each town in the county had received blank petition forms. If not, the annexed petitions should be copied and conveyed to a "suitable person" in the town with a request that they be returned to the person who copied them.[40]

The last section of the circular was devoted to details of handling the petitions and was titled "Small, but Necessary Matters." The person who received the circular and the attached blank forms was asked first to cut the petitions apart and to paste each one at the top of a half-sheet of paper. Next they were to fill in the first blank in the body of the petition, which described the persons who were submitting it with the words "citizens," "inhabitants," "legal voters," "women," or whatever the case may be. In the second blank they were to write, if the memorial was directed at a state legislature, the name of the city or town in which the petition originated; if the petition was aimed at Congress, they were to write the city or town and the county. Volunteers were instructed to make sure that signatures were written on only one side of the paper and to paste on more sheets if needed. The circular emphasized that everyone should write his or her own name: "Names should not be *copied* on—it might lead to a suspicion that they were forged."[41]

The last instructions detailed how to submit the completed petitions to Congress or the state legislature. It was important, the circular emphasized, that the names on each petition be counted and that the number be written clearly at the top before it was forwarded. The completed petitions were to be sent by each town with a letter to a member of Congress or to the state legislature, though in some cases arrangements could be made to paste together all the petitions from one county to send in a large roll. Volunteers were also told that petitions of any size as well as letters under two ounces could be sent postage free. Even better, the circular advised, signed petitions could be handed to congressmen before they departed for Washington. All petitions relating to Texas were to be submitted at the beginning of the special congressional session starting in September 1837, while the other memorials were to be sent at the beginning of the regular session in December.[42]

In addition to circulars, personal letters were employed to send blank petition forms to women who could be trusted to put them into circulation in their towns. Letters enclosing blank petitions were sometimes sent to women whom organizers knew through family or other social networks. At other times organizers sent letters and forms to women with whom they were completely unacquainted. On July 10, 1837, just two months after the convention, a member of the Philadelphia Female Anti-Slavery Society composed a letter to a woman in Bedford County, Pennsylvania, on the back of a blank petition. "Although an entire stranger," prefaced the writer, "I take the liberty of requesting you to hand this to any lady who is willing prove her christian principles (which enjoin love to all), her patriotism, and her sympathy, for the oppressed by exerting herself to circulate these petitions." The correspondent explained how the society had taken charge of petitioning in each county and asked the recipient to reply promptly, stating whether or not she would circulate the petition. "Deeply reflect on it before you refuse to act" on behalf of the slave, the writer urged, "for we are commanded not only to remember them that are in bonds bound with them, but to do unto others as we would they should do unto us." Like other personal letters aimed at encouraging petitioning, this missive repeated female antislavery rhetoric from petitions, addresses, and other abolition literature. Apparently its entreaties succeeded, for the petition was circulated throughout Bedford County and sent to Congress.[43]

Personal letters were also used to gather lists of women to whom petitions could be sent and to instruct volunteers how to circulate petitions. Henrietta Sargent, a member of the Boston Female Anti-Slavery Society, agreed to distribute blank forms in Worcester County, but she ran into difficulty because she knew not "a single individual of fidelity to address" with the exception of Abby Kelley. So Sargent wrote a letter to Kelley asking, "Will you have the goodness to furnish me with such names as you can recommend, with the town where each person resides, and help me by inquiry to a full list." In like manner Mary G. Chapman addressed a letter to John O. Burleigh and enclosed a blank form asking him to have the "goodness to place this memorial in the hand of a friend who will exert herself to obtain signatures to its petitions from the women of Oxford." She reminded Burleigh that after signatures were obtained, the volunteer should count the names and put the figures at the top of the petition before sending it with a letter to the representative of her district or town.[44]

As effective as personal letters were in persuading individual women to circulate petitions, abolitionists knew that creating a massive persuasive campaign around the right of petition required the power of the anti-slavery press. Abolition newspapers provided male and female petition coordinators the opportunity to report on the progress of signature gathering, to offer tips, and to remind volunteers of deadlines. On July 14, for example, Amos A. Phelps offered a few suggestions in response to inquiries he had received regarding the simultaneous circulation of memorials to Congress and to state legislatures. He described two ways to go about the task. Volunteers could either circulate both state and national petitions simultaneously or circulate them separately. For those employing the first method, Phelps recommended trying to get each individual to sign every petition. "If, however, the individual should be unwilling to write his name so many times, precedence should be given to those petitions of greatest importance—those for instance which refer to Texas and the abolition of slavery and the slave-trade in the District of Columbia." Volunteers were instructed that if the person being solicited refused to sign these petitions, they should have others ready. "Some, for example, will sign a memorial for the abolition of the inter-state trade, who will not sign one for the abolition of slavery in the District of Columbia." If volunteers chose to circulate the petitions separately, Phelps asked that memorials designed for Congress be circulated first and "those for the *State Legislature . . . carefully preserved,* for circulation at another time."[45]

The abolitionist press aided in the petitioning effort by printing further inducements, instructions, and reminders. In mid-August, for example, the *Emancipator* ran an article headlined "How to Do It," which included a form of petition against the annexation of Texas. The reader was urged to put the petition into circulation and to "get every man and woman in your neighborhood to sign it." Volunteers were to attach long rolls to each petition and to take care that men and women signed in separate columns. The number of each class of signers was to be counted and marked on the back, and the petition was to be sent to Washington, D.C., by September 1. The next week the newspaper suggested that "sometimes it is advantageous to petition Congress in classes. For instance, ministers of the gospel in a certain district; lawyers in a county, the merchants of the village, and so on." In September volunteers were further encouraged by a letter from a member of the legislature of New York who proclaimed the new system to be a success. "I am glad a system has been fixed upon for petitioning the state and national legislatures at the approaching sessions," he said. "Hitherto, what has been done has been at haphazard, especially in this state." The legislator reported that a man in his city who was calling on every family with ten different petitions he received from the antislavery office was meeting with great success. "*Very few* refuse to sign."[46]

Constant reminders in abolition newspapers and personal letters aimed at increasing the efficiency of signature-gathering efforts also strengthened connections among women. These reminders accomplished on a broader scale what women had managed to do at the first female antislavery convention. The convention fulfilled a need, stated a report of the Dorcester Female Anti-Slavery Society, for "woman [to] consult with woman" even though participants became subjects of public "ridicule and contempt." The gathering, explained the Dorcester society, enabled women to join men in bearing a "united, public testimony against the brutalizing system of slavery." The convention inspired Abby Kelley, who after meeting with other abolition women became "even more energetic in her activities."[47]

Part of Kelley's enthusiasm may have come from the fact that the convention provided a crucial setting for women to express their frustration over limits on female activism and to devise a rationale to justify expansion of their role. Mary G. Chapman's letter to the convention illustrated the centrality of this issue: "The present state of the world demands of woman the awakening and vigorous exercise of the power which womanhood has allowed to slumber for ages," wrote Chapman. "She has been oppressed, kept in ignorance, degraded—not in vain if she has thereby learned active sympathy for the enslaved—not in vain, if her sufferings contribute to her salvation." Indeed, as Elizabeth Cady Stanton wrote years later, the 1837 meeting and subsequent female antislavery conventions were "the initiative steps to organized public action and the Woman Suffrage Movement *per se*."[48]

*   *   *

Historians have recognized that passage of the first gag rule proved a godsend to the abolition movement by wedding the unpopular cause with the sacred right of petition. Yet approval of Pinckney's resolution also had a profound effect on the rhetoric of female abolitionists, who began to articulate natural rights arguments to justify their petitioning and to claim that they were citizens. Passage of a second gag rule, moreover, created an urgency that led female antislavery leaders to call an unprecedented convention to organize a systematic plan of petitioning and to alter the petition forms. In the process women asserted an increasingly bold political stance grounded in their standing as republican citizens rather than in their moral and religious duties. So drastically did women expand their petitioning to influence public opinion about slavery that jealous conservators of traditional female roles soon attempted to put women back in their place. Yet as we shall see, traditionalists succeeded only in forcing women to develop even bolder defenses of their right to petition and to participate in political decision making.

CHAPTER 5

It's None of Your Business, Gals

A young woman who with her friends went door-to-door gathering signatures for antislavery petitions in a town neighboring Boston during the
summer of 1837 described an incident in which "a certain Mr. —— met
us at the door of his own house." When she and her colleagues asked
him if there were any ladies within who would be interested in signing an
antislavery petition, "he answered in a very decided, contemptuous manner, 'NO'—without even so much as asking them." Punning on the notion
that Congress possessed exclusive control over slavery in the District of
Columbia, the petitioner concluded that he "apparently belonged to that
class of men who claim the right to 'possess exclusive jurisdiction in all
cases whatsoever' over their wives' consciences." After leaving that house,
the signature gatherers walked to another house, where a father met them
at the door and declared that he hoped no one in his house would sign
their petitions, proclaiming it "an insult to the public to send such papers
to Congress, and a very great imposition, altogether too bad, to send young
people about in that manner, on such despicable business." At that point
the young abolitionist explained that no one had sent her out and that she
and her companions were engaged in their task "because we thought it our
duty to do what was in our power for the oppressed." The man remained
unmoved and ordered them to "be gone and to mind and never bring *such
a thing to his house again.*" The petition circulator refused to relent and proceeded to explain that she had no intention of insulting anyone but only
wished to give the women of the house a chance to do their duty. That was
too much. The man sent the canvassers on their way, saying, "It's none of
your business, *gals*, and you'd better go *right straight home.*"[1]

As women's antislavery petitioning entered its second major phase,
more women than ever lent their names to the cause. Signing petitions
marked a significant transformation in the women's political identities,
for in performing this act, they entered public dialogue, in effect developing from private individuals into public actors who operated independent of male guardians. By circulating petitions, moreover, antislavery

women agitated public opinion and exercised skills of political influence. As participation in the petition campaign continued to expand the political activism of antislavery women, defenders of male political dominance and traditional gender roles attempted to halt their progress. Their attacks only pushed women abolitionists to develop stronger arguments about their right as citizens to petition, to take the unprecedented step of threatening to unseat congressmen who ignored them as constituents, and to link the right of petition with the right of suffrage.

*   *   *

By signing petitions, women employed their literacy—a fairly recent acquisition for American women as a group—to influence public opinion, in effect transforming their identities from isolated individuals to public actors. The presence of female signatures indicates that by the mid-1830s many women possessed a level of literacy at least sufficient to write their names. This was no small matter, for among the first generation of Americans approximately half of white men and only a third of white women were able to sign their names. While by the end of the colonial period about 80 percent of white men could write their signatures, only 40 to 45 percent of white women could do so. This percentage increased to about half during the Revolutionary period. A major spurt in white women's literacy occurred between 1790 and 1830, during which time nearly 400 female academies were established in the United States and the female readership and sales of novels increased dramatically. By 1840 almost all white New England women could sign their names.[2] Literacy, both the ability to sign one's name and to read, was a crucial step in women's development to communicate with and influence others as well as to expand the ways they thought about themselves. For antebellum women, Mary Kelley has argued, reading books sometimes "confirmed an already familiar identity. Sometimes they became catalysts in the fashioning of alternative selves." Interestingly, women frequently signed their names to the endpapers and covers of the novels they read, often doing so as many times as they read and reread a book, in a sense claiming "that the text was uniquely theirs." As marks of an individual identity made by oneself, female signatures on endpapers suggest that for antebellum women novels were a vehicle to achieving "a distinctive personality, a particular address to the world, a way of acting and thinking."[3]

Antebellum women also employed their signatures as marks of spiritual transformations and religious identities. Drawing on the notion that God writes the names of the saved in "the lamb's book of life," Charles Finney and his disciples called forth sinners to the anxious bench during revivals and urged them to repent. Christian converts, the vast majority of whom were women, then signed their names to a church membership roll. Finneyite exhortations to "let your names be enrolled" were adopted by abolitionists, many of whom themselves had undergone conversion and several of whom, such as Theodore Weld, had worked with Finney. Women and men who joined antislavery societies signed the constitutions of the local organization, a practice also common among temperance activists, whose signatures confirmed their identities as totally devoted to temperance— "Teetotalers."[4] All of these practices involved women employing their literacy to sign their names, an act that in some way marked transformations in their commitments and identities after being interpolated by discourse (novels, revivals, or temperance rhetoric). Likewise, women's signatures on antislavery petitions signaled not only an abolitionist identity but also the identity of a woman who believed that religious conviction justified political action.

One aspect of the transformation of women's political identities implied by women's signatures on petitions was engagement with, rather than withdrawal from, knowledge and discussion of public affairs. Willingness to learn about a public issue and potentially express one's opinion about it was a major step in becoming a public actor. Yet due in large part to social strictures against women's involvement in politics, many women knew little about national issues and had no particular interest in learning. One signature gatherer reported soliciting a signature from a woman who said that as for the subject of slavery, she "*didn't know* nothing about it, and didn't *care* nothing about it; it never troubled her any way; she never thought nothing about it, nor never wanted to: slavery never hurt her at all."[5] After circulating petitions in New York City, Juliana Tappan bemoaned the apathy of women. "I have left many houses ashamed of my sex," she wrote in a letter to Anne Weston of Boston. "Ladies sitting on splendid sofas looked at us as if they had never heard of the word Texas and I presume some of them would have been unable to say whether it was north or west or south of Louisiana, or whether or not it belongs to the United States."[6] Whether they decided to sign petitions as a result of personal reading, attending abolition lectures, or being persuaded by canvassers or family members, women who lent their names exercised skills of decision making on a political issue and entered public debate by making known their opinions.

Another aspect of the changing political identity of female petition signers was their apparent willingness to defy prohibitions against petitioning grounded in norms of respectable middle-class women's behavior. Those who inscribed their names managed to overcome the notion that signing petitions "is an odd and unladylike thing to do," which deterred many women from signing for fear their reputations would be compromised. Other women who declined to sign petitions stated that slavery was a political issue best left to "our rulers" with which women ought not meddle. A solicitor recalled being met at the door by a woman to whom she explained the antislavery petition only to be told that the inhabitant "didn't want to have anything to do with any paper of the kind." Rhode Island abolitionist Harriet Peck, as Deborah Bingham Van Broekhoven has described, succeeded in winning several hundred names despite encountering "various objections" to signing an 1836 petition circulated in Kent County. "Some ladies seemed to consider it a departure from their proper place, and excused themselves by saying they did not wish their names to appear in Congress," Peck recounted.[7]

When married women signed petitions, they defied not only general prohibitions against women expressing political opinions but also the belief that there was no need for women to speak independent of their husbands, an act that challenged biblical and legal doctrine. Widely accepted biblical teachings required wives to submit to their husbands. As Elizabeth Cady Stanton characterized the relationship in *The Woman's Bible*, for women, marriage "was to be a condition of bondage," and the wife was to abide "in silence and subjection." For all her material wants, she was to remain "dependent on man's bounty," and "for all the information she might desire on the vital questions of the hour, she was commanded to ask her husband at home." Biblical teachings of the wife's submission in marriage were formalized in the legal doctrine of coverture. Originating in English common law, coverture was the legal assumption that when she married, a woman's identity became submerged, or covered, by that of her husband. As Blackstone explained, "By marriage, the husband and wife are one person in law; that is, the very being or legal existence of the woman is suspended during marriage, or at least incorporated and consolidated into that of the husband, under whose wing, protection, and *cover*, she performs every thing." Unmarried daughters were also expected to submit to the control of their fathers or brothers.[8]

Based on accounts written by female signature gatherers, these tenets of submission to male relatives influenced women's decisions about signing antislavery petitions. Sarah Grimké, an experienced signature gatherer, complained, "I have sometimes been astonished and grieved at the servitude of women, and at the little idea many of them have of their own moral existence and responsibilities. A woman who is asked to sign a petition for the abolition of slavery in the District of Columbia . . . not infrequently replies, 'My husband does not approve of it.'" The servility of women also bothered Hannah H. Smith, who lamented, "Women have been taught to depend on men for their opinions." Smith had made this observation while she and her daughter collected signatures for petitions and concluded that "it was the men generally, who needed free discussion, for the women would not act contrary to the ideas of the male part of their family." A similar frustration was reported by a young lady petitioning in Boston who was told by one woman, "I can not sign it for my husband is a colonizationist!"[9]

When women affixed their signatures to petitions, making a mark that authorized petitions as statements of their opinions, they threw off the cover of their husbands or fathers and asserted their existence as political individuals. For some women, lending their signature to a petition may have involved rejecting the notion that the signature of their husband, father, or brother adequately represented their opinion. For other women, signing a petition was an act of defiance against the wishes of male protectors, who might have opposed abolitionism or opposed women petitioning or both. It is worth noting, moreover, that throughout the campaign the vast majority of women eschewed the use of marital titles and signed petitions as, for example, Chloe F. Metcalf, Lydia W. Fairbanks, and even Philomela Johnson Jr. rather than Mrs. Metcalf, Mrs. Fairbanks, and Mrs. Johnson.[10] Given that in 1890 Frances E. Willard was still urging women to write their names as individuals rather than as the wives of someone else, the petitioners' decision to drop "Mrs." during the 1830s appears to radically defy gendered signature norms. Female signatures on antislavery petitions, then, constituted affirmations of the right of women to express their opinions as individuals, as independent from male protectors, and provide evidence of women exerting political agency.[11]

Not only signing but also circulating petitions effected a transformation in women's political identities, for it provided practical experience in carrying out a campaign to influence public opinion. Female canvassers developed strategies specially suited to win women's signatures by incorporating women's daily routines and the spaces they inhabited into patterns of circulating petitions. Upper-class antislavery women, for instance, adapted the rituals associated with social visiting to the political activity of circulating antislavery petitions.[12] But this manner of circulating petitions was open only to affluent women, not to middle-class and working-class members of female antislavery societies. Middle-class women relied on family and religious networks in addition to other female associations, such as sewing circles, in order to circulate petitions. Hundreds of women of varying class and religious backgrounds went door-to-door seeking signatures from strangers. After analyzing the signatures on petitions circulated during 1837 and 1838, Gerda Lerner observed that the strategies women employed to collect signatures differed from those of men. On petitions circulated by women she found clusters of signatures of the canvasser's female relatives. After collecting signatures from family members, explained Lerner, women would probably go house-to-house to gather other women's names. Men went about the task differently. On their petitions, family names were randomly scattered among the signers, indicating that men circulated their petitions at the workplace or perhaps at meetings. Men also tended to place petitions in stores, banks, and barbershops and often passed them around gatherings such as logrollings and camp meetings. Only later, if at all, did men include male family members. We can assume, Lerner says, that petitions signed only by women were circulated by women because widespread opposition to women's involvement in public affairs would deter men from soliciting women's signatures. If men did solicit women's signatures, she concludes, they did so within the family circle.[13]

Petition circulators also gained experience in practicing their skills of interpersonal persuasion, which involved internalizing arguments they read and heard as well as sharpening their skills of oral argumentation. Such skills are evident in a female signature gatherer's account of her interaction with an older woman who was reluctant to sign a petition. "My *darter* [daughter] says that you want the niggers and whites to marry together," the elder woman reportedly said. Yet when pressed by the petition circulator, the woman admitted that she did not understand abolitionists to condone amalgamation and asked if indeed they did. "Why, no—that's no business of ours," the abolitionist assured her. "We leave all to do as they please with regard to it." The canvasser then explained that the petition simply asked Congress to free slaves in the District of Columbia. After making clear the goal of the petition, the circulator stated, "I suppose you know that the colored people in the District are held as property, bought and sold like beasts, and treated very cruelly. Now what we ask is, that Congress, which 'possesses exclusive jurisdiction' there, should give all those slaves their freedom and place them under the protection of law." The older woman responded in agreement and lamented the fact that her daughter was so mistaken.[14]

Although signature gathering "engendered self-confidence and assertiveness" and "led many women toward increased participation in the public sphere," the resistance they encountered understandably led female abolitionists to regard circulating petitions as an unpleasant duty. Maria Weston Chapman recalled that when the fall rolled around, it was time for abolition women to overcome "the reluctant pain of accosting the hostile circles in our neighbors' drawing rooms with antislavery petitions." Several members of the Providence Rhode Island Female Anti-Slavery Society reported that although they had won many signatures, they found petitioning to be a "self-denying, and unpleasant task." Lydia Maria Child wrote to Ellis and Louisa Loring that she had been treated with "a great deal of politeness" in Northampton, Massachusetts, but predicted that would change as soon as she started circulating abolition petitions. "Then I shall be, as I have before been, like the man who had spent a night, that seemed years." Yet she pledged that "even in the disagreeable task of carrying around petitions, it will not cost me a very severe struggle to obey the 'Stern Daughter of the Voice of God.'" About five months later Child's prediction had come true. She wrote to Henrietta Sargent, "My husband and I are busy in that most odious of all tasks, that of getting signatures to Petitions. We are resolved that the business shall be done in this town more thoroughly than it has heretofore. But, 'Oh, Lord, sir!'"[15]

The burden of petitioning was worsened by denunciations from the press and the pulpit. Clergy and other traditionalists anxious about male political dominance were alarmed to see women encouraging one another to express publicly their opinions separate from those of their husbands. The *Boston Religious Magazine*, the *New York Commercial Advertiser*, and the *Providence Journal* all "sharpened their pens and brightened up their wits" to attack the idea of women circulating and signing petitions to Congress. These newspapers, the *Emancipator* claimed, questioned whether women knew anything about slavery and despised the idea that women should meddle with politics. They scolded "female petitioners" for the "impertinence" of "undertaking to teach Congress their duty."[16]

As bad as the editorial condemnations were, they were nowhere near as punitive as those issued by clergymen such as Pastor Albert A. Folsom of the Universal Church in Hingham, Massachusetts. It is "irreverent and unbecoming," he proclaimed, "to threaten incessant application, until Congress shall grant the *stale prayer* of the *misguided petitioners,* who are made up of all classes, characters and *colors.*" Petitioning and speaking publicly against slavery, said Folsom, were "peremptorily" forbidden by "the simplicity of Christ," as was "all interference in the concerns of state, on the part of the female portion of the community." Folsom spelled out the unfortunate consequences that would befall a woman who petitioned with the "clamorous" abolitionists. Such a woman, he said, would begin by seeking "relaxation too often from her domestic obligations." Then she would leave her children and become a slave to her "appetites and passions" while she interested herself "with wonderful zeal in the cause of the Southern negro." Besides suggesting that women petitioners were sexually involved with male slaves for whom they advocated, Folsom predicted that abolition petitioning would poison women's souls, embitter their affections, and exasperate their feelings. "She, who is naturally amiable and modest, . . . is imperceptively transformed into a bigoted, rash, and morose being. . . . Self-sufficiency, arrogance and masculating boldness follow naturally in the train."[17]

Equally brutal were the reproaches proclaimed by Hubbard Winslow, pastor of Boston's Bowdoin Street Congregational Church. He rebuked women who sent "their names up to gentlemen holding official stations, gravely declaring their own judgment in regard to what they ought to do." Women who went so far as to petition their representatives, Winslow declared, had lost the graces of modesty, deference, delicacy, and sweet charity that distinguished the character of woman. Instead these female petitioners displayed the unsavory qualities of boldness, arrogance, rudeness, and indelicacy. As if these accusations were not damning enough, Winslow concluded by declaring that women who petitioned were guilty of sinful behavior. "They have stretched themselves beyond their measure and violated the inspired injunction that saith: . . . 'Let the woman learn in silence with all subjection, but I suffer not a woman to teach, not to usurp authority over the man, but to be in silence.'" In another sermon Winslow referred to "the bustling and obtrusive applications which are now daily made in this city, by an organized company of females, to obtain signatures to memorials designed to instruct the Congress of the United States in relation to their duty." Winslow characterized women petitioners as masculine by calling them "female brethren," and he dismissed their arguments as unreasonable "tirades."[18]

Similar condemnation hailed down on Sarah and Angelina Grimké, who, immediately after the first female antislavery convention adjourned, set out on a lecture tour to convince women to sign petitions and to form new antislavery societies.[19] Early in the tour the sisters promoted petitioning by visiting John Quincy Adams, who, although not an abolitionist, was fighting the petition battle in Congress in the face of tremendous opposition from southerners and with little help from northerners. During the sisters' interview with the aging statesman on June 6, 1837, Angelina asked Adams whether there was anything women could do to bring about the abolition of slavery. Adams replied, "If it is abolished, *they* must do it."[20] The sisters proceeded to speak in towns throughout New England, where men and women jammed galleries to hear their various arguments about why northerners were responsible for fighting slavery. Angelina painted the slavery question as "the great moral struggle between liberty and despotism, now plaguing this country."[21] Audience members commended their efforts, and they won converts to the antislavery cause. When on June 1 Angelina and Sarah addressed the Boston Female Anti-Slavery Society, for example, they convinced thirty-five women to join the organization on the spot.[22]

Despite the Grimkés' successes in persuasion, or perhaps because of the sisters' oratorical powers, clergymen denounced their public lectures. In July the General Association of Congregationalist Clergy published a pastoral letter that warned against the "dangers which seem at present to threaten the female character." Although it never mentioned the Grimkés specifically, there was no doubt that the pastoral letter, written by antiabolitionist Nehemiah Adams of Boston, aimed to condemn the sisters for their public speaking and for encouraging other women to petition. It decried women who assumed "the place and tone of man as a public reformer" and professed regret for "the mistaken conduct of those who encourage females to bear an obtrusive and ostentatious part in the measures of reform." Deploring the "intimate acquaintance and promiscuous conversation of females with regard to things which ought not to be named," the pastoral letter extolled the "mild, dependent, softening influence of woman upon the sternness of man's opinions" and praised the "unostentatious" efforts of women to advance religion in the home and through foreign missions. About a month after the Congregationalists' pastoral letter was published, another attack on female antislavery activism was leveled in the "Appeal of Abolitionists, of the Theological Seminary, Andover, Mass." The young men of Andover complained that some abolitionists, namely Garrisonians, were bringing about "*disorgani-*

zation and anarchy" by "unsettling the domestic economy, and removing the landmarks of society." The Andover men decried "the *public lectures of females*" and were annoyed that the cause of emancipation had been "surrounded with so many foreign and repulsive associations," such as women's rights.[23]

It was no coincidence that the burst of female petitioning and public activism on behalf of the petition campaign kindled such vehement opposition. Petitioning and public speaking were means through which women expanded their influence over an issue of political importance during a time when the boundaries of what was considered political behavior were changing rapidly. "As women claimed new terrain, both literally and metaphorically," Glenna Matthews writes, "they frequently faced what we would now call turf wars." Some men warned women against petitioning and speaking in public because they were jealously guarding their monopolization of public persuasion and, by extension, of political power in general. Angelina Grimké readily apprehended that the clergy were denouncing the sisters' lecturing because "if it can be fairly established that women *can lecture*, then why may they not preach, & if *they* can preach, then woe! woe be unto that Clerical Denomination which now rules the world."[24]

Traditionalists were upset not only because antislavery women, by petitioning, were exerting a greater degree of political influence than their predecessors, but also because the female petitioners espoused the despised cause of immediate abolition. Contradictions resulting from the combined distaste for abolition and women's increasing efforts to influence public opinion were exposed in a letter to the *Emancipator* signed "A FEMALE PETITIONER." The writer observed that typically men praised the brave efforts of their grandmothers during the Revolutionary War as well as more recent exertions by women on behalf of the Seaman's Aid Society, the Baptist Female Bible Association, and the fair for the blind. But when women turned their attention to the dreadful subject of slavery and petitioned Congress for its abolition, the writer complained, "we immediately overstep the bounds of female delicacy and propriety!" She continued,

> A chart of "the appropriate sphere of woman," then, is laid down thus: for Burmah, China, and Arabia, Africa and the islands of the sea, you may feel deep interest, and exert yourselves to support missionaries. For the exercise of domestic charity, you have home missions to sus-

tain, tracts to distribute from house to house, Bibles to circulate, the "oppressed" seamen to succor, the blind to assist, and the sick to visit. But the dark spot of slavery must not be assailed; that is a private affair altogether. True, public discussion and light on the subject might convince slaveholders of their sin; and reiterated petitions to Congress might induce them to exercise a power which they have a perfect right to do: but it is altogether out of your sphere to tell Congress what to do; it is usurping authority.

To further illustrate the inconsistencies of attacking women for petitioning against slavery, the writer asked if, should women lose their husbands in the "imminent war for Texas," it would be "overstepping the bounds of female delicacy and propriety to petition Congress for pensions."[25]

Male editors and clergy were not alone in condemning the political activism of antislavery women generated by the petition campaign. Early in 1837 the well-known reformer and female educator Catharine E. Beecher launched her attack on abolitionists and female activism through publication of *An Essay on Slavery and Abolitionism with Reference to the Duty of American Females,* which she wrote in response to Angelina Grimké's *Appeal to the Christian Women of the South.* In the process of encouraging women to petition and take action to abolish slavery, Grimké's *Appeal* advocated a radical expansion of women's role in reform work. Particularly alarming to Beecher was the fact that in carving out a role for women in the abolitionist movement, Grimké had described a model woman as deeply interested in political issues, critical of the clergy, resistant to social norms, confident of her authority to interpret the Bible, unwilling to subordinate herself to men, and defiant of the law. Beecher responded in her *Essay* that the plan of "arraying females" in the abolition movement was "unwise and inexpedient." Engaging in antislavery activity, she feared, would draw women "forth from their appropriate retirement" and thrust them into the "arena of political collision." Once woman entered the political sphere, Beecher predicted, she would be corrupted by power and would lose her "aegis of defence": her moral purity. Consequently she would forfeit "all the sacred protection of religion, all the generous promptings of chivalry, all the poetry of romantic gallantry." Rather than embracing Grimké's model of the active woman, Beecher pleaded with readers to preserve the status of woman by retaining "her place as dependent and defenceless, and making no claims, and maintaining no right but what are the gifts of honour, rectitude and love."[26]

Especially upsetting to Beecher were Grimké's entreaties for women to petition. "Petitions to congress, in reference to the official duties of legislators, seem, IN ALL CASES, to fall entirely without the sphere of female duty," Beecher retorted. The only proper persons to make appeals to rulers, she maintained, were those who appointed rulers: men. Women's role was not to petition legislators but to influence male friends and relatives to address legislators. "But if females cannot influence their nearest friends, to urge forward a public measure in this way, they surely are out of their place, in attempting to do it themselves." Nor would Beecher accept the argument that it fell within woman's duty to petition for her suffering slave sister. The probable effect of women petitioning against slavery, she claimed, would be to exasperate congressmen, and consequently women would be deemed "obtrusive, indecorous, and unwise." Even worse, Beecher predicted that petitioning would be "the opening wedge, that will tend eventually to bring females as petitioners and partisans into every political measure that may tend to injure and oppress their sex." Beecher concluded that it was "neither appropriate nor wise, nor right, for a woman to petition for the relief of oppressed females." [27]

Beecher's essay struck a serious blow to efforts to persuade women to petition and to join antislavery societies, and her criticism could not be ignored. Angelina Grimké, with encouragement from Theodore Weld, responded by writing a series of letters addressed to Beecher, which were printed in three major abolitionist newspapers during the summer and fall of 1837 and published the next year as a book. Grimké devoted two letters to countering Beecher's prescriptions on female activism and defending the propriety of women's petitioning. In response to Beecher's claim that women who sent petitions to Congress would be deemed "obtrusive, indecorous, and unwise," Grimké held that women should be governed by principles of duty, not by concerns about the response their petitions would evoke from congressmen. Worrying about being criticized as improper, she advised, was nothing more than obeying man rather than God. Grimké countered Beecher's warning that petitioning would draw women into political matters that would "injure and oppress their sex" with the hope that both women and men would avoid becoming partisans. Then, in remarkably political language that both echoed and extended arguments in her *Appeal to the Women of the Nominally Free States,* Grimké shifted from issues of gender propriety to principles of natural rights political philosophy. "The right of petition is the only political right that women have," she wrote. "Why not let them exercise it whenever they are aggrieved?"

Equating denial of women's right of petition with the hallowed impetus for the American Revolution, Grimké stated, "Our fathers waged a bloody conflict with England, because *they* were taxed without being represented. This is just what unmarried women of property now are." America's revolutionary ancestors "were not willing to be governed by laws which *they* had no voice in making," she explained, "but this is the way which women are governed in this Republic." "If, then, *we* are taxed without being represented, and governed by laws *we* have no voice in framing, then, surely, we ought to be permitted at least to remonstrate against every political measure that may tend to injure and oppress our sex."[28]

At this point Angelina Grimké was prepared to carry the argument one step further. "The fact that women are denied the right of voting for members of Congress," she wrote, "is but a poor reason why they should also be deprived the right of petition. If their numbers are counted to swell the number of Representatives in our State and National Legislatures, the *very least* that can be done is to give them the right of petition in all cases whatsoever; and without any abridgment. If not, they are mere slaves, known only through their masters."[29] Although Grimké did not say that the logical conclusion of her argument was that women should be given the right to vote, she moved just short of it. According to Grimké, petitioning was a meager right—"the *very least*"—that women unquestionably possessed. She implied that if petitioning was the "least right" accorded women, surely they deserved greater rights, including that of suffrage.

Angelina Grimké's defense of women's petitioning was bolstered that same summer by Sarah Grimké in her *Letters on the Equality of the Sexes and the Condition of Women.* Sarah responded to attacks on female petitioning by recounting that she had heard of instances in which women had signed petitions secretly because they feared the consequences if their husbands learned of the deed. Decrying the notion of women seeking to please man before seeking to please God, she asked why women should be "*governed* by the opinion of man, any more than man by the opinion of woman." She advised women, "Never deceive a man by a *show* of submission. Tell him that you cannot obey him, rather than God, and that it is your intention to sign that petition."[30]

Despite the efforts of the Grimkés to defend female petitioning, the clergy's constant vilification intensified differences between the Garrisonian wing of the antislavery movement and more conservative abolitionists. The executive committee of the American Anti-Slavery Society tried to quell the commotion, and to this end Whittier pleaded with the

Grimkés to keep the issue of women's rights out of their lectures. He wrote the sisters on August 14 that their lectures were "powerful assertions of the right and the duty of woman to labor side by side with her brother for the redemption of the world." Why, then, was it necessary for them to raise the subject of women's rights? Weld likewise opposed saddling the cause with any issue that would detract from the goal of achieving abolition of slavery. In response to Whittier and Weld, Angelina Grimké argued that it was not they who had begun the discussion of women's rights, but the pastoral letter, which "roused the attention of the whole country to enquire what *right* we had to open our mouths for the dumb." Grimké attempted to convince Weld that it was necessary to discuss the issue of women's rights in order to justify female activism on behalf of abolition: "Can you not see that women *could* do, & *would* do a hundred times more for the slave if she were not fettered? Why! we are gravely told that we are out of our sphere even when we circulate petitions." She warned, "If we surrender the right to *speak* to the public this year, we must surrender the right to petition next year & the right to *write* the year after &c. What *then* can *woman* do for the slave, when she is herself under the feet of man & shamed into *silence?*" Grimké insisted that if women were to do any good for the antislavery cause, their "*right* to labor in it *must* be firmly established . . . on the only firm bases of human rights, the Bible." In the course of the exchange Grimké refuted Weld's position that discussing women's rights was inexpedient for the abolition cause by establishing that women could not fight for human rights when their own rights were denied. At the conclusion of this epistolary debate Weld did not reprise his objections to the sisters' discussions of women's rights.[31]

Despite criticism from clergy, newspapers, and fellow abolitionists, the Grimkés continued their speaking tour through New England. They maintained a grueling schedule and, as the tour went on, faced persistent public criticism. All of these factors wore away at the sisters' health. Eventually typhoid fever struck Angelina and forced the sisters to cease lecturing on November 3. During the six months from May to November 1837 they had addressed more than 40,000 people in 88 meetings in 67 towns. The fruits of their labors were signatures on petitions. In fact, Lerner has found a direct correlation between the sisters' lectures and petitions sent to Congress in the months after their visits. Of the 44 petitions sent from Massachusetts to the session of Congress that convened after the tour, 34—77 percent—came from towns in which the sisters had lectured, and more than half the towns they visited sent a petition. "The old societies and the new were spurred in their petitioning activity by these lectures," wrote Lerner. Likewise, Larry Ceplair concluded that the Grimkés' New England lecture tour "made an immediate, concrete contribution to a very important area of the antislavery cause—petitioning, which built antislavery strength in communities by strengthening organization, enhancing fundraising, and more widely distributing literature."[32]

*   *   *

Amid the controversy over the Grimkés' lecture tour and increased numbers of female petitioners, Congress convened in September 1837 at a special session called by the new president, Martin Van Buren, to deal with the financial panic seizing the nation. When they arrived in Washington, congressmen were faced with a mass of petitions signed by more than 200,000 people opposing the annexation of Texas. All of the memorials were "discarded from consideration" after the House voted to suspend activity on all subjects other than the panic. The enormous pile of antislavery petitions, therefore, was left for the regular session.[33]

When the regular session of Congress convened on December 4, 1838, members were overwhelmed with antislavery petitions signed by more than 414,000 Americans. The average number of signatures on petitions sent to Congress had increased from 32 in 1836–37 to 59 during the second session of the Twenty-fifth Congress (December 4, 1837–July 9, 1838). Petitions asking for abolition in the District of Columbia sent in 1837–38 were signed by more than 78,880 women, and petitions against the annexation of Texas were signed by 77,419 women. In all, some 201,130 women signed petitions addressed to the special session and first regular session of the Twenty-fifth Congress. By comparison, 34,000 signatures—15,000 of which were women's—had been sent to the House during the second session of the preceding Congress. In other words, the organized petition campaign instituted in May 1837 generated a net increase of 380,630 petition signatures. On women's petitions alone there was an increase of 286,130 names.[34]

Presentation and debate over the mass of abolition petitions during the new session of Congress began tumultuously. On December 20 William Slade of Vermont, perhaps the most outspoken antislavery member of the House, threw that body into chaos when he moved to refer an antislavery petition to a select committee with instructions to compose and present a bill for abolishing slavery in the District of Columbia. During Slade's speech in support of his motion, Representative Henry A. Wise led an exodus of the Virginia delegation from the floor, as did Representative Hopkins Holsey for Georgia and Representative R. Barnwell Rhett for South Carolina. All told, fifty or sixty slaveholding members exited the chamber. After a sufficient number of southern members returned to form a quorum, the House voted to adjourn. As members prepared to exit, a representative from South Carolina requested men from slaveholding states to attend a meeting in one of the committee rooms. They were joined by slaveholding members from the Senate to prepare a gag rule. The next day Representative John Patton of Virginia offered a resolution similar to previous gags, with an added prohibition against discussing slavery in the territories. Over the protests of Representative John Quincy Adams, the measure was approved by a vote of 122-74. For the rest of the session all petitions relating to slavery were laid on the table without debate.[35]

While Congress tabled antislavery petitions for the rest of its session, throughout the first months of 1838 the Massachusetts legislature received abolition memorials and established a special committee to hear testimony on the issue of abolishing slavery in Washington, D.C. Among the abolitionists slated to speak was Henry B. Stanton, who "half in jest and half in earnest" asked the Grimké sisters to testify because "the names of some thousands of women were before the Committee, as signers of petitions." Having recovered from the strain of the lecture tour, the sisters accepted the invitation. When the day scheduled for their speeches arrived, however, Sarah was ill with a severe cold, so the responsibility fell to Angelina alone.[36]

On the day of Grimké's speech, February 21, 1838, people began to fill the House chamber soon after one o'clock in the afternoon. By two o'clock, wrote Maria Weston Chapman, one of only a few women present, every space in the room was "filled to a similitude of the 'middle passage.'" Every seat and every bit of standing room was occupied. "The alleys were thronged—the staircases choked up. Men clustered in the windows and around the pillars, and seized upon every coign of vantage. The lobby and grand stair-case were full, and a tide of people, after standing patiently for an hour, swept homeward disappointed." As Grimké walked to the podium, a loud hiss rose from the audience. Each time she attempted to speak, the crowd drowned her words with hisses.[37]

When finally the audience relented and Grimké was able to speak, she attended immediately to the task of defending the right of women to speak to "promiscuous" audiences. "I stand before you," she told the committee, "as a moral being, endowed with precious and inalienable rights, which are correlative with solemn duties and high responsibilities. . . . As a moral being I feel that I owe it to the suffering slave, and to the deluded master, to my country and the world" to overturn slavery. Grimké then proceeded to her primary task, that of presenting petitions and justifying women's petitioning. Grimké said,

> I stand before you as a citizen, on behalf of the 20,000 women of Massa-chusetts, whose names are enrolled on petitions which have been sub-mitted to the Legislature, of which you are the organ. These petitions relate to the great and solemn subject of American slavery—a subject fraught with the deepest interest to this republic, whether we regard it in its political, moral, or religious aspects. And because it is a *political* subject, it has often been tauntingly said, that *women* had nothing to do with it. "Are we aliens, because we are *women?*" Are we bereft of citi-zenship, because we are the mothers, wives and daughters of a mighty people? Have women *no* country—*no* interests staked in public weal—no liabilities in common peril—no partnership in a nation's guilt and shame?

Grimké made no attempt to distance women's petitioning from what was understood as political action. On the contrary, she insisted that politi-cal activity was entirely proper for women. In another passage Grimké stated forcefully that it was right for American women to be involved in the slavery debate "not only because it is moral and religious, but because it is *political*, inasmuch as we are citizens, of this republic, and as such, *our* honor, happiness, and well being, are bound up in its politics, government and laws." [38]

* * *

Congress was still in session and the Patton gag was still relegating peti-tions to the table when the Second Anti-Slavery Convention of American Women convened in Philadelphia's Pennsylvania Hall, May 15–18, 1838. Much of the discussion on the first day of the convention was devoted to petitioning. Juliana Tappan moved that "whatever be the sacrifice," abo-lition women should continue to maintain the right of petition "until the slave shall go free, or our energies, like Lovejoy's, are paralyzed in death." Tappan also proposed that for every petition Congress had rejected dur-ing the preceding year, "*five* should be presented during the coming year."

The convention expressed its anger at Congress by declaring that petitioning was the "refuge of the most humble and powerless" and by scolding that "*true greatness* would never turn away from such appeals."[39]

A major event during the convention was Angelina Grimké's speech on the evening of May 16, which was aimed at inspiring listeners to take action against slavery, especially to petition. That evening some 3,000 people crammed into Pennsylvania Hall to hear Grimké and Garrison. Around the perimeter of the new building formed a noisy mob, which barraged the windows with stones. Not one to shrink in the face of violence, Grimké seized the actions of the mob as a rhetorical resource. "What if the mob should now burst in upon us, break up our meeting and commit violence upon our persons—would this be anything compared with what the slaves endure?" she demanded. Indeed, Grimké insisted, she knew what the slaves suffered. "As a Southerner, I feel that it is my duty to stand up here tonight and bear testimony against slavery," she stated. "I have seen it—I have seen it. I know it has horrors that can never be described. I was brought up under its wing: I witnessed for many years its demoralizing influences, and its destructiveness to human happiness." Slaveholders and slaves themselves had become numb to the evils of slavery, observed Grimké, and this blunting of the sensibilities was spreading northward. But, she warned, northerners must rise and fight slavery before they are consumed by moral lethargy. They could no longer remain silent about this national sin, or they would be punished by God: "God swept away Egypt with the besom of destruction, and punished Judea also with a sore punishment, because of slavery. And have we any reason to believe that he is less just now?"[40]

To save themselves from the wrath of God, Grimké recommended that northern men and women read books on slavery, discuss the subject with their neighbors, and give money to the abolitionist cause. But above all, she said, "let me urge you to petition." Women must petition, she stressed, because although "*men* may settle this and other questions at the ballot box," women have no such right. "It is therefore peculiarly your duty to petition." Knowing that many women were discouraged by the repeated tabling of the petitions they had worked to send, Grimké dispelled any notion that no good came from their efforts. "The South already turns pale at the number sent," she argued, and the petitions had called southerners' attention to the issue of slavery. "The fact that the South looks with jealousy upon our measures shows that they are effectual." What more could women expect, she asked, when slaveholders dominate Congress and deny "our right to petition and to remonstrate against abuses of our sex and of our kind." She urged women to remember that "we have these rights" not from man but "from our God." In a further effort to inspire women to sustain their petitioning, Grimké offered the example of the women of England. Not only had English women done much of the work to abolish slavery, but they continued to gather signatures for a petition to the queen to abolish apprenticeship. Grimké reported that one petition the English women sent to the throne measured two and a quarter miles in length. She promised that when women of the United States would send such a petition to Congress, "our legislators will arise as did those of England, and say, 'When all the maids and matrons of the land are knocking at our doors we must legislate.'" When that moment arrived, when "the zeal and love, the faith and works of our English sisters" were duplicated in America, then the slaves would "shout deliverance" and "we may feel that satisfaction of *having done what we could.*"[41]

The morning after Grimké's speech, delegates to the women's convention held an official session in one of the smaller rooms of Pennsylvania Hall. According to the *Proceedings*, Lucretia Mott "made some impressive remarks respecting the riot the preceding evening, and exhorted the members of the convention to be steadfast and solemn in the prosecution of the business for which they were assembled." The convention adopted other resolutions spelling out the obligations of women with respect to abolition and agreeing with Grimké's entreaty that women ought to petition. Not long after this meeting ended and the women had left Pennsylvania Hall, the rioters broke into the building and set it aflame, claiming that it was a "temple of amalgamation."[42] The *Emancipator* noted the irony that the Liberty Bell, which had been rung when the Declaration of Independence was read in 1776 and was inscribed with the words "Proclaim Liberty throughout All the Land, to All the Inhabitants Thereof," sounded the alarm of fire. "It must have seemed like ringing the knell of liberty when this ancient bell rang on occasion of the mob-fire by which the new Hall of Freedom was consumed!"[43]

* * *

The burning of Pennsylvania Hall did not prevent the female antislavery convention from issuing its customary address. The body of women voted to take the unprecedented step of directly instructing northern senators and representatives to heed the opinions of their constituents and to present antislavery petitions. *An Address to the Senators and Representatives of the Free States, in the Congress of the United States* carefully enumerated a string of events that purportedly proved the existence of a conspiracy by slaveholders to destroy northerners' civil rights in order to perpetuate slavery. According to the *Address*, the northern people had seen and were "laying up in their memories" a chain of incursions upon their rights, including the entrance of Missouri into the Union, which "gave new vigor to the internal slave-trade, and augment[ed] the slaveholding power in our national councils," and the admittance of Arkansas "with perpetual slavery for her Bill of rights." Both of these acts occurred, the *Address* argued, due to the passivity of northern congressmen. This same timidity had allowed slaveholders to get away with disrupting the federal mails, threatening the lives of citizens opposed to slavery, and requiring northerners to send fugitive slaves back into bondage. Alluding to the gag rule, the *Address* warned that although slaveholding congressmen and their colluding northern colleagues had "commanded us to give up freedom of discussion and the right of petition," the citizens of the North were becoming "roused to the conviction, that their own rights are closely involved with those of the slave, and they will not be threatened into a surrender of those rights." The *Address* concluded by cautioning in no uncertain terms that the people would wreak retribution on unsympathetic congressmen: "We would respectfully warn you, that the free states will not long tolerate the existence of slavery and the slave-trade in that District. If you will not utter the conscientious remonstrance of a free people, they will choose more courageous and far-sighted servants."[44]

A remarkably bold statement for antebellum women, the *Address* did little to conceal its political nature and went so far as to threaten to unseat officeholders who failed to comply with women's demands. Indeed, the very act of women collectively lobbying elected officials on an issue of national controversy through a political pamphlet was so brazen that the *Address* opened with a defense of women approaching their congressmen. It insisted on women's right to plead their case "as human beings interested in the cause of universal humanity." Although the *Address* stressed the inclusion of women in the human family and implied that they had a natural right to instruct their representatives, it also insisted on woman's moral superiority: "As mothers training the consciences of youth, we are wielding a power stronger than political parties; and it will not be the fault of women engaged in this sacred cause, if apologies for slavery do not cease with the present generation." The pamphlet also justified women's right to address senators and representatives on the subject of slavery because congressmen had "insulted" their petitions and because women were "*peculiarly* degraded" by the "polluting system" of chattel slavery.[45]

*   *   *

The signing and circulating of antislavery petitions by women transformed their political identities by leading hundreds of thousands of them to engage in public dialogue and to defy social norms by expressing their opinions separate from male relatives. The burst of female activism that occurred in the wake of the 1837 women's antislavery convention alarmed those who jealously guarded male dominance of the public sphere, as well as those who feared that by descending into politics, woman would lose her claim to moral purity. Intense criticism aimed at stifling female petitioners and speakers brought into relief for many women the injustice of the historical denial of their right to petition and speak freely on political subjects. Because of the intensely public nature of their activism, the Grimké sisters bore the brunt of the attacks, but clergymen and the antiabolition press also berated the thousands of women who circulated and signed petitions. In response, antislavery women were impelled to develop new defenses of their right to attempt to influence their political representatives.

On one hand, defenders of women's right of petition clung to the argument that female moral superiority rendered women uniquely suited to petition. On the other hand, advocates employed bolder arguments that women possessed a natural and constitutional right of petition and that they were endowed with equal responsibilities and therefore equal rights with man. Angelina Grimké went so far as to argue that the fact that women were denied the right to vote provided no reason to deny them the right of petition. Republican principles demanded that women be heard in some way, she maintained, or Congress would be guilty of taxation without representation. The same reasoning, she implied, also led to the conclusion that women possessed the right to vote. Grimké was not alone in defending women's right to petition and connecting it to the franchise. In the course of defending the right of women to petition against slavery, John Quincy Adams would question, on the floor of the U.S. House of Representatives, the practice of denying women the right to vote.

Although the flood of antislavery petitions that swept into Congress when it convened on December 7, 1837, was sandbagged by the Patton gag, those pertaining to the annexation of Texas continued to seep onto the floor of the House of Representatives. On March 5, 1838, the House referred all memorials relating to the Texas question to the Committee on Foreign Affairs, which was charged with composing a report about the content of the petitions and the expediency of granting their requests. On June 14 the report was presented by the committee's chairman, Benjamin Howard of Maryland. Annoyed by the preponderance of petitions from females, Howard expressed his "regret" that so many of the memorials were signed by women. It was inappropriate for women to petition their legislators, he said, because females were afforded ample opportunity for the exercise of their influence by approaching their fathers, husbands, and children in the domestic circle and by "shedding over it the mild radiance of the social virtues, instead of rushing into the fierce struggles of political life." By leaving their proper sphere, Howard charged, women were "discreditable, not only to their own particular section of the country, but also to the national character."[1]

Although few northern representatives during the 1830s defended abolitionists' right of petition, especially that of abolitionist women, John Quincy Adams rose to the occasion. "Sir, was it from a son—was it from a father—was it from a husband, that I heard these words?" demanded the former president. "Does this gentleman consider that women, by petitioning this House in favor of suffering and distress, perform an office 'discreditable' to themselves, to the section of the country where they reside, and to the nation?" Adams offered Howard a chance to retract his assertion: "I have a right to make this call upon him. It is to the wives and to the daughters of my constituents that he applies this language." Howard stood his ground. Adams retorted with a four-day harangue defending the propriety of women involving themselves in political matters and of exercising their constitutional right of petition.

As the exchange between Howard and Adams illustrates, ongoing debates over the reception of petitions not only linked northern civil rights with the issue of slavery but led congressmen to discuss women's participation in politics. Given the large proportion of antislavery petitions signed by women, in the course of defending abolitionists' right to petition in general, it became necessary for Adams to defend women's right of petition in particular. Having violated traditional norms of respectable gender behavior, the womanhood of female petitioners was especially vulnerable to attack by those who hoped to indict the character of petitioners as grounds for rejecting the petitions in order to silence discussion of slavery. Indeed, opponents spurned the petitions' conservative characterizations of women's prayers on behalf of the slave as extensions of Christian duty, recognizing them instead as radical attempts to justify women's incursion into the exclusively male realm of congressional debate. Conflating acceptable gender behavior with constitutional rights, adversaries argued that because it was improper for women to petition Congress, they had no right to petition Congress. Women, they argued moreover, could not reason logically or act independently—basic qualifications for republican citizenship—and therefore their petitions should not be seriously considered. Adams responded to attacks on female antislavery petitions, which were leveled for the most part by southern members and a handful of northerners, by exposing the conflation of acceptable gender conduct with the exercise of natural rights. There was no doubt, he argued, that women possessed a constitutional right of petition, and exercise of that right should not be contingent on the character of petitioners. Yet not only did Adams attempt to safeguard women's right of petition, but he insisted that women were citizens and, remarkably, questioned whether women might not also possess the right to vote.

*   *   *

Despite female abolitionists' conservative rhetoric that portrayed their petitioning as an extension of Christian duty, opponents characterized their efforts as an attempt to intrude into the exclusively male political domain of congressional debate. Representative Henry Wise of Virginia proclaimed that religion should have nothing to do with the issue of slavery because it was "a delicate political question," and "those only should deal with it who have some common sense as well as experience as statesmen, and who are honest patriots." "Neither women nor priests are politicians, except in the intrigues of court," Wise declared. "What sort of a Government are we to have if women and priests are to influence our legislation!" Kentucky's Representative Joseph Rogers Underwood recommended facetiously that since "the motives of the petitioners in this case are so pure," then they should be heard "in the cause of religion and freedom!" "The Saviour of man did not propagate his religion by petitioning legislative assemblies," he declared. Southerners' attempts to remove slavery from the realm of religion and morality, a realm in which female signers claimed that their judgment reigned supreme, and to place it into the arena of politics, recognized as the province of man, undercut one of the major justifications advanced in women's petitions for involvement in the slavery debate.[2]

Members who wished to silence discussion of slavery could argue, furthermore, that female petitions should be disregarded because abolition women were improperly interfering with the business of Congress. Representative Jesse Bynum of North Carolina preached, "It was not in the field, nor is it in the cabinet, where the counsel of lovely woman has been found most potent; to adorn her sex, she is destined for a different sphere." Though he claimed to pay "cordial homage to the fair sex," Wise stated that he believed woman's sphere of action was drawn clearly and that she should not move beyond it: "Woman in the parlor, woman in her proper sphere, is the ornament and comfort of man; but out of the parlor, out of her sphere, if there is a devil on earth, when she is a devil, woman is a devil incarnate!" Another Virginian, Representative J. Garland, confessed that he did not like to see women "madly shooting out of their proper sphere, and undertaking to control national politics. I do not like to see them become politicians." For their own good, Representative Patton of Virginia directed women petitioners, most of whom he believed to be single, to find "something else to do." He hoped they would find good husbands and "that they may spend their days and their nights in some employment more likely to give them pleasure, and do the world a benefit than drawing their petitions, so well calculated to produce effects so little likely to give them satisfaction or comfort after they are produced." William Cost Johnson of Maryland recommended that northern representatives instruct their women petitioners "to attend to knitting their own hose and darning their stockings, rather than come [here] and unsex themselves, be laid on the table, and sent to committee to be reported on."[3]

Having castigated female petitioners for violating norms of acceptable gender behavior, opponents criticized the petitioners for lacking womanly virtues. "Women become most mannish grown" when they "assume the part that men should act alone," pronounced Bynum poetically. Wise branded them "devils," "demons," and "furies" who were "hissing rage, and rapine, and rape, and murder, on our lives and property, and matrons and maids, of the South." Maintaining that by sending petitions, abolition women were attempting to incite slaves into insurrection that would endanger the lives of southern women and "hazard the life and safety of the dear and tender offspring clinging to the bosoms of their own sisterhood," Patton condemned their heartless behavior as unwomanly. He compared what he perceived as the hostile actions of northern women to the restrained behavior of southern ladies, stating that "they must be very different from their sex of any class that I have been acquainted with, if they would persevere in any course that went to hazard everything dear to their sex." Patton professed to be certain that if northern women were informed as to the effect they were producing "upon the helpless, defenceless objects of their blind charity, they, being Christians, (as all women are, or should be) would leave the thing to God."[4]

Southern congressmen also attempted to block reception of female petitions by claiming that women lacked the qualifications for participation in public deliberation. Representative Robertson of Virginia insisted that the "offensive memorials" be returned to members who presented them (he did not want them "to be preserved forever among the archives of the nation") because in many cases they had been "signed by women and children ignorant of the institutions under which we live, and not knowing, it is to be hoped, the consequences of their folly." The Constitution "went no further than to declare the right of petition," Bynum contended, because if it had, the dignity of Congress would have been endangered. "The most frivolous petitions from women, children, boys, or lunatics, might be received, at a great consumption of the time of this House, and at an enormous expense to the people." Bynum's arguments for excluding female antislavery petitions echoed a rationale formulated by Thomas Jefferson during the early national period to curtail demands for extended political representation. Jefferson had classed women with infants and slaves among those "who had no will [and who] could be permitted to exercise none in the popular assembly; and of course, could delegate none to an agent in a representative assembly." Not only did Bynum, like Jefferson, refuse the possibility that women could apply reason to the discussion of important questions, but he warned that if their irrationality were allowed to seep into Congress, the consequences would be dire. If the House were to receive petitions from females, he cautioned, the whole body "might be converted into scenes of levity and frivolity totally destructive of the dignity and character of wise legislation." Here again Bynum argued along the same lines as Jefferson, who in 1816 had rationalized excluding women from "the public meetings of men" to prevent "depravation of morals and ambiguity of issue." Bynum said he "could not conceive a more degrading condition than this House would be placed in, by consuming its time, at an enormous expense to the Treasury, in receiving and listening to the petitions and memorials of old grannies and a parcel of boarding-school misses, in matters of state and legislation. . . . The Congress of the United States was no place for them." Bynum then explicitly connected fears of women's irrationality with denial of their right of petition. It could never have been the intention of the framers of the Constitution to allow the reception of petitions from women, Bynum postulated. "In that august body there was too much wisdom, dignity, and patriotism, to presume it."[5]

In addition to disdaining the irrationality of female antislavery petitioners, opponents denied women's ability to act as independent agents, dismissing the petitions as the scribblings of "unthinking" women who had been duped by "cowardly" ministers. Garland charged that "the abolition priests of the North" had led "pious females so unwarily into their schemes." Bynum denounced female petitioners as "weak" and "deluded" creatures upon whom "an ambitious, cunning, designing, but dastardly priesthood" had cast a trance. Employing anti-Catholic rhetoric common to that time, he confessed that southerners understood full well "the unholy ambition of the priesthood" who had "kindled up" the flame of abolitionism and "who were now engaged in taking the advantage of the ignorant women and boys throughout the country." "Look at the petitions; what one was not headed by a priest of some denomination or other, and filled up in part of women and children, adults and boys?" Bynum complained that women, led by power-hungry "priests" as in the days of the crusades, were on the verge of starting a religious war. The Christians of the South, "whose religion it is to hold slaves," vowed Bynum, would not "yield in their love for their religion and piety to those of the North, who have thus undertaken to pass sentence of condemnation on them." Wise, too, charged that women petitioners did not act on their own volition but had been corrupted by ministers, whom he also branded as "priests."[6]

Congressmen should squelch women's petitions without a hearing, went another line of argument, because women could not bear the responsibility of the effects of their pleas. Representative Garland lamented that the female petitioners "have not brought themselves to contemplate the awful consequences of their rash proceedings." Bynum predicted that when agitation over slavery resulted in civil war, female abolitionists and their allies would flee the scene: "Where, then, will be found their women and children, who crowd this House with silly petitions? Where their priests? In the tented field? No, sir, but skulking, shivering, shrinking from danger and responsibility, and even then denying the part that they had once taken in getting up this tragic drama. Will their women then be seen in the field, amid the clangor of arms and the shouts of victory, or heard in the cabinet with the cries of their children around them?" Because women by their nature could not defend the Union, Bynum argued, their petitions that were likely to incite a war should be disregarded. Fundamentally, the representative denied women the right to participate in public deliberation because they could not fulfill a major obligation of citizenship: risking one's life in military service to defend the republic.[7]

Taken as a whole, the case for discarding female abolition petitions amounted to a two-tiered attack on women who attempted to expand their participation in politics. Opponents denied that petitioning against slavery was an extension of female moral duty, instead labeling it a clearly political action related to a clearly political subject. By bursting into congressional debate over the political issue of slavery, detractors maintained, northern females acted in such an unbecoming, unwomanly manner that their reputation, if not their sanity, was doubtful, and the House had no obligation to hear the requests of such deluded individuals. This objection amounted to denying women the right of petition because exercising that right fell outside norms of respectable womanly behavior. Slaveholders also developed a second level of arguments to build a republican rationale for denying women the right of petition and, more generally, claims to citizenship. Women, they maintained lacked the requisite virtues of republican citizenship: they could not deliberate rationally, act independently, or fulfill a citizen's obligation to serve in the military. Not unlike the scenario in which the representatives formally abrogated the right of slaves to petition and questioned that of free blacks, members suggested that women possessed no citizenship rights. "Have women, too, the right of petition?" asked Wise at one point in the debates. "Are they citizens!"[8]

* * *

In the 1830s few northern members were willing to defend abolition petitions, and even fewer were willing to bulwark women's right of petition. Yet several, including John Dickson of New York and Caleb Cushing and

Levi Lincoln of Massachusetts, followed Adams's lead in answering attacks on female petitioners. Although detractors insisted that female antislavery petitioning constituted overt political action and improper behavior for true women, upon presenting the petition from the 800 ladies of New York, Dickson emphasized the benevolent nature of women's memorializing. "In the Jewish, Greek, and Roman histories," he recalled, "female remonstrance" heard in public councils "were the cause of 'enlargement and deliverance,' of 'light, and gladness, and joy, and honor,' to a despised and an oppressed people." They were, he said, "all-powerful in expanding and extending the principles of charity, humanity, and benevolence, and in breaking the chains of oppression." Likewise in the war for American independence, he said, "the influence of woman was talismanic over the heart of man, and roused to action all of his noblest energies." Women's honor should be credited, for "all her remonstrances, petitions, and entreaties, and all her influence, have ever been exerted in favor of humanity, benevolence, and liberty." Dickson characterized female antislavery petitions as motivated not by political gain but by benevolence. "Surely," he hoped more than believed, "the chivalry of this House will never permit it to turn a deaf ear to the remonstrance of ladies, pleading, as they believe, for the wronged and oppressed."[9]

Given the obstreperous attacks southerners leveled against female petitioners, it was necessary for northern members to do much more than deny that antislavery women harbored political motivations. They had to defend the character of female petitioners. As Adams complained, the petitions had been treated with contempt, and "foul and infamous imputations" had been "poured upon a class of citizens as pure and virtuous as the inhabitants of any section of the Union": females. Likewise, Lincoln represented petitioners from his district as "pure, elevated, and [of as high] intellectual character as any in the world, men and women, kind and generous, and of tenderest sympathies, who would no sooner do an injury or an act of injustice to any human being than the most chivalrous or true-hearted of the sons or daughters of the South."[10]

Yet at issue in the arguments over the character of female antislavery petitioners was more than their reputations as women. At issue was their status as citizens. Adams readily apprehended that attacks on the character of female petitioners effectively denied women's right of petition, and he took Howard to task for representing the exercise of the right of petition as disgraceful to women as well as to their section of the Union and the nation as a whole. "Now to say, respecting women, that any action of theirs was disgraceful, was more than merely contesting their legal right so to act," Adams averred; "it was contesting the right of the mind, of the soul, and the conscience." This was no "light question," no mere quarrel over the honor of a few women, he emphasized. It concerned "the very utmost depths of the Constitution of the country" and affected "the political rights of one half of the People of the nation."[11]

Throughout the debates over reception of female petitions in which southerners repeatedly indicted the womanhood of petitioners, Adams maintained vehemently that there was no legal or constitutional principle linking the right of petition with the character of petitioners. When Adams presented a petition purportedly signed by nine ladies of Fredericksburg, Virginia, Representative Patton, who had lived in that city, assailed Adams for bringing before the House a petition from "mulatto" women of "infamous character." Patton said he could not permit himself to believe that "the gentleman from Massachusetts would have persisted in being the organ through whom such a petition should be presented." He swore "on his honor and veracity as a man" that he did not believe that there was the signature of "any decently respectable individual in Fredericksburg" attached to the petition, that the only name he recognized was that of "a mulatto free woman of infamous character," and that he believed that other names were those of "free negroes, all of whom he believed to be bad." He insisted, therefore, that the petition be taken from the table and returned to Adams.[12]

Patton's insinuation that the petition emanated from prostitutes, disclosed Adams, influenced him not a wit in deciding whether or not to present the paper. Rather than worrying over the character of the petitioners, Adams said that he "adhered to the right of petition."

> Where is your law which says that the mean, and the low, and the degraded, shall be deprived of the right of petition, if their moral characters is not good? Where, in the land of freemen, was the right of petition ever placed on the exclusive basis of morality and virtue? Petition is supplication—it is entreaty—it is prayer! And where is the degree of vice or immorality which shall deprive the citizen of the right to supplicate for a boon, or to pray for mercy? Where is such a law to be found? It does not belong to the most abject despotism. There is no absolute monarch on earth who is not compelled by the constitution of his country to receive the petitions of his people, whosoever they may be. The Sultan of Constantinople cannot walk the streets and refuse to

Johnny Q, Introducing the Haytien Ambassador to the Ladies of Lynn.

A petition urging the Massachusetts legislature "to repeal all laws which make any distinction among its inhabitants, on account of color" provoked the press to ridicule the 785 ladies who signed the form circulated by the Lynn Female Anti-Slavery Society. This 1839 cartoon also pokes fun at Representative John Quincy Adams for his role in presenting women's petitions to Congress. (Courtesy of the Library Company of Philadelphia)

ABOLITION FROWNED DOWN.

This 1841 cartoon depicts the tone of the debate over antislavery petitions in the House, when Representative John Quincy Adams persisted in defending abolition petitions despite passage of a stronger gag rule. Representative Waddy Thompson Jr., a South Carolina Whig, glowers at Adams, saying, "Sir the South loses caste whenever she suffers this subject to be discussed here; it must be indignantly frowned down."
(Courtesy of the Library of Congress)

receive petitions from the meanest and vilest in the land. This is the law even of despotism. And what does your law say? Does it say that, before presenting a petition, you shall look into it, and see whether it comes from the virtuous, and the great, and the mighty? No, sir, it says no such thing; the right of petition belongs to all. And, so far from refusing to present a petition because it might come from those low in the estimation of the world, it would be an addition incentive, if such incentive were wanting.[13]

Although he held steadfast to the belief that the right of petition was absolute no matter the character of memorialists, Adams grasped the opportunity afforded by Patton's attack on the reputation of the petitioners to turn the table and question the character of opponents of women's petitions. When in the course of debate Patton disclaimed actually "knowing" the "bad" women who had signed the petition but stated that he "knew of them," Adams said he was glad to hear it, for otherwise he would ask "if they were infamous women, then who was it that had made them infamous?" Not their own color, he judged, but their masters. Adams said he was inclined to believe this because "there existed great resemblances in the South between the progeny of the colored people and the white men who claimed the possession of them. Thus, perhaps, the charge of being infamous might be retorted upon those who made it, as originating from themselves."

Adams's comments threw the House into great agitation, for he had stabbed brutally at the honor of southern gentlemen. Despite the fact that in February 1837 he faced formal censure for casting character aspersions on southerners in return for the imputations against the Fredericksburg women, he persisted in the strategy of questioning the character of representatives who opposed female petitions. Adams shamed representatives who would turn a deaf ear to women's petitions, asking each member to suppose that his own mother was one of the petitioners: "Would you reject and turn the petition out of doors, and say that you would not even hear it read?" "Every member of the House has, or had, a mother," he observed, adding that "in the whole class of human affections, was there one sentiment more honorable, or more divested of earthly alloy, than that which every man must entertain for his mother." He hoped that Representative Thomas Glascock of Georgia would withdraw his objection to the reception of a female petition "for the sake of that gentleman's character as a man; [and] for the sake of his character as a son."[14]

Indictments of the character of southern members as well as defenses of the virtue of female petitioners seemed to depart from the principle that all people, blacks and women included, possessed a constitutional right of petition. Yet understanding as he did the common connection between what were perceived as women's duties and the rights these duties entailed, in his 1838 speech Adams focused on extending the reach of women's duties to include political affairs. Unlike the majority of women's antislavery petitions in the first phase of their campaign, Adams did not shy away from characterizing the actions of female petitioners as political. Rather, he endeavored to alter the meaning and connotation of that term. In response to Howard's claim that women had no right to petition Congress on political subjects, Adams asked rhetorically, "What does the gentleman understand by 'political subjects'?" Adams answered that "every thing which relates to peace and relates to war, or to any other of the great interests of society, is a political subject. Are women to have no opinions or action on subjects relating to the general welfare?" Fellow Massachusetts representative Caleb Cushing bolstered Adams's statements, maintaining that "it seems to me a strange idea to uphold, in this enlightened age, that woman, refined and educated, intellectual woman, is to have no opinion, or no right to express that opinion." [15] While Adams answered imputations that women had breached the political domain by broadening the definition of politics to encompass concerns acknowledged to reside within the province of woman, Cushing vouched for women's capability to participate in rational deliberation, to act like citizens.

Contrary to repeated allegations that it was "discreditable," "unbecoming," and "masculinizing" for women to involve themselves in political matters, Adams maintained that there were plenty of instances in which "the action of women was held up as the highest virtue, and their interference in politics was recorded with praise." Endeavoring to show that Howard's principle that women should have nothing to do with political affairs possessed no grounding in the Bible, he cited the case of Deborah, a judge and prophetess during the infancy of the Jewish nation; of Jael, who slew the enemy of her nation; and of Esther, who saved the Jews by petitioning. Adams also mentioned Abigail, Huldah, and Judith. Indeed, he said, he could go through the entire history of the Jews and find innumerable examples of women who "not only took an active part in the politics of their times, but who are held up with honor to posterity because they did so." Turning to secular history, Adams challenged Howard to "find there that it is 'discreditable' for women to take any interest or any part in political affairs." Adams bid opponents of female petitioners to examine the character of Aspasia, an Athenian woman whom Socrates praised as "an excellent mistress of the art of rhetoric." Invoking a historical example cherished by southerners, Adams asked whether they had "forgotten that Spartan mother, who said to her son when going out to battle, 'My son, come back to me *with* thy shield, or *upon* thy shield.'"

Hoping to take advantage of patriotic sentiments, Adams also invoked heroines of the American Revolution. After recalling the work of the "ladies of Philadelphia" who outfitted Washington's troops when they were destitute of clothes, he praised the women of Charleston who petitioned for the release of Lt. Col. Isaac Hayne. In the midst of adducing this example, Adams shouted, "Where is the chairman of the Committee on Foreign Relations?" But Howard was not in the House. Adams railed, "I want him to discuss this point. Here were women who entered deeply into concerns relating to their country, and felt that they had other duties to perform, besides those to the domestic comforts of their husbands, brothers, and sons. They petitioned! I want him to listen to their petition, all glorious to their memories as it is!" He then proceeded to read the rather lengthy petition. But Adams did not stop there. He called up the example of Deborah Gannett, who had adorned herself in men's clothes, joined the patriot army, and fought for three years until she was wounded. Members of the House were aware of Gannett's feats because within recent memory they had voted to give her husband a military pension based on the services of his wife and had praised her on the grounds that she had "fought and bled for human liberty." After commending Gannett's actions, which involved rushing physically into "the vortex of politics," Adams asked how Howard could conceivably think it wrong for women to petition on a matter of politics. Aiming his last example from the Revolution directly at Howard, who had returned to the chamber, Adams recounted that the ladies of Baltimore won praise from all over the country by making summer clothing for the army of Lafayette. "Sir," said Adams, "was it from the lips of a son of one of the most distinguished of those ladies of Baltimore—was it from the lips of a descendant of one of the most illustrious officers in that war that we now hear the annunciation that the political and public services of women are to be treated with contempt? Sir, I do hope that honorable gentleman, when he shall reply to this part of my argument, will modify his opinions on this point."[16]

Howard was not about to wait for a chance to reply. He rose and begged permission to speak. Adams yielded the floor. Howard protested vociferously against classifying the generous and patriotic ladies of the Revolution with the female petitioners on Texas annexation, stating that he saw "not the slightest resemblance" between the conduct of the ladies of Baltimore during the Revolution and that of the women who were petitioning Congress against the admission of Texas: "When the relatives and friends of women are in the field, struggling amidst perils and sufferings for the independence of the country, undergoing all sorts of hardships and privations, without sufficient food or raiment, nothing could be more becoming to the female character than that, by the exercise of their needle, or influence, or industry, they should try to alleviate the toils of their gallant defenders." In his rejoinder Adams accused Howard of harboring an opinion about women much like that entertained by the Turks: women have no souls. This opinion, said Adams, was not shared by the nation generally, and it reflected cruelly on the conduct and character of the women of the republic.[17] While Howard attempted to contain women's political participation to actions linked directly with their domestic duties, Adams sought to stretch those links to political concerns.

Although Adams redefined politics to include all subjects relating to the general welfare and adduced numerous historical examples of women's involvement in politics, he was far from ready to "countenance the general idea that it is proper, on ordinary occasions, for women to step without the circle of their domestic duties." Instead he recommended a three-pronged test by which one could determine whether it was proper for women to deviate from the custom of remaining distant from politics. When presented with such a circumstance, prescribed Adams, one must inquire "into the motive which actuated them, the means they employ, and the end they have in view." Adams then applied this test to the case at hand, the petitions against annexation of Texas. As for the motive, he said, it was of the "highest order" of purity: "They petition under a conviction that the consequence of the annexation would be the advancement of that which is sin in the sight of God, viz: slavery." The means were appropriate, Adams said, because it was Congress who must decide the question, and it was Congress to whom the women must petition. Echoing a justification offered by the female petitioners themselves, he stated, "It is a petition—it is a prayer—a supplication—that which you address to the Almighty Being above you. And what can be more appropriate to their sex?" As for the end sought by female petitioners, it, too, was virtuous, pure, and of the most exalted character: "to prevent the perpetuation and spread of slavery through America." In contrast to Howard's condemnation, Adams concluded, "the correct principle is, that women are not only justified, but exhibit the most exalted virtue when they do depart from the domestic circle, and enter on the concerns of their country, of humanity, and of their God." Thus Adams repeated the argument employed in the women's appeals, addresses, circulars, and petitions that it was the moral duty of women to speak for those who could not speak for themselves and to help those who could not help themselves. In fact, Adams believed that benevolent activity was a particularly feminine trait: "I say that woman, by the discharge of her duties, has manifested a virtue which is even above the virtues of mankind, and approaches to a superior nature."[18]

Adams coupled his arguments expanding the scope of women's duties with defenses of their constitutional rights. During the controversy over the petition from the nine women of Fredericksburg, he held that the right of petition was absolute, and during the uproar over the preponderance of female petitions against Texas annexation, Adams did the same, maintaining that his stance reflected the beliefs of the majority of Americans. "I will ask not whether it is the judgment of this House, but whether it is the sober judgment of the People of these United States, that the right of petition itself is to be denied to the female sex? to WOMEN? Whether it is their will that women, as such, shall not petition this House?" Furthermore, Adams characterized Howard as denying women the right of petition because they had no right to vote. Then he asked, "Is it so clear that they have no such right as this last? And if not, who shall say that this argument of the gentleman's is not adding one injustice to another?" In a few short breaths Adams, son of the woman who in 1776 threatened that "the ladies . . . will not hold ourselves bound by any laws in which we have no voice, or representation," went so far as to suggest that women did, in fact, possess the right to vote and that it was an injustice that they were denied the practice of that right. In so doing he embraced a position more radical than that of many women's rights advocates of his time. On the floor of the House of Representatives he questioned the assumption that the Constitution denied women the right to vote. He suggested that the reason women did not vote was custom rather than lack of a right to the franchise. He declared that outright denial of women's right to vote was an injustice, as was the denial of women's right of petition. It would be another eight years before the women of New York petitioned their legislature for the vote, a decade before the National Woman's Rights Convention would assert that women possessed the right of suffrage, and eight decades before an organized movement of women persuaded Congress and the public to adopt the position Adams began to articulate on Friday, June 29, 1838.[19]

Women who had signed petitions were particularly pleased to read Adams's defense of their actions and showered praises upon him. When he returned to Massachusetts after Congress had adjourned, Adams was greeted by expressions of approbation in the form of several celebratory events hosted by women in towns of his congressional district. On September 4, 1838, the ladies of Quincy hosted a formal picnic and ball to honor him for defending their rights. The event was held on the "Hancock lot," a piece of land donated to the town of Quincy by John Adams and on which still remained the cellar of the house in which John Hancock was born. Adams's wife, Louisa, and other ladies of the family joined the party, but Adams remained behind until a deputation of men arrived to escort him to the company. There he was received, he recalled, "by six young unmarried ladies, between whom I was conducted to the large lime-tree in the centre of the lot, there received by two married ladies." He was then presented to the "lady hostess" of the party and conducted, with his wife, to chairs under an arch of evergreens. Gathered around was a circle of about 200 women. When everyone was in place, the Reverend Peter Whitney, speaking for the ladies, addressed Adams by name and said that he had been invited to the party in token of the ladies' respect for his long and eminent public services.[20]

When Adams addressed the group, he thanked the women for their kind celebration and acknowledged the large number of petitions he had received from females of the district. Reviewing scenes from the two most recent sessions of Congress, he recalled that Howard had committed a "violent outrage . . . upon the [female] petitioners, and [an] insult upon the sex." Adams explained that he felt himself "called upon to repel" the insult and that thereupon ensued his "defence of the rights and fair fame of women." Adams said that he believed questions about the duty of women to participate in public affairs should be left to women's own discretion, and he felt assured "there was not the least danger of their obtruding their wishes upon any of the ordinary subjects of legislation," such as banks, tariffs, and public lands, "all which so profoundly agitate the men of this country." Women, he trusted, were concerned with other kinds of matters. In fact, he believed that "far from being debarred by any rule of delicacy" from petitioning, by the "law of their nature," which rendered them kind, benevolent, and compassionate, women were "fitted above all others" for the exercise of this right.[21] Adams could not bring himself to endorse unlimited exercise by women of the absolute right of petition. Instead he trusted—or perhaps urged—that they would act only on public matters related to woman's moral duty and would take no interest in purely political matters such as banks and tariffs. In other words, Adams expected female moral duty to guide the exercise of women's natural rights.

* * *

Debates over the reception of female antislavery petitions provoked what was perhaps the first sustained discussion of women's political rights and the status of women as citizens in the history of the U.S. Congress. Although during the Revolutionary period women's rights were discussed in private correspondence and, during the post-Revolutionary period, in ladies' magazines, as Rosemarie Zagarri has observed, these discussions "did not occur within official political institutions." While the Supreme Court considered women's rights in *Martin v. Commonwealth* and state constitutional conventions contemplated extending the franchise to women, no sustained examination of women's political rights took place in Congress until the debate over female antislavery petitions. The petition debate, then, constituted a significant moment in the ongoing negotiation of women's citizenship. Like debate over the petitions of slaves, whose right of petition was denied, and those of free blacks, whose right of petition was called into doubt, presentation of female petitions raised the possibility that women could be stripped of their tenuous claims to First Amendment rights and citizenship. At the core of the southern case against receiving female petitions was the indictment that the petitions constituted not good works resulting from women's Christian duty but, rather, politically motivated machinations controlled by fanatical ministers and wholly improper actions for women. Conflating notions of female duty with political rights, southerners argued that the women's petitions should be ignored because, having transgressed beyond their proper duties, these women were not respectable, and the House was not obligated to accept petitions from people of questionable character.[22]

Adams remained steadfast in his conviction that women possessed a natural right of petition and perhaps a natural right to vote, yet he linked the exercise of women's civil rights to their duties as women. In this sense Adams's defense of women's right of petition replicated a pattern Zagarri has identified in periodical literature expostulating on political rights from 1792 to 1825 in which interlocutors employed separate philosophies to delineate the rights of men and women. Men's rights, she explains, were grounded in Lockean philosophy, which in American practice reified political liberty. Women's rights, by contrast, were grounded in Scottish Enlightenment philosophies, which made rights interchangeable with duties. Zagarri writes, "By performing their God-given role, women laid claim to their appropriate rights; their appropriate rights became synonymous with their womanly duties." The conflation of women's rights and duties served the conservative goal of rationalizing the exclusion of women from direct participation in politics by acknowledging that women possessed rights but limiting their rights to those that flowed directly from domestic duties.[23]

Yet Adams construed women's concerns and duties as reaching beyond the household to "every thing which relates to peace and relates to war, or to any other of the great interests of society" or "the general welfare."[24] These, he said, were rightly women's concerns. Furthermore, Adams placed these concerns in the category of political subjects, implying that women's duties extended to participation in political affairs. In this way Adams pushed the logic of Scottish natural rights philosophy in a direction that enhanced women's social and political equality. However, he was not ready to defend women's rights by applying Lockean notions that secured universal rights and freedoms to all humanity. Nor was he willing to abandon the notion that men and women possessed different natures and therefore different duties. But Adams did attempt to use political philosophies associated with women's rights to expand significantly the entailments of women's duty into what many considered the male political realm. For as Zagarri has observed, the acknowledgment that women did possess natural rights, even though exercise of those rights was circumscribed by gendered notions of duty, amounted to a "discursive key that unlocked the possibility of women's social and political equality." A decade before the organized women's rights movement began to "exploit rights discourse" to claim universal rights for women, Adams moved in that direction with his defenses of women's antislavery petitioning.[25]

Yet while Adams championed the right of women to petition and to express openly their views on slavery, there were those among the antislavery ranks who disagreed entirely. Petitioning, conventioneering, and public speaking by women, they feared, were compromising the goals of abolitionism and casting a pall over the movement. The woman question, as it was called, combined with doubts about the efficacy of moral suasion, contributed to growing dissension in the antislavery movement that would result eventually in the disintegration of organized abolition and significant changes in the petition campaign.

During the summer of 1838, while John Quincy Adams defended the right of women to petition and demanded proper consideration of memorials opposing Texas annexation, abolitionists began to express serious doubts about the efficacy of petitioning as a means of influence. Four sessions of Congress had sent antislavery petitions to the table, where, volunteers lamented, they were gathering dust. Fearing a drastic decline in the number of signatures sent to the next session of Congress, the New England Anti-Slavery Society, in its May 1838 annual report, found it necessary to answer "all who question the propriety and expediency of our continuing to petition Congress on the subject of slavery, inasmuch as our petitions are treated only with contempt." The New Englanders emphasized that petitioning had proved successful in the battle to prevent Texas annexation and that petitions were an important means of educating the people of the United States about the sins of slavery. The report stated, moreover, that the "petition is the only mode of access which the women of this country have to Congress, and to shut against them this door is to blot them out of a civil existence."[1]

The New Englanders' entreaty reflected not only concern over the future of the petition campaign but anxieties caused by widening rifts among organized abolitionists. Congressional disregard for antislavery petitions, obsolescence of the committee charged with overseeing the campaign, and ideological feuds plagued the American Anti-Slavery Society (AASS). Tearing at the seams of the abolitionist fabric were two major issues: whether to abandon moral suasion and adopt a strategy of direct political action, and whether to permit women to participate fully in the national organization—the "woman question." No agreement could be reached on either score, and by 1840 what was once the AASS was rent into two separate organizations. Despite the division and its fallout, petitions flowed into Congress in numbers greater than ever before. Neither of the national antislavery organizations could take credit for this feat, for while the abolitionists squabbled, Representative John Quincy Adams assumed the helm of the petition campaign and developed an antislavery lobby in Congress.

The split in organized abolition resulted in a significant decline in the organized petitioning activities of female abolitionists. The dramatic decrease in women's petitioning, scholars have explained, likely was caused by abolitionists' change in strategy from moral suasion to direct political action. Theodore Weld, James G. Birney, and the Tappan brothers led a faction of abolitionists who saw little use in attempting to convert slaveholders and, recognizing that immediatism was both unpopular and unworkable, advocated gradual emancipation begun immediately. To accomplish this end, political abolitionists embraced the ballot and advocated electing abolition candidates to form an antislavery party. In effect, however, they joined opponents of women's petitioning in defining the slavery issue as primarily political rather than moral, making it difficult for women to continue to claim that their petitions were nonpolitical, moral pleas. Many women who had petitioned Congress in previous years became reluctant to do so for fear that engaging in what was now defined more clearly as a political act would compromise their respectability. Women became reticent also because political abolitionists discouraged female petitioning, preferring that only electors seek congressmen's attention to promote abolition.[2]

While the height of women's collective abolition petitioning, conventioneering, and publishing occurred from 1835 to 1839, women continued to petition against slavery through the 1860s. From 1840 to 1854, in the third major phase of women's antislavery petitioning, thousands of women continued to sign petitions aimed at repealing the gag rule and the Fugitive Slave Act and opposing the annexation of Texas. During the fourth and final phase of their petitioning, from 1861 to 1865, in fact, women inscribed an even greater number of signatures than they had at the height of their efforts in the 1830s to petitions calling for complete emancipation and passage of the Thirteenth Amendment.

Women who sent their names to Congress in these later phases of the campaign engaged in activities that had become understood as more overtly political than in previous years. Indeed, these women joined antislavery men in transforming what was during the 1830s a despised, radical, nongovernment protest movement into, by 1860, a major political party that won the presidency. Reflecting the increasingly political nature of their petitioning and their transformation into overt national political actors, women altered the manner in which they signed petitions as well as the rhetoric of their requests. As they became involved in electoral politics and saw themselves as constituents to whom congressmen were accountable, some women ceased to accept the notion that men's names should be allowed to stand out on petitions and began to mix their signatures with those of men. Their petitions instructed representatives about specific federal legislation, such as the Kansas-Nebraska Bill, in remarkably bold republican language. By the mid-1850s women's petitioning on the clearly political issue of slavery had become so acceptable that even one of the most outspoken critics of this practice during the 1830s, Catharine E. Beecher, signed her name to a petition. Acceptance of the propriety of women exercising their right to petition on political subjects, even a subject so political as amending the U.S. Constitution, was crucial to the success of 1860s petition campaigns, which were dominated by women, to win passage of the Thirteenth Amendment.

*   *   *

Throughout the summer and autumn of 1838 conservative abolitionists voiced loud opposition to the abolitionist movement's devoting its time and energy to defending women's right to petition and speak out publicly against slavery. "I know they were *helpers* to the apostles," stated O. Scott of Lowell, Massachusetts, in a letter published in the *Liberator*, "but they were not *leaders.* The most careless reader of the Bible must see, that women were never designed for the performance of the same public duties as men are." If women were destined to act so boldly, why, asked Scott, did not Jesus choose women as apostles? Although Scott claimed to support women's rights as well as men's rights, he did not believe that any essential scriptural rights were being withheld from women in the free states. He scolded Garrison for promoting the "woman question" and declared that he believed no good would grow out of "urging women forward to public action and office in promiscuous assemblies." Garrisonians' defense of women's rights so angered Amos A. Phelps that he resigned his seat on the Board of Managers of the Massachusetts Anti-Slavery Society, complaining in his letter of resignation that "the Society is no longer an *Anti-Slavery* Society *simply,* but in its principles and modes of action, has become a *woman's rights, no-government-Anti-Slavery Society.* While it remains such, I cannot consistently co-operate with or sustain it."[3]

Garrison defended his stance on the inclusion of women in abolition societies by congratulating the Second Anti-Slavery Convention of American Women, which met in May 1838, and praising their resolutions, which "would do honor to any philanthropic body." In the work of abolition, he claimed, there should be "neither male nor female." Putting his philosophy into practice, Garrison advocated that there should be "no Conventions of an exclusive character, but that all should meet together as moral beings on the broad platform of human rights." The Haverhill, Massachusetts, Anti-Slavery Society agreed with Garrison's position, and at its annual meeting on July 4 resolved that "the cause of American emancipation commends itself especially to the mothers, and daughters of our land; and that we are therefore justified in calling them to *participate* in our *deliberations* and *measures,* for the liberation of the oppressed." In speaking to this resolution, the Reverend Sylvester Brown of Amesbury commended the Grimké sisters on their Massachusetts lecture tour and berated ministers who, "to enlist woman in some favorite scheme of their own," denigrated the sisters for stepping "an inch beyond [their] appropriate sphere." He assured listeners that women speaking in public would neither cause "the order of nature to be reversed" nor lead woman to part with "a particle of her native modesty."[4]

Despite objections to women's public activism, in 1838 Angelina Grimké took up her pen to defend female activism and to encourage women to persevere in their petitioning in her *Appeal to the Women of the United States.*[5] Explicitly addressing her remarks to women but knowing that they would be read by male abolitionists, Grimké sternly reminded readers to view women as citizens and petitioning as an important constitutional right: "We urge upon you, women of America, the duty of petitioning . . . because your voices as citizens of this republic can be heard only through this medium. It is your solemn duty as citizens of the United States to throw a saving influence into the councils of our nation." Reluctant to build her case entirely on natural rights claims, Grimké further argued that women were uniquely suited to petition. Unlike men, she wrote, when women petitioned, it was "not because they are swayed by selfish considerations, personal interest, or party spirit." Women, she said, were "impelled by the loftier and more enduring motives of humanity, justice and love." Like John Quincy Adams in his 1838 *Speech on the Right of Petition,* Grimké asserted women's status as citizens and their natural right of petition but justified exercise of that right on the basis of woman's moral duties.[6]

In the spring of 1839 antislavery women gathered in Philadelphia for their third national convention, at which they reaffirmed their commitment to petitioning Congress. Although Sarah Grimké and Angelina

Grimké Weld were in Philadelphia, they did not attend. Angelina, who had married Theodore Weld the year before, was pregnant and exhausted from a flow of house guests as well as from her work with Sarah and Theodore on *American Slavery as It Is*. Sarah Lewis of Philadelphia, rather than Mary Parker, who had presided over the previous conventions, assumed the president's chair to direct the business of the 102 delegates gathered in the Hall of the Pennsylvania Riding School. Despite these changes at least one thing remained the same: the abolitionist women made a commitment to petitioning. On the first day of the convention Abby Kimber stated that because petitions had excited discussion of slavery in Congress and had called forth "some who have nobly defended both the cause of abolition and the right of petition," women should resolve to continue petitioning. In addition, the Business Committee was charged with composing a circular to urge antislavery women to continue to petition.[7]

The circular acknowledged that for several successive years women had "willingly and cheerfully expended their time and strength" in procuring signatures to memorials to Congress but had witnessed no results proportionate to their efforts. "It is possible that some of you are almost discouraged, and ready to say, 'We have labored in vain, we have spent our strength for naught,'" the circular admitted. Yet it urged women to repeat "with increased fidelity and perseverance" the arduous work of circulating petitions, for "thousands, since we last circulated petitions, have commenced their dreary life of bitter bondage." Petitioning, it reminded readers, was "peculiarly incumbent" upon women, who would not be suspected of "party motives," for congressmen "will believe in our *sincerity*, and this belief will be greatly advantageous to the success of our memorials." Given their moral power, women were obligated to exercise "our only means of direct political action." "It is not ours to fill the office of government, or to assist in the election of those who shall fill them. We do not enact or enforce the laws of the land. The only direct influence which we can exert upon our Legislatures, is by protests and petitions. Shall we not, then be greatly delinquent if we neglect *these?*"[8]

Reading the circular was for many of the customary female delegates their only link to the third women's convention, for they decided instead to attend the AASS meeting in New York to aid Garrison in defending the rights of women to participate and vote in the national organization. Advocates of increased power for women opposed the New York committee, and especially the Tappan brothers, who prescribed a limited role for females and espoused for the movement as a whole a strategy of increased political activity. Although the majority of the men present opposed allowing women to vote, Garrison and his female allies shepherded through a resolution granting women the right to vote in the convention. This feat was achieved largely because the women insisted that they be allowed to vote on the resolution. Yet despite the fact that the Garrison faction won for women the right to vote at national conventions, the meeting was controlled by the conservative executive committee.

The degree of women's participation in the antislavery movement was jeopardized by the executive committee's annual report, which argued that it was the duty of all abolitionists to use the ballot to protect the slave. Of course, not *all* abolitionists could use the ballot, because women and some blacks, not to mention slaves, were denied suffrage. The committee also issued a direct challenge to those who advocated petitioning and other less direct political activities. "The power of influencing Congress by mere petition has already failed," said the report. "Four times have the ears of the popular branch been hermetically sealed. In both houses are the petitions regularly delivered over unopened to the dust and cobwebs of oblivion." Events in Congress did little to restore abolitionists' faith in the time-honored practice. Despite hopes that the third session of the Twenty-fifth Congress, which convened in December 1838, would treat antislavery petitions with more respect, just the opposite occurred. Determined to suppress any opportunity for presentation of abolitionist petitions or speeches, from the very beginning Democrats moved to implement a gag rule. Just eight days into the session Representative Charles G. Atherton, a Democrat from New Hampshire, introduced a resolution based in large part on states' rights principles that immediately tabled petitions pertaining to slavery. The Atherton gag was passed on December 12 by a vote of 126-78. The *Democratic Review* heralded it as "one of the most skillful, prompt and energetic parliamentary movements that we have ever witnessed" and a "sudden and total extinguisher" of party agitation within the halls of Congress. But passage of the Atherton gag enraged abolitionists in no small part because the measure was proposed by a northerner.[9]

Foiled in 1839, the next year Garrison again tried to win control of the AASS. By this time the executive committee had raised enough money to retire the society's debts and planned to dissolve the organization at the convention. But Garrison was determined to keep the society alive and under his power. Lacking supporters, he chartered a steamboat and offered the residents of Lynn, Massachusetts, an outing to New York for a nominal fee if they would agree to attend the convention and follow his lead when voting. Some 500 people took him up on the offer. Garrison's tactics were less than admirable, but supporters of the New York committee also recruited delegates, though not as many as Garrison. The decisive moment of the convention occurred when the vote was taken on whether to appoint a woman, Abby Kelley, to the AASS business committee. The Garrison brigade won the vote but not the battle, for the New York committee responded by withdrawing from the convention and the society.[10]

The "old organization," composed of individuals loyal to Garrison and based in Massachusetts, maintained their insistence on immediate abolition, nonresistance, moral suasion, and supporting women's efforts to win equality. Opponents of Garrison formed the American and Foreign Anti-Slavery Society (AFASS), which came to be called the new organization. The AFASS was headed by members of the former executive committee of the AASS, who wanted to keep the question of women's rights separate from the issue of emancipation and denounced as improper much of women's previous antislavery activism. Having lost faith in the efficacy of moral suasion, the new organization embraced political action and sought to form an antislavery party. Although both the AASS and the AFASS existed through the Civil War, after 1840 neither could muster a significant national constituency.[11]

The feud raging in the national society disrupted the activities of female abolitionists, and the fourth convention of antislavery women, which had been planned to convene in Boston in May 1840, never occurred. Many women who customarily attended the women's convention decided instead to join Garrison's ranks at the tumultuous AASS convention in New York. Other women were deterred from attending because their local societies were besieged with the same issues that were ripping apart the AASS. The situation was most acute in Boston, where the Female Anti-Slavery Society could not elect an impartial president because all candidates were either supporters of the new or the old organization. By April 1840 dissension among the Boston women ran so deep that one of the few things on which they could agree was a motion to dissolve their organization.[12]

A similar fate befell the centralized petition campaign; by spring 1839 it, too, was disintegrating. Once state and local societies realized that they could operate the petition campaign on their own, the national organization seemed like a distant body that debated esoteric points at yearly conventions. Recognizing that their help was no longer desired, the AASS committee charged with running the petition campaign (Henry Stanton, John G. Whittier, and Weld) disbanded and shifted responsibility for petitioning to the local organizations. New campaign organizers faced an increasing number of abolitionists who had lost faith in petitioning. Alvan Stewart, president of the New York State Anti-Slavery Society, went so far as to repudiate petitioning altogether. He complained that despite the fact that thousands of petitions had been sent to Congress, they resulted in nothing except insults hurled at the petitioners. "We might as well send the lamb as an ambassador to a community of wolves," Stewart said. "I would not lift my hand to sign a petition to Congress, to be insulted by that body."[13]

* * *

While abolitionists wrangled over moral suasion and the woman question, a significant change in the nature of the gag rule occurred during the politically charged first session of the Twenty-sixth Congress. The session started in disorder on December 2, 1839, because the Whigs were poised to win control of the House, and due to disputed election results, New Jersey sent two delegations, one Whig and one Democrat. It took almost a month to elect a Speaker, adopt rules, and get to House business. The impending presidential election, moreover, infused the workings of the body with intense partisanship. Whigs sensed victory in the upcoming 1840 presidential election, but they knew their chances would be hurt if the party were perceived to favor abolition. Southern Whigs, in particular, were eager to demonstrate intolerance for antislavery agitation. Thus on December 30 Representative Henry A. Wise, a Virginia Whig, called for a permanent rule to gag petitions relating to slavery. This effort failed, and the session proceeded without gagging discussion of antislavery petitions. As was his custom at the beginning of each Congress, Representative William Slade of New York delivered on January 18 and 20, 1840, a prepared speech against slavery. To the horror of slaveholding representatives and northern Whigs alike, in the most radical antislavery speech yet made in Congress, Slade requested immediate abolition of slavery throughout the United States.

Slade's speech supplied plenty of ammunition for Wise and indignant southerners to enact a gag. After a week of squabbling, Representative William Cost Johnson of Maryland introduced a permanent gag rule, which passed 114-108. The Johnson gag reigned as the most extreme method of silencing antislavery petitions that ever was or would be imposed in the House. Whereas the Pinckney and Hawes resolutions had sent abolition petitions immediately to the table, the Johnson rule stated that no petition or memorial praying for abolition "shall be received by the House, or entertained in any way whatever." The Johnson gag was more than a resolution, which would have expired at the end of the session; it was a rule that remained in effect for the remainder of the first session and for the upcoming second session of the Twenty-sixth Congress. Indeed, House Rule 21 was so difficult to displace that similar standing rules that immediately rejected abolition petitions were enacted by every Congress until 1844.[14]

Yet despite the decline in antislavery organization and the strengthened gag rule, in 1840 the number of petitions sent to Congress increased. The escalation resulted from the fact that control of the campaign had switched from the national antislavery office to the able hands of John Quincy Adams. Although Adams never identified himself as an abolitionist, the fact that volunteers sent him thousands of petitions each year established his sovereignty as a leader of the movement. Indeed, Adams wrote in his journal that he regarded the antislavery movement as "almost exclusively committed" to his trust. Recognizing in May 1839 that the AASS no longer fairly represented an antislavery constituency, he drove the final nail into the coffin of the organization's petition campaign by publishing a public letter to the "Citizens of the United States, whose Petitions, Memorials and Remonstrances have been intrusted to me." In his letter Adams chided abolitionists who held out hope for persuading slaveholders of the immorality of slavery as naive. He condemned abolitionists' insistence on immediatism as preposterous—as a moral and physical impossibility—and scolded them for their many internal disagreements. Adams's letter to the petition volunteers was published throughout the nation and created a sensation. But there was little abolition leaders could say in response to his criticisms because Adams had risen to the status of antislavery hero.[15]

While the national abolitionist organization was collapsing, antislavery supporters in Congress began to solidify into a voting bloc. Due in large part to the efforts of Joshua Leavitt, who was working in Washington early in 1841 as a correspondent for the *Emancipator,* northern Whigs were persuaded to place slavery at the top of their agenda. As a result, Whig congressmen gradually took charge of the petition campaign. They developed a new strategy to pressure members who succumbed to southern power and refused to present petitions. The *Emancipator* told volunteers to send their petitions to a representative of their choice and also to send a letter to antislavery representative Seth M. Gates indicating the congressman to whom the petition had been entrusted. Thus members who failed to present petitions could no longer remain anonymous. Key antislavery congressmen also formed what Joshua Giddings called "a Select Committee on Slavery." This committee developed a strategy for the upcoming session of Congress that involved presenting resolutions and bills that would circumvent the gag and allow discussion of slavery. Antislavery speeches would be delivered, polished, then printed in the *Congressional Digest* for national circulation. With such an aggressive agenda, the committee realized they would need help in researching and writing speeches. For these tasks they turned to Weld, who arrived in Washington on New Year's Day, 1842, to complete the formation of the abolition lobby.[16]

* * *

That the petition campaign was being run by congressmen and Washington lobbyists rather than by grassroots activists in local antislavery societies was a clear sign of the politicization of abolitionism during the 1840s. During this period, after the split of the AASS, there occurred a significant decline in female antislavery petitioning. In her study of antislavery petitioning in Oneida County, New York, Judith Wellman observed that while the total number of extant petitions from 1850–51 is more than one and one-half times the number for 1838–39, the percentage sent by women was significantly smaller. According to Wellman, women signed only 2.3 percent of the petitions in 1850–51, compared with the 69.4 percent they had signed in 1838–39. Likewise, Jean R. Soderlund found that the number of signatures gained by the Philadelphia Female Anti-Slavery Society declined from 1,483 names in 1840 to 678 in 1841. "After 1846," says Soderlund, "the women solicited signatures from door-to-door much less frequently, if at all. They circulated some petitions, particularly those drawn up by the state society, but most of their own petitions were undersigned by only the president and the secretary." As early as 1841, in fact, rather than circulating a petition throughout town, the Philadelphia society spoke with a corporate voice in its petition signed only by its president, Sarah Pugh, and secretary, Anna M. Hopper.[17]

Although female antislavery societies invested less energy in gathering signatures and the number of female signatures on petitions declined drastically, during the 1840s women as individuals and members of other groups organized petition drives in their communities. For example, the same year that the Philadelphia Anti-Slavery Society sent a petition signed only by its officers, more than 675 women of Pennsylvania affixed their names to a single petition asking Congress to alter the laws so that "the revenue derived from taxation upon articles of food and clothing consumed by us, may not in any degree be appropriated to aid in the holding of human beings in slavery." In the spring of 1842 Pugh added her name along with 41 other women to a petition calling for repeal of the Fugitive Slave Law. Starting in 1843 the women of Pennsylvania gathered nearly 100 petitions, including one signed by 208 women, urging Congress to release the people of the free states from all obligations supporting slavery.[18]

In Boston, where the female antislavery society had disbanded, in 1841 and 1842 women gathered thousands of names by concentrating their efforts on petitions against the gag rule and admission of slave states. Charlotte Hartford won the names of 178 women to her petition calling for repeal of the gag rule, topping Sarah B. Litch, who gathered 100 names, only to be outdone by Sarah Chapman's monster petition boasting 722. Petitions instructing Congress to reject proposals admitting Florida, Texas, and other territories into the Union as slave states were equally popular and won names of women from Hubbardston, Upton, Willbraham, Braintree, Southboro, and elsewhere in the state, such as Abington, where 241 women signed such a petition. Most impressive was the petition begun by Louisa Loring in Boston, signed by herself and 635 other women. In addition to circulating petitions against the gag rule and extension of slavery, Massachusetts women lent their names to "The Great Petition to Congress," a statewide effort asking Congress to forever separate the citizens of Massachusetts from all connections with slavery. When Adams attempted to present this petition to the House in February 1843, it bore the signatures of 51,863 men and women of Massachusetts and, according to a reporter for the *Congressional Globe*, was arrayed on "a large wooden framework" that resembled "a gigantic reel, or juvenile waterwheel."[19]

Nor did women cease petitioning in New York. Hundreds of them joined men from the state during 1844 in signing petitions calling for an end to slavery in the District of Columbia. Noteworthy among the petitions signed by New York women that year is one from 1,111 citizens of Oneida County titled the "Welsh Petition," in which petitioners made their request for abolition in the capital first in Welsh, then in English. "A sense of oppression and a desire for more enlarged freedom induced us or our ancestors to leave our country and emigrate to this," it explained, arguing that "what we seek after ourselves we can not but desire for all men." The next year Sarah H. Wicks and 85 other women of Oneida County once again petitioned against slavery in the District. Also during 1845, when the pro-annexationist James K. Polk assumed the presidency, 298 female inhabitants of Lewis County and 197 ladies of the town of Norway, among scores of other women, remonstrated against the annexation of Texas.[20]

While petitions continued to stream from women in the antislavery strongholds of New England, there was a noticeable increase during the early 1840s in petitioning activity among women of the western states and territories. Hannah Hartley, Prudence Coffin, Caroline Stubbs, and hundreds of other women throughout sparsely populated Indiana signed and circulated a popular form of petition opposing the annexation of Texas. In 1844 more than 100 women of Randolph County, Illinois, joined men in requesting abolition of slavery, and in 1846 Amy Newburn gathered the names of 180 women in Putnam County who sought the same goal. In Ohio, a Western state with a well-established abolitionist network and history of petitioning, women continued to send in names as they had throughout the 1830s. In 1842, for example, Lydia R. Finney and 254 other women of Oberlin signed a petition asking members of the House to repeal the gag rule. The next year 175 Oberlin women followed their work with a memorial for abolition in the District of Columbia. Also in 1843 women of Mount Pleasant signed on to protests against the war in Florida and admission of a new slave state, while in 1844 ladies of Marion County numbering 120 prayed for abolition in the District.[21]

Not only did women continue to petition Congress during the 1840s, but at this time a significant change occurred in the manner in which they signed petitions. Rather than keeping their names separated in a column labeled variously as "females," "ladies," "women," or "inhabitants," women began to mix their signatures indiscriminately with those of men. One of the earliest instances of women interspersing their names with men is a petition from the citizens of Pennsylvania protesting the gag rule, which was presented in the House on December 15, 1841. Family names were clumped together on this petition, but they were not separated by sex as had been the custom. This change is particularly evident in the 1842 Great Petition to Congress from the Citizens of Massachusetts that asked representatives to separate forever the petitioners from all connections with slavery. Rather than placing all men's names in the left column and all women's in the right, men and women mixed their names in the same column, again usually in family groups. Also that year, when the inhabitants of the town of Nantucket petitioned for abolition in Washington, D.C., women mingled their names with those of men. Nor was this trend toward combining the names of men and women limited to residents of Massachusetts. When signing a petition for abolition in the District of Columbia in 1841, the women from Ashtabula, Ohio, an area where five years earlier the obsequious Fathers and Rulers petition form had been particularly popular, felt no compulsion to separate their signatures from those of men. The fact that women were signing their names to petitions without clearly distinguishing their signatures from those of men indicates that during the 1840s women had become increasingly comfortable with petitioning and no longer internalized the notion that their opinions were less important than those of men.[22]

These new assertions of women's political authority coincided with Whig women's increasing involvement in electoral politics. During the 1840 presidential campaign, Whigs incorporated women into audiences of political rallies hoping that as symbols of morality their presence would associate candidates with virtue. "In sharp contrast to Democrats, whose demonstrations remained exclusively male and often rowdy affairs," describes Michael F. Holt, "Whigs ostentatiously invited their wives, sisters, and daughters to rallies to testify to the party's family-oriented respectability." Yet Whig women were more than "conspicuous, but passive" audience members; they also gave speeches, conducted political meetings, and wrote pamphlets for the Whig Party. Gaining women's support for William Henry Harrison's bid for the presidency was so important to the Whigs that during his campaign swing through Virginia, party leader Senator Daniel Webster took the time to deliver a special address to the ladies of Richmond. Women's participation in the election of 1840, Elizabeth Varon has demonstrated, set in motion a transformation in women's civic role from "marginal to the discourse and rituals of partisan politics" to active in the polity. As Whig women (and the vast majority of those who signed antislavery petitions were Whigs) exerted growing political power by supporting or withholding support from candidates for public office, there is no wonder that they expected politicians to pay greater heed to their requests.[23]

Another indication that women had become more accustomed to exercising their right of petition to influence political deliberation can be found in the language of the petitions. Petitions sent by women from 1831 to 1836 employed a humble tone, emphasized woman's moral superiority, and sought to disassociate the signers from politics. But beginning with the introduction of short forms in 1837, petitions from women became far less supplicatory. During the 1840s women embraced even bolder language. Most remarkable for its strong language is a petition sent to Congress on December 22, 1842, by Rebecca Buffum and 27 "female citizens" of Cincinnati. Acknowledging that women have been "taught to regard our male fellow Citizens, as our national protectors," they chastised Congress for making laws that protect men and "dumb animals" while they have left "their Mothers, Wives, Sisters, Daughters" completely unprotected from "the ruthless invader," the slave hunter. Echoing antislavery rhetoric that preyed upon anxieties that the slave power sought to destroy northerners' rights, the petition explained that the Fugitive Slave Law authorized any man who called himself a slaveholder to "seize us without warrant, and to carry us to the land of manacles, whips and despair." In such cases, they complained, women would be denied the right of a jury trial, though such a right is guaranteed when a man lays claim to a pig. In a letter to Adams accompanying the petition, Amos Buffum explained that the "highly respectable white ladies" who signed the petition had seen "frequent advertisements for white runaway Slaves." Thus the women prayed Congress "to pass such laws as will give us the same security against all such claims, as is enjoyed by women, under the various governments of Europe." The assertion that the monarchical governments of Europe afforded women better protection than the free institutions of America was particularly biting in 1842, a moment when the United States teetered on the brink of a third war with Great Britain. Yet the petition's most insolent request was reserved for its conclusion, where the female citizens asked that if Congress were unable to fully protect women against claims of the slaveholders, it would at least grant women the "same protection, which by the laws of the land you now have, for your dumb animals." [24]

The largest female petitioning campaign of the 1840s was sparked by the election in 1848 of General Zachary Taylor, a Louisiana slaveholder who would be responsible for resolving the question of slavery in the lands ceded by Mexico in the Treaty of Guadalupe Hidalgo. A committee of antislavery women in Ohio conceived of a drive to amass a "Ladies Mammoth Petition Against Slavery" opposing "the farther extension of American Slavery." Hoping to win signatures from women throughout the North, organizers enlisted the aid of the reform press to print the form and instructions to send the signed petition to Representatives Giddings, J. G. Palfrey, or Amos Tuck, who had agreed to take charge of presenting the memorials. Recognizing that if California were to be admitted as a slave state, the balance between slave and free states would favor slavery, thousands of women answered the call by signing the Women of America petition.

Absent from the Women of America petition was the deferential language characteristic of the Fathers and Rulers petition and other forms used during the mid-1830s. Instead of calling themselves the ladies of Philadelphia or the women of Putnam, Ohio, the signers identified themselves as women of America. This change in the naming of the female petitioners reflects a transformation in women's political consciousness whereby they no longer conceived of themselves only as members of local populations but as citizens of a national community. The transformation in the political consciousness of women who continued to petition suggests a connection between the abolition movement as a whole and individual women who affiliated with that movement. Abolitionists became more political during the 1840s in order to adapt to changes in American political culture, such as the emergence of the party system and the growth of electoral politics. "By 1850 the very definition of citizenship itself originated no longer in the religious and cultural network of family and community life on a local level," writes Wellman, "but in the newly dominant realities of life in a national state." Given this new meaning of citizenship and the fact that they called themselves Women of America, when antislavery women persisted in petitioning Congress after 1840, it is quite possible that they viewed themselves as political beings very different from those who petitioned during the 1830s. They were not so much local church members engaged in the work of reform as citizens of a national community concerned about the justice and expediency of federal legislation. Though they might have understood themselves as national citizens, nevertheless women's citizenship differed from that of white men, for women were nonvoters in a political milieu in which the franchise reigned supreme. The right of petition, then, provided the sole means through which women could enact their national citizenship.[25]

The transformation of women's political identity from one rooted in localities and religious duty to one of national citizenship and natural rights was further enacted in the Women of America petition through the use of republican, patriotic language. "In this AGE OF LIGHT, while the great principles of LIBERTY are animating the nations," it stated, referring to the European revolutions of 1848, "the government of these United States—this 'Model Republic'—should use all its constitutional power to eradicate, within its own bounds, an evil which is being repudiated by the civilized world as its direst curse." Not only did the petition attempt to capitalize on widespread popular sympathy for European refugees, as Deborah Van Broekhoven has noted, but it also, in essence, exposed the hypocrisy of Americans who embraced Austrian and German freedom fighters while slavery persisted in their own nation. The petition forthrightly asked that Congress devise measures to prevent the further extension of slavery, that the government withdraw protection for the slave trade, and that Congress abolish slavery in those sections in which it had "competent jurisdiction," meaning the District of Columbia. The predominance of appeals to humanitarian philosophy, republican principles, and national pride rather than to religious duty in the Women of America petition indicates that when the antislavery movement embraced political activism, women did not shy away from politics but, rather, became more political along with their male colleagues. Indeed, the same year the Women of America petition was put into circulation, women and men from throughout the northern states met in Seneca Falls, New York, to call for women's political rights, including the right to vote in federal elections and to organize a campaign to win those rights. Reflecting an identity of national citizenship, they articulated their opposition to slavery in the United States in terms of national honor in the concert of world politics.[26]

By the close of the Thirtieth Congress in March 1849, the Committee on the Judiciary had received 125 Women of America memorials (judging from extant documents), some of which were signed by hundreds of women. This was three times the number of petitions sent by men, and many times the number of signatures. The returns from New York were particularly impressive: 780 women of Utica signed, only to be outshone by New York City women who gathered 805 names to a single petition. The petitions, presented unrestrained because after nine years of protracted debate the gag rule was rescinded on December 3, 1844, intensified already deepening sectional rifts, preventing congressional efforts to establish civil government in California and New Mexico.[27]

The Women of America petition campaign was only the beginning of women's opposition to the extension of slavery into new states. During the fiery debates over the Compromise of 1850, massive numbers of women signed petitions expressing their disapproval of measures introduced by Senator Henry Clay of Kentucky. When Congress reconvened in December 1849, southern apprehension that new free states would be added, upsetting the sectional equilibrium, had crystallized into defiance against submitting to the Wilmot Proviso, which excluded slavery from the lands won from Mexico. Meanwhile, northerners clung steadfastly to the proviso, despising the idea of spreading slavery westward and of swinging the balance of power in Congress to slaveholders. So divided was the House that it took fifty-nine ballots to elect a Speaker. Despite his moniker of "Old Rough and Ready," President Zachary Taylor lacked the political acumen and support to salve the wound, which festered until it threatened the Union.[28]

Seeking to quiet repeated cries for disunion, near the end of January 1850, Clay, a respected statesman, after obtaining Webster's support, proposed a series of measures aimed at abating the crisis. These measures admitted California on its own terms as a free state (not under the Wilmot Proviso); organized New Mexico as a territory under the issue of popular sovereignty; asked Texas to relinquish its western boundary claim to the Rio Grande, which would have made much of New Mexico part of the slave state of Texas, in exchange for $10 million from the federal government (which amounted to the federal government assuming the public debt of Texas); organized Utah as a separate territory; abolished the slave trade in the District of Columbia but reaffirmed the continuation of slavery; and passed a new Fugitive Slave Act that placed federal enforcement agencies at the disposal of slaveholders and deprived any person accused of being a runaway slave the right of trial by jury.[29]

Abolitionists reacted immediately to the events in Congress. In February 1850 the executive committee of the AFASS issued a circular in the form of a handbill and in newspapers throughout the North urging renewed petitioning. "The time has arrived," heralded the circular, "when the people of the United States are called in the providence of God to decide for themselves and their latest posterity, whether human bondage, with its terrible evils, shall be suffered to extend itself from the Atlantic to the Pacific." It warned that "the Slave power" was making a desperate effort to prevent the admission of California and New Mexico as free states in order "to secure its permanent ascendency on the North American continent." Deploring "the cruel and arbitrary manner in which alleged fugitives from slavery are seized and carried away," abolitionists warned that the success of the Compromise of 1850 would equal "the triumph of evil." It would, they predicted, subject northern interests to the "aristocracy of the South" and "a mighty empire to the various curses attendant upon human bondage." It was no surprise that passage of the compromise in September outraged abolitionists.[30]

A particularly disagreeable aspect of the compromise was the strengthening of the Fugitive Slave Law, which abolitionists characterized as legalizing the hunting of human beings through the streets and hills of the North and compelling northerners to participate in slavery. Petitions against the law poured forth from throughout the North; a great number were signed by women. Among those angered by the law was Elizabeth Rodman of New Bedford, Massachusetts, who in the fall of 1850 put into motion a petition signed by 1,728 ladies calling for repeal of the Fugitive Slave Law. In Abington 1,193 citizens of Massachusetts, 587 of which were women, signed the same form of petition against the law. Indeed, petitions against the Fugitive Slave Law were signed by women from cities and towns throughout the state of Massachusetts. The same was true in Ohio, where among many others, 2,833 women and men of Portage County prayed for repeal of the law.[31]

While the vast majority of antislavery petitions to Congress throughout the campaign were signed by whites because free blacks tended to memorialize state legislatures to preserve their civil rights, 400 free blacks of Allegheny County, Pennsylvania, petitioned Congress in 1850 to repeal the Fugitive Slave Law. Their petition was more than ten times longer than the one printed by the AFASS, which was a short form. The petitioners, who identified themselves only at the very end of the petition as "colored people," constructed a long, elaborate case against the Fugitive Slave Law, describing how it left African Americans in the nonslaveholding states particularly vulnerable to enslavement. "In the event of the absence of record-proof and the demise of those having personal knowledge of the transactions, any such person claimed under the Act of 1793, would be left to the mercy and discretion of the claimant, and therefore without any recourse or redress whatever," the petition explained. These terrible circumstances would "subject our hearths and firesides to dismay and desolation, our wives, our children, and ourselves to outrages against which all other Americans are most sacredly and securely protected." The petition, which was signed by men and women who mixed their signatures, expressed their opposition to the 1793 Fugitive Slave Law and every act introduced thereafter that infringed on "our liberties as American Citizens."[32]

Introduction early in 1854 of the Kansas-Nebraska Bill once again sparked the indignation of northerners, who expressed their anger by sending Congress droves of petitions. The bill, conceived by Senator Stephen A. Douglas of Illinois and augmented by Calhounites, explicitly repealed the Missouri Compromise and thus made possible the introduction of slavery north of the 36°30' line. So obnoxious was this proposal to antislavery congressmen Salmon P. Chase, Joshua Giddings, and Charles Sumner that on January 24, 1854, they issued *An Appeal of the Independent Democrats,* which attacked the Kansas-Nebraska Bill "as part and parcel of an atrocious plot to exclude from a vast unoccupied region immigrants from our own states, and to convert it into a dreary region of despotism, inhabited by masters and slaves." The *Appeal*'s effect was electric, sparking renewed fervor for antislavery and turning public opinion decidedly against Douglas. As the Illinois senator would later admit, the public was so enraged by his bill that he could have traveled from Washington to Chicago by the light of his own burning effigies.[33]

During the five months in which Congress wrangled with the Kansas-Nebraska Bill, public meetings were held throughout the North to galvanize opposition to the measure and to organize protest, mostly in the form of petitioning. One such meeting in Youngstown, Ohio, forwarded a series of resolutions denouncing Douglas's bill as "a usurpation of power, at variance with the spirit and letter of the Constitution, contrary to the legitimate interests and prosperity of the country, and in direct and open violation of every principle of honor, in the observance of a compact made by the opposing interests of different States in the Compromise of 1820." Women joined in petitioning on this pressing national issue, and the confidence with which they attempted to influence the outcome of federal legislation stands in remarkable contrast to the attitudes exhibited in petitions of the 1830s. "We are informed the subject of establishing a territorial government for Nebraska is now before your honorable body," stated the women of Greece County, Ohio, expressing their dismay at the hypocrisy of Congress "leaving the way open for slavery and that too after it had been positively prohibited." They firmly instructed congressmen "not to extend such an enormous evil as slavery into territory now free." Elsewhere in Ohio more than 480 ladies from Oberlin and some 640 ladies from Ohio City signed petitions against repeal of the Missouri Compromise. Solemnly protesting against the Kansas-Nebraska Bill as fatal to prosperity and the existence of the nation, and as "opposed to every human impulse," 104 women of Elgin, Illinois, petitioned against the measure introduced by the senator from their state.[34] Anti-Nebraska petitions were also signed by midwestern women, especially from Michigan and Wisconsin.[35]

Once again Massachusetts women produced an outpouring of petitions, such as the one begun by Lucia Merrill and signed by 136 other women of Montague. Most impressive was the petition remonstrating against the repeal of the Missouri Compromise sent by 1,100 women of Andover. The petition was noteworthy because of the large number of signers, including Mary Stuart, Sarah B. Edwards, Harriet Lee, and a number of other women of Andover. But one name scrawled tightly at the top of the second column stood out from the rest. It was the signature of the woman who twenty-four years earlier had shrouded in secrecy her involvement in the petition campaign against removal of the Cherokee and seventeen years earlier had written a scathing public letter in which she had stated, "In this country, petitions to congress, in reference to the official duties of legislators, seem, IN ALL CASES, to fall entirely without the sphere of female duty." It was the signature of Catharine E. Beecher. That an individual who had so publicly scorned women petitioning Congress on political issues signed a petition against federal legislation suggests that by 1854 there was growing acceptance, even among persons espousing conservative notions of gender decorum, of women petitioning their representatives.[36]

* * *

The crisis of 1850, northern outcry against the Fugitive Slave Law, and division along party lines in the vote that passed the Kansas-Nebraska Bill in May 1854, as we know from hindsight, presaged the ultimate rending of the Union. Pushed over the edge by the election of Abraham Lincoln, a free-soil Republican, on December 20, 1860, a convention at Charleston dissolved "the Union now subsisting between South Carolina" and the United States of America. Georgia, Alabama, Mississippi, Florida, Louisiana, and Texas seceded by February 1, 1861, and delegates from these states formed the Confederate States of America. Despite Abraham Lincoln's inaugural assurances to southerners that he would respect slavery and enforce the Fugitive Slave Law, on April 12, 1861, the guns were fired at Fort Sumter and the nation was thrown into civil war. Based on its advantage in population and resources, the North expected a short conflict, but those hopes were dashed by embarrassing Federal defeats early in the war. Mounting military casualties moved the women of Iowa to express that they were "appalled at the loss of life and the bereavements that flow from the civil war that is now waging in our country," and they asked Congress to cease hostilities and to consider terms of peace. Close to 38,000 men

GREAT MASSACHUSETTS PETITION.

To the Senate and House of Representatives of the State of Massachusetts:

The undersigned citizens of the State of Massachusetts, earnestly desiring to free this commonwealth and themselves from all connection with domestic slavery and to secure the citizens of this state from the danger of enslavement, respectfully pray your honorable body,

1. To forbid all persons holding office under any law of this state from in any way officially or under color of office, aiding or abetting the arrest or detention of any person claimed as a fugitive from slavery.

2. To forbid the use of our jails or public property of any description whatever within the Commonwealth, in the detention of any alleged fugitive from slavery.

3. To propose such amendments to the Constitution of the United States as shall forever separate the people of Massachusetts from all connection with slavery.

NAMES.

THE GREAT MASSACHUSETTS PETITIONS have been sent to Postmasters and known friends of human liberty in every town in the State. Many thousands have been printed. Let every freeman into whose hands they may fall, constitute himself an agent to obtain signatures. See that your own town and all the neighboring towns are supplied. Return them by forefather's day, Dec. 22d, or at any rate by Jan. 1, 1843. Hold your town meetings on the 22nd of December, and your county meetings on the first of January, throughout the state. Direct to the Latimer Committee, at their Head Quarters No. 3, Amory Hall, Boston. Let the parcels come, if possible, post paid, or free of expense. Sign under the word names, in a SINGLE Column.

GREAT PETITION TO CONGRESS.

To the Senate and House of Representatives of the United States of America:

The undersigned citizens of the State of Massachusetts, earnestly desiring to free their commonwealth and themselves from all connection with domestic slavery and to secure the citizens of their state from the danger of enslavement, respectfully pray your honorable body,

To pass such laws and to propose such amendments to the Constitution of the United States as shall forever separate the people of Massachusetts from all connection with slavery.

NAMES.

Massachusetts women lent their names to the Great Petition to Congress, a statewide effort asking Congress to forever separate the citizens of Massachusetts from all connections with slavery. When Representative John Quincy Adams attempted to present this petition to the House in February 1843, it bore the signatures of 51,863 men and women of Massachusetts and was arrayed on "a large wooden framework" that resembled "a gigantic reel, or juvenile water-wheel." (Courtesy of the Boston Athenæum)

Feb. 10th, 1854.

To the Senate and House of Representatives of the United States in Congress assembled. The undersigned, Women of the town of Andover, in the Commonwealth of Massachusetts, do most respectfully and earnestly petition the Congress of the United States, to maintain inviolate the plighted faith of the nation, by making effective provision for the exclusion of slavery from all territory North of the geographical limit usually known as the "Missouri Compromise Line."

In 1854 the women of Andover, Massachusetts, submitted to Congress this petition opposing repeal of the Missouri Compromise. It was signed by 1,100 women, among them Catharine E. Beecher (first signature in right column), who in 1837 had publicly decried the idea of women sending petitions to Congress. The petition was also signed by her sister Harriet Beecher Stowe (first signature in the left column), author of Uncle Tom's Cabin.

and women of New York signed another petition urging measures of reconcilement.[37]

With the onset of the war, Lincoln hesitated to touch the slavery question, while antislavery Republicans became more adamant in their insistence that the war should end the issue of slavery once and for all. Hoping to sway Lincoln and moderate Republicans, antislavery northerners doubled their petitioning efforts for emancipation. These petition campaigns for emancipation and passage of the Thirteenth Amendment, which lasted from 1861 to 1865, constitute the fourth major phase of women's antislavery petitioning. By far the most popular petition praying for the abolition of slavery from 1861 to 1862 was prepared by a "committee of gentlemen in Boston" for general circulation among northerners. Headed with the directive "Proclaim Liberty throughout all the land, to all the inhabitants thereof," it in no uncertain terms blamed the South for the war. The "present formidable rebellion" found its "root and nourishment in the system of chattel slavery at the South," the petition stated, adding that the leading conspirators were slaveholders, "who constitute an oligarchy avowedly hostile to all free institutions." The petition contended that "no solid peace can be maintained while the cause of this treasonable revolt is permitted to exist." Consequently the petitioners asked that Congress employ its war powers to liberate "unconditionally the slaves of all who are rebels" and, "while not recognizing the right of property in man," to provide slaves of Union men a "fair pecuniary award." Doing so, they asserted, would "facilitate an amicable adjustment of difficulties" and "bring the war to a speedy and beneficent termination."[38]

Although both men and women signed this form of petition, in Pennsylvania, at least, another form was composed specifically for the signatures of women. In contrast to the general petition that identified signers as citizens but explicitly separated the signatures as voters and nonvoters, the female petition identified signers as women of Pennsylvania. It attempted to heighten the political ethos of women signers by emphasizing their contribution to and interest in the war as the "mothers, wives, and daughters of those who go forth in their country's defence." About half the length of the form written by the Boston gentlemen, the women's petition did not argue about the faults of the South or mention the war powers of Congress. Rather, the women pleaded for abolition and compensation to end the war out of "our love for our country, and for those who go forth to fight its battles, as well as by our love of liberty for ourselves and for all."[39]

Resulting in large part from the constant pressure placed on him by abolitionists in Congress and by northern public opinion, on January 1, 1863, Lincoln finally and reluctantly decreed that slaves in the rebel states were free. Dissatisfied that the Emancipation Proclamation freed slaves only in areas still in rebellion, Susan B. Anthony and Elizabeth Cady Stanton, abolitionists and women's rights activists, founded the Woman's National Loyal League, which aimed to achieve emancipation of slaves in all southern states. The organization's strategy, they announced, was to amass a petition to Congress calling for immediate emancipation signed by 1 million people from every state of the Union. Their drive began with Stanton announcing the founding convention of the league and issuing *An Appeal to the Women of the Republic,* which was printed in the *Liberator* as well as other antislavery periodicals. Employing patriotic appeals and reminding women of their moral duty, Stanton urged women to speak out against slavery just as their foremothers had spoken out for liberty during the American Revolution.[40]

The first convention of the Loyal League met in New York City on May 14, 1863, and the list of its participants reads like an honor roll of female abolitionists and women's rights activists. Angelina Grimké Weld, who had ceased public lecturing in 1839, served as a vice-president and returned to the podium to deliver a stirring address. Other major participants included Martha Coffin Wright, sister of Lucretia Coffin Mott and one of the organizers of the first women's rights convention in 1848; Ernestine Rose, who in 1840 had circulated petitions in New York state for the women's property bill and who was a leading female orator; and Antoinette Brown Blackwell, a Unitarian minister who throughout the 1850s lectured on abolition and women's rights. The Loyal League was by and large a white organization that did little to encourage the participation of blacks, but black women in Philadelphia, Chicago, Ohio, and likely elsewhere nonetheless took active roles in the campaign.[41]

At its founding convention in May 1863, the Loyal League agreed to use a single, short petition form in hopes of compiling a massive petition bearing 1 million signatures from every state in the Union to visibly demonstrate that the majority of the public favored emancipation. The petition read,

The Undersigned, Women of the United States above the age of eighteen years, earnestly pray that your Honorable Body will pass, at the earliest practicable day, an Act emancipating all persons of African descent held in involuntary service or labor in the United States.[42]

As the wording of the petition written by the convention indicates, Loyal League leaders, all of whom were women, initially envisioned a petition signed exclusively by women. But on June 11, 1863, the membership voted to permit men to sign the petition. The next year the Loyal League changed the wording of the mass petition:

> The undersigned, citizens of _____ believing slavery the great cause of the present rebellion, and an institution fatal to the life of Republican government, earnestly pray your honorable bodies to immediately abolish it throughout the United States, and to adopt measures for so amending the Constitution, as forever to prohibit its existence in any portion of our common country.[43]

The language of the petition was changed because men wished to sign an emancipation petition and Garrisonian abolitionists wanted a constitutional amendment freeing the slaves.[44]

During the months after the convention, leaders put in place a system of petitioning in which canvassers collected, in addition to names, a contribution of at least one penny from each signer. Besides drawing on women's prewar petitioning experience, the league recruited children to circulate the petition by offering a badge and membership to the league to anyone who collected at least fifty names and fifty cents for the cause.[45] After returning to the lecture platform at the league's founding convention, Grimké Weld contributed to the campaign by writing an "Address to the Soldiers of Our Second Revolution," which was published in the antislavery press. She venerated Union soldiers for their "sufferings, daring, heroic self-devotion, and sublime achievements" and greeted those who were homeward bound with "joy and admiration." Amid her praises Grimké Weld defined the war "not, as the South falsely pretends, a war of races, nor of sections, nor of political parties." It was, she insisted, "a war of PRINCIPLES," a war to win rights for free laborers as well as slaves and to protect the rights of free speech, free schools, free suffrage, and free government. She entreated the men who were returning home to finish the work they had begun on the battlefield by signing the league's petition for emancipation: "Your country needs your power of soldierly endurance and accomplishment, your hard-earned experience, your varied tact and trained skill, your practiced eye and hand—in a word, all that makes you veterans, ripe in discipline and education power. Raw recruits *cannot* fill your places. Brave men! Your mission, though far advanced, is *not* accomplished."[46]

One of the major obstacles to convincing women to participate in the Loyal League was that they were already engaged in the work of benevolent and charitable societies to aid in the relief of soldiers and their families. A good number of women believed, moreover, that the business of amending the Constitution should be left to political representatives— that is, to men. To ameliorate these hesitations, Stanton published *An Appeal to the Women of the Republic*, dated January 25, 1864, which was sent out with petition forms and published in reform journals. Reminding women that they could neither vote nor fight for their country, Stanton stated, "Your only way to be a power in the Government is through the exercise of this, one, sacred, *Constitutional* 'RIGHT OF PETITION;' and we ask you to use it NOW to the utmost." Stanton praised northern women for showing "true courage" and "self-sacrifice" in their benevolent work as "angels of mercy to our sick and dying soldiers in camps and hospitals, and on the battle-field." But she hoped women would expand their activism beyond benevolence: "Let it not be said that the women of the Republic, absorbed in ministering to the outward alone, saw not the philosophy of the revolution through which they passed; understood not the moral struggle that convulsed the nation—the irrepressible conflict between liberty and slavery. Remember the angels of mercy and justice are twin sisters, and ever walk hand in hand." Stanton asserted that once slavery was ended, the brothers, husbands, and sons of northern women would never again be called for the sake of the freedom of the nation to die on the battlefield or starve in rebel prisons. Toward this goal, Stanton concluded, women must sign the petition.[47]

In February 1864 the league sent its first signed petition to Charles Sumner, senior U.S. senator from Massachusetts, for presentation to Congress. The petition was made up of 6,000 forms glued end to end and rolled into bundles. The finished product bore the signatures of 100,000 Americans—65,601 women and 34,399 men. Workers in the state of New York gathered the most signatures (17,706); Illinois, the home state of President Lincoln, had the second largest total (15,380). The successful campaign was due in many cases to the work of organizations such as the Ladies' New York City Anti-Slavery Society and the Philadelphia Female

Anti-Slavery Society. But in other cases the work was less organized and succeeded due to the efforts of key individuals. In Wisconsin, for example, a rural widow who had lost her husband and two sons in the war collected 1,800 signatures. So driven was this woman that she also recorded the names of those who refused to sign, so "they may be handed over to the future scorn they so well deserve."[48]

Sumner presented the massive petition on February 9, 1864, in a highly orchestrated performance that involved two tall black men carrying the enormous bundles into the Senate chamber. In his speech of presentation, which became known as "The Prayer of One Hundred Thousand," Sumner emphasized that the petition was signed by 100,000 men and women from all parts of the Union and from varying backgrounds. Their prayer, he said, was simple: "They ask nothing less than universal emancipation; and this they ask directly at the hands of Congress. No reason is assigned. The prayer speaks for itself. So far as it proceeds from the women of the country, it is naturally a petition, and *not* an argument. But I need not remind the Senate that there is no reason so strong as the reason of the heart. Do not all great thoughts come from the heart?" Sumner's speech was printed by the Loyal League and distributed throughout the country to inspire further petitioning.[49]

When on April 8, 1864, the Senate approved the Thirteenth Amendment, the Loyal League responded by immediately sending out an additional 15,000 petition forms to be used in an effort to get the amendment approved by the House. Yet month after month the House failed to act. Sumner, as the Loyal League's chief spokesman in Congress, continued to present petitions such as one signed by 4,362 women of Maine, another from the women of Pennsylvania with 6,336 signatures, another from New York signed by 6,857 women and 6,492 men, and yet another from Wisconsin signed by 2,391 women. By the time Congress recessed for the summer of 1864, the number of names on Loyal League petitions totaled nearly 400,000. According to Wendy Hamand Venet, based on the 1860 census about one in every twenty-four Americans living in the northern states signed petitions circulated by the Woman's National Loyal League on behalf of the Thirteenth Amendment. The House finally approved the Thirteenth Amendment on December 18, 1865. It was the first constitutional amendment to be passed as a result of a mass campaign to bring public opinion to bear on Congress, a campaign initiated by and sustained largely by women.[50] What is particularly remarkable about the Loyal League's accomplishment is that despite the fact that women were denied suffrage, through the use of the right of petition they managed to win an amendment to the U.S. Constitution.

*   *   *

Notwithstanding the decline of organized abolition at the state and national levels in 1839, women continued to petition throughout the 1840s, 1850s, and 1860s, sending massive abolition petitions to Congress on the most pressing political issues of the day. When abolitionists shifted from moral suasion to political action, rather than backing away from overt political activity, some antislavery women embraced this change. By the 1840s they had begun to mix their signatures with those of men; no longer did women accept the notion that men's names should be allowed to stand out because their opinions meant more to representatives. Moreover, the language of women's petitions during this later period dropped deferential overtures characteristic of the memorials of the 1830s and took on a bolder tone. By the 1850s female petitioning had grown so much more acceptable and abolitionist sentiment so much more popular that even its most outspoken critic of the 1830s—Catharine E. Beecher—signed her name at the top of a petition. Acceptance of the propriety of women exercising their right to petition was crucial to the success of the petition campaign to win passage of the Thirteenth Amendment. Finally, after three decades of petitioning and due in large part to the ongoing efforts of women who signed and circulated petitions, abolitionists secured their ultimate goal of emancipating the slaves. In the process of petitioning to end slavery, many women transformed their political identity from humble subjects to national citizens.

We Can No Longer Be Neglected or Forgotten

Over the course of their efforts from 1831 to 1863, women supported abolitionist goals of influencing public opinion and pressuring legislators by sending millions of signatures on petitions to Congress. In 1836, even before an organized plan of petitioning was implemented, Congress received petitions signed by 15,000 women. In 1837, after women met in an unprecedented national convention to coordinate their efforts, 201,130 women affixed their signatures to antislavery petitions. Combined with the roughly equal number of men's names sent that year, the antislavery petitions were so numerous that they would have filled, from floor to ceiling, a room twenty feet wide by thirty feet long by fourteen feet high. When someone suggested to the clerk responsible for these petitions that they be printed, he was "nearly frightened out of his wits." In the years 1838–39 women alone signed 14.5 percent of abolition petitions, and women together with men signed 54.9 percent. That means that women by themselves or with men signed nearly 70 percent of the petitions received by Congress during those two years in the early period of the antislavery movement. (The remaining 30 percent were signed by men only.) During the 1840s, 1850s, and 1860s women continued to petition, and during this time the most massive petitions—the ones bearing the most names—were sent to Congress by women.[1]

It is impossible to know exactly how many names women sent to Congress because the volume of petitions received by Congress became so immense that many were destroyed. Stories about the massive piles of petitions have become archival legends. Gilbert Barnes wrote that at one time there were several truckloads of petitions "stored here and there about the Capitol." The current whereabouts of these petitions are unknown. Barnes also reported that C. H. Van Tyne, who composed a guide to the National Archives, used to tell his classes at the University of Michigan that during a visit to the Capitol, he came upon a caretaker fueling a stove with antislavery petitions. The caretaker reportedly said there were so many of these bundles of paper that he figured those he burned would never be missed. Whether this tale is truth or fancy, I found amidst the hundreds of folders of petitions a note from the clerk indicating that large numbers of petitions had been carted out of the depository. There were so many antislavery petitions, he scrawled in 1864, "that they have been removed to the Store Room." Fortunately he provided a state-by-state inventory of the number of signatures on the petitions that were removed. According to his calculations, the displaced petitions bore more than 90,000 names.[2]

Because so many documents are missing, it is impossible to know for certain how many antislavery memorials were sent to Congress by women, but it is possible to estimate. Based on the fact that from 1837 to 1863 women signed petitions at the conservative rate of 15,000 per year (the number sent in 1836 before the petition campaign was formally organized), the total number of female signatures gathered from 1831 to 1863 would amount to well over three quarters of a million. But this figure is assuredly too small, for women's petitioning increased dramatically after 1836. If even half as many women who signed petitions during 1837 did so from 1838 to 1863, the total number of female signatures gathered from 1836 to 1863 would amount to almost 3 million. This total does not include the more than 65,000 female signatures gathered by the Woman's National Loyal League in 1864 to secure passage of the Thirteenth Amendment.

But the number of signatures alone does not tell the full story of the impact of women's antislavery petitioning. When they sent 15,000 signatures in 1835 and 1836, women swelled to a flood what was previously a trickle of memorials submitted almost exclusively by men. As day after day petitions continued to flow into the House, representatives became increasingly irritated and finally, in June 1836, passed the gag rule. The rule provided just the issue abolitionists needed to expand their appeal among the public by linking the popular right of petition with the unpopular cause of immediate abolitionism. It provided evidence, moreover, for abolitionists' claim that the South was conspiring to destroy northerners' civil rights in order to perpetuate the peculiar institution. Whether or not they were genuinely concerned about the plight of the slave, more northerners became sympathetic to abolitionism when the gag rule demonstrated that slavery threatened their own civil rights.[3]

Another important effect of women's efforts was that they enabled abolitionists to send enough petitions to Congress to provoke senators and representatives to debate the question of slavery, a feat petitioning by men alone had failed to accomplish. According to William Lee Miller, the debates in the House over the right of petition were nothing less than "a nation-defining argument between . . . two parts of the founders' legacy": human slavery and human freedom. Not only did the petitions lead Congress to discuss slavery, but the debate over slavery and suppressing petitions stirred indignation and discussion of antislavery issues among the public at large. The congressional debate over slavery, concluded an 1836 report of the Starksborough (Vermont) Anti-Slavery Society, was "extending an irresistible moral influence" over the entire nation. "Wherever the reports of the proceedings in Congress are circulated and read," the Vermont abolitionists explained, "there will be a knowledge of the doings in relation to those petitions extended; and this circumstance will serve to stir up the spirit of inquiry in relation to our objects, our principles, and measures, in many places where the merits of the Anti-Slavery Society have heretofore been but little known."[4]

Petitioning also enabled abolitionists to reach people who would remain untouched by other forms of abolitionist rhetoric. Indeed, the petitions were probably read by more people—congressmen, abolitionists, and members of the public to whom appeals were made for signatures—than were any other form of antislavery literature. Unlike antislavery lectures, newspapers, and pamphlets, which often reached only persons already converted to the cause, petitions brought abolitionists into contact with "the pro-slavery, the indifferent, with those who are as much as ourselves opposed to slavery, . . . so that many who would not otherwise think at all about it are induced to give it a little place in their minds." The strategy of discussing slavery face-to-face allowed petition circulators to speak with people who would never go to hear an abolitionist lecturer and who could not read an abolitionist tract. Often the signing of petitions resulted in the formation of a new antislavery society. One abolitionist explained that a signature on a petition served a "three-fold purpose" in converting people to abolitionism: "You not only gain the person's name, but you excite inquiry in her mind and she will excite it in others; thus the little circle imperceptibly widens until it may embrace a whole town."[5]

*   *   *

By petitioning, women not only helped bring about an end to slavery, but they also made important strides toward securing their own rights and transforming the political identity of woman into that of active national citizen. Participation in the petition campaign, which involved running meetings, writing appeals, holding conventions, persuading neighbors, and speaking in public, led women to exercise forms of political communication previously reserved exclusively for men. Women would apply these skills of political organizing in a host of postbellum political activities. Petitioning Congress, which due in large part to the struggles of female abolitionists had become an acceptable means of influence for women, continued to be a crucial and persistent outlet employed by women determined to participate in politics despite the fact that neither the Constitution nor custom recognized them as full citizens. As Gerda Lerner concludes in her study of the activities of female abolitionists, "Many women, once they had become habituated to political activity through [antislavery] petitioning, transferred this activity to causes more directly connected with their self-interest." During political battles for women's rights such as equal property legislation and suffrage, Lerner writes, "the ancient method of trying to influence legislators and change public opinion by means of memorials was raised to new levels of significance." These petitions, she concludes, were equally important "in helping to mould an ideology of feminism around which women's political activities could be rallied."[6]

After 1863 and well into the twentieth century, millions of women petitioned Congress on issues such as granting pensions to Civil War nurses, aiding freedwomen and -men, outlawing lynching, controlling the sale of alcohol, attacking and defending Mormon polygamy, and demanding suffrage for women. Recognition of the numerous issues for which women petitioned after the Civil War as well as the magnitude of their efforts not only sheds light on women's use of this right but also disproves David C. Frederick's claim that congressional reaction to the antislavery petition campaign so weakened the right of petition that "never again would any group exercise the right of petition on so grand a scale to engage in a dialogue with Congress on an important social issue."[7]

On the contrary, women played a major role in mass petition campaigns that significantly influenced, for example, Congress's decision to take action against polygamists. When in 1898 Brigham H. Roberts, a reputed polygamist, was elected to Congress, hundreds of thousands of women petitioned against his seating and for a constitutional amendment outlawing polygamy. Organizations such as the Women's Board of Home Missions of the Presbyterian Church, the National Congress of Mothers, the National Council for Women, and the American Female Guardian Society were especially active in the campaign. Mrs. R. H. Murray, Mrs. Alex Watson, and dozens of other members of the Woman's Missionary Society of the Central Presbyterian Church of Michigan, for example, called on the Fifty-sixth Congress to propose an amendment to the Constitution that would define legal marriage to be "monogamic" and to make "polygamy, under whatever guise or pretense, a crime against the United States, punishable by severe penalties." Likewise the Woman's Home Missionary Society of the Methodist Episcopal Church, Philadelphia Conference, "urgently" petitioned Congress to "secure, as soon as possible, an Amendment to the Constitution of the United States, forever prohibiting the practice of polygamy and polygamous cohabitation in any part of the United States."[8]

The petition drive demanding that Congress deny Roberts his seat garnered 7 million signatures from both women and men. According to the *New York Evening Journal,* which played an active role in the campaign, women jostled in the House galleries to witness presentation of the petition, which was laid on the Speaker's desk in twenty-eight rolls, each two feet in diameter, wrapped together in an American flag. The mass petition won its goal, for the House voted by a great majority to exclude Roberts. The *New York Times* concluded that "the vast mob" of women who "bawled for the shutting out of Roberts" had won their way.[9]

Women also played leading roles in petition drives to educate the public about lynching and to press for federal antilynching laws. In 1892, a year in which 230 blacks were lynched, Ida B. Wells set in motion an antilynching campaign and urged others to join her. The next year prominent African American leaders Mary Church Terrell, Frederick Douglass, Francis J. Grimké, and Walter H. Brooks joined other blacks in signing a petition asking senators to instruct the Judiciary Committee to grant a hearing on "the lawless outrages committed in some of the Southern States upon persons accused of crime, but who are denied the ordinary means of establishing their innocence by due process of law." Exactly six months after reception of the petition, Republican congressman Henry W. Blair of New Hampshire introduced a joint resolution to provide $25,000 to investigate lynching and all alleged rape cases since 1884 that had resulted in unlawful violence against the accused "by whipping, lynching, or otherwise." Despite the fact that on four separate occasions Blair presented petitions from African Americans in support of his resolution, it was strenuously opposed by southern members and expired in committee. In 1900 more than 2,400 men and women of Massachusetts, members of the National Afro-American Council, petitioned the House of Representatives requesting a bill that would make lynching a federal crime and require the president to send national troops to rescue any person from the hands of a mob in any state of the Union. On January 20 Representative George H. White, a black Republican of North Carolina, introduced the first federal antilynching bill, which deemed all parties tried and convicted of "participating, aiding, and abetting" lynching guilty of treason against the U.S. government and punishable by death. Despite a national petition campaign to support the bill, it languished in the Judiciary Committee.[10]

Neglect of the bill did not end antilynching petitioning, which was reignited in 1917 by a bloody race riot in East Saint Louis, Illinois, that left thirty-nine African Americans dead. Among the outpouring of petitions to Congress was that of the 368 members of the Young Ladies Protective League of Washington, D.C., who petitioned against "the outrages perpetrated upon American citizens in East St. Louis" and who requested Congress to punish those guilty of the "massacre" and, furthermore, to make lynching a federal crime punishable by death. The next year Representative Leonidas C. Dyer, a Missouri Republican, introduced a bill that imposed heavy penalties on counties where lynchings occurred. The National Association for the Advancement of Colored People was largely responsible for organizing lobbying efforts, including petitioning, to support the Dyer bill. Although the House approved the Dyer bill three times, southern Democrats repeatedly blocked its passage in the Senate, claiming that the measure would violate states' rights. In the end no federal legislation against lynching was ever passed, but the frequency of lynching declined gradually after 1920. Yet lynching persisted, and both blacks and whites continued to petition Congress on the subject through 1944.[11]

In addition to social reforms such as antipolygamy and antilynching efforts, women initiated mass petition campaigns to agitate for the right to vote. The decision to employ petitioning as a major means of persuasion was based on suffrage leaders' years of experience in the antislavery and temperance movements in which they had gained organizational skills and had become accustomed to public activism. The Declaration of Sentiments of the 1848 Woman's Rights Convention, modeled on the American Declaration of Independence and the 1833 Declaration of Sentiments of the American Anti-Slavery Society, specifically listed petitioning among its principal means of agitation. The women and men present at the convention pledged that in order to win for women all the rights and privileges of citizens, they would "employ agents, circulate tracts, petition the state and national legislatures, and endeavor to enlist the pulpit and press in our behalf." During the 1840s and 1850s women organized several petition campaigns aimed at state legislatures. In 1846 New York women petitioned their state legislature for the right to vote. In 1850 the women's rights convention held in Worcester, Massachusetts, implemented a systematic petition campaign in eight states, and the powerful orator Lucy Stone implored delegates to diligently circulate petitions. In 1854 Susan B. Anthony headed a campaign in New York state that circulated petitions requesting that women be granted the right to control their own wages, to maintain custody of their children after divorce, and to vote. With their efforts further coordinated by sixty "captains," one in each county, the women succeeded in gathering more than 10,000 signatures in the course of a few months.[12]

Yet it was not until after the Civil War that women's rights advocates began to petition Congress. Believing optimistically that women's contributions to abolitionism and the Union war effort had demonstrated female patriotism, feminist leaders fully expected radical Republicans to introduce a measure calling for universal suffrage. But their hopes were dashed in December 1865 with the presentation of the Fourteenth Amendment. The amendment mandated that any state that denied suffrage to male citizens—meaning men born or naturalized in the United States and having reached the age of twenty-one years—would lose representation in Congress proportionate to the number of male citizens denied the right to vote. While it required Confederate states to grant the vote to black men before those states would be readmitted to the Union, the amendment strengthened the disfranchisement of women by guaranteeing suffrage only to male citizens, thus implying a separate form of citizenship for females. If the Fourteenth Amendment were to pass as written, Stanton and Anthony foresaw, it would take another constitutional amendment to secure for women the right to vote in federal elections. "If that word 'male' be inserted," Stanton predicted, "it will take us a century at least to get it out."[13]

Women's rights leaders reacted to introduction of the Fourteenth Amendment by calling for unification of the black suffrage and woman suffrage movements and by starting a petition campaign for universal suffrage. Stanton and Anthony composed a form titled "A Petition for Universal Suffrage," which asked Congress to "prohibit the several States from disenfranchising any of their citizens on the ground of sex" and implied that women were more deserving of the vote than slaves by characterizing the signers as "intelligent, virtuous, native-born American citizens" who were continually denied political recognition.[14] Stanton wrote a letter published on January 2, 1866, to the *National Anti-Slavery Standard* denouncing the Fourteenth Amendment as an attempt by Republicans "to turn the wheels of civilization backward." The audacity of the measure, she declared, "should rouse every woman in the nation to a prompt exercise of the only right she has in the Government, the right of petition." By the end of the 1865–66 congressional session, solicitors had collected 10,000 signatures for the petition, which was presented in the Senate by Senator Gratz Brown, a Democrat from Missouri.[15] Another mass effort was organized in May 1868 by the American Equal Rights Association, which was formed in 1866 at the first women's rights convention since the Civil War and whose primary goal was to win universal suffrage. The printed petitions put into circulation by the association requested Congress to pass "an Amendment to the Constitution of the United States, prohibiting all political distinction on account of Sex." Notwithstanding these efforts, when the Fourteenth Amendment was ratified in June 1868, it extended the vote to black males but not to women.[16]

Those seeking suffrage for women continued to use petitioning to achieve their goal. On November 10, 1876, the National Woman Suffrage Association (NWSA) published *An Appeal to the Women of the United States for a Sixteenth Amendment,* which resembled appeals issued by female abolitionists during the 1830s.[17] Besides urging men and women to sign a petition entreating Congress "to adopt measures for so amending the Constitution as to prohibit the several States from Disenfranchising United States Citizens on account of Sex," the *Appeal* provided instructions for circulating the petition—instructions quite similar to those attached to antislavery petitions some four decades earlier. State societies were to "send out petitions to reliable friends in every county, urging upon all thoroughness and haste." After the petitions were returned to state organizers, Stanton instructed, "they should be pasted together, neatly rolled up, the number of signatures marked on the outside, with the name of the State," and forwarded to the chairman of the association's congressional committee in Washington, D.C.[18]

In response to the *Appeal,* during the first half of January 1876 petitions poured in from twenty-two states at the rate, according to the NWSA, of a thousand names per day. The signatures were divided into columns based on sex to emphasize that men as well as women supported woman suffrage. Not only did men sign these petitions, but in spite of Stanton's racist rhetoric of the late 1860s, among the masses of petitions there is one from

A PETITION

FOR

UNIVERSAL SUFFRAGE.

--→·←--

To the Senate and House of Representatives:

The undersigned, Women of the United States, respectfully ask an amendment of the Constitution that shall prohibit the several States from disfranchising any of their citizens on the ground of sex.

In making our demand for Suffrage, we would call your attention to the fact that we represent fifteen million people—one half the entire population of the country—intelligent, virtuous, native-born American citizens; and yet stand outside the pale of political recognition.

The Constitution classes us as "free people," and counts us *whole* persons in the basis of representation; and yet are we governed without our consent, compelled to pay taxes without appeal, and punished for violations of law without choice of judge or juror.

The experience of all ages, the Declarations of the Fathers, the Statute Laws of our own day, and the fearful revolution through which we have just passed, all prove the uncertain tenure of life, liberty and property so long as the ballot—the only weapon of self-protection—is not in the hand of every citizen.

Therefore, as you are now amending the Constitution, and, in harmony with advancing civilization, placing new safeguards round the individual rights of four millions of emancipated slaves, we ask that you extend the right of Suffrage to Woman—the only remaining class of disfranchised citizens—and thus fulfil your Constitutional obligation "to Guarantee to every State in the Union a Republican form of Government."

As all partial application of Republican principles must ever breed a complicated legislation as well as a discontented people, we would pray your Honorable Body, in order to simplify the machinery of government and ensure domestic tranquillity, that you legislate hereafter for persons, citizens, tax-payers, and not for class or caste.

For justice and equality your petitioners will ever pray.

NAMES.	RESIDENCE.
Elizabeth Cady Stanton,	New. York
Susan B. Anthony	Rochester — N.Y.
Antoinette Brown Blackwell	New York
Lucy Stone	Newark N. Jersey
Joanna S. Morse	48 Livingston. Brooklyn
Ernestine L. Rose	New York.
Harriet E. Eaton	6. West. 14th Street N Y
Catharine C. Wilkeson	83 Clinton Place New York
Elizabeth R. Tilton.	48 Livingston St. Brooklyn
Mary Trowler Gilbert	295 W. 19" St New York
Mary E. Gilbert	New York
M Griffith	New York.

Responding to the introduction of the Fourteenth Amendment, passage of which would introduce the word "male" into the Constitution and create a significant barrier to woman suffrage, in 1865 Elizabeth Cady Stanton and Susan B. Anthony launched a petition campaign for universal suffrage. This petition, presented in Congress on January 29, 1866, was signed by Stanton, Anthony, Antoinette Brown Blackwell, Lucy Stone, Ernestine Rose, and other New York women's rights advocates. (Courtesy of the National Archives)

PETITION FOR
WOMAN SUFFRAGE.

TO THE SENATE AND HOUSE OF REPRESENTATIVES,

IN CONGRESS ASSEMBLED:

The undersigned, Citizens of the United States, Residents of the ~~State of~~ *Dist- of Col,*
County of _____, Town of *Union Town* earnestly pray your Honorable Body to
adopt measures for so amending the Constitution as to prohibit the several States from
Disfranchising United States Citizens on account of Sex.

Colored
MEN:

Colored
WOMEN:

Fredk. Douglass Jr	Mrs. Fredk Douglass Jr.
Nathan Sprague	Mrs Nathan Sprague
Ignatius Dorsey	Mrs. Juila Dorsey
Matthias H. Hunter	Mrs. Elizas A. Spencer
Jacob Moore	Mrs Delphia Spazinbury
Mr. R H Jones	Mrs Sarah A Kyne
Mr Solomon G Brown	
Mr H. Hillkerson	Mrs Mary v berry.
Edward Brown	Harriett H. Lee
John A Louden	Caroline Burnett
Milton Bayles	Jane Lawson
Thomas G Hill	Alice Scott
James A Shaw	Rozie Harris
H. Lansdale	Miss Celia Gray
B. Frazier	Miss Elizabeth Chase
John H Dennington	Mrs Caroline Chase

African American women and men, among them Frederick Douglass Jr.
(first signature in left column) and his wife (first signature in right column), participated
in the National Woman Suffrage Association's 1876 petition campaign urging passage of
an amendment enfranchising women.

the District of Columbia signed by Frederick Douglass Jr., Mrs. Frederick Douglass Jr., and some thirty other "colored" citizens, as they identified themselves. The signers, of whom eighteen were women, according to Rosalyn Terborg-Penn, probably belonged to the African American elite living in the affluent Anacostia section of Washington, D.C. In all, more than 10,000 names were presented to Congress during January and February 1876. The following year the NWSA issued a letter "To the Friends of Woman Suffrage" to put into motion another campaign to amass "NEW MAMMOTH PETITIONS TO THE FORTY-FIFTH CONGRESS." Members of both the NWSA and the American Woman Suffrage Association gathered signatures, which were presented in February 1878.[19]

The 1876 petition campaign was unsuccessful in winning a constitutional amendment granting women the franchise, and women would continue to organize, propagandize, and petition into the twentieth century in hopes of winning the ballot. In 1890 the NWSA and the American Woman Suffrage Association merged into a single organization, the National American Woman Suffrage Association, which thereafter spearheaded the suffrage campaign. At its 1908 annual convention the association voted to launch a campaign to collect a million signatures on a petition to Congress for a woman suffrage amendment to the Constitution. When the petition was presented in the spring of 1910, it bore the names of more than 404,000 Americans. Although the association fell short of reaching its goal of 1 million names, it was an impressive accomplishment nonetheless, especially during a period of the woman suffrage movement known as "the doldrums." Suffragists undertook another petition drive in 1913, at which time they also organized pilgrimages to bring the petitions to Washington, D.C., from the localities in which they originated. The effort culminated on July 31, 1913, with an automobile procession to the Capitol and presentation of suffrage petitions bearing 200,000 names to a group of senators. Two years later suffragists succeeded in collecting a half-million signatures. On May 9, 1915, after a rally at a Washington theater and a march to the Capitol, a delegation presented the petition to President Woodrow Wilson. The last great suffrage parade, held in New York City on October 27, 1917, featured some 2,500 women waving placards that enumerated the signatures of more than 1 million women to a suffrage petition.[20]

On January 10, 1918, the House of Representatives voted in favor of the woman suffrage amendment. But just when the franchise seemed within reach, it was snatched away by the Senate, which failed to pass the measure by two votes, even after an eloquent plea by President Wilson. On

February 10, 1919, despite the fact that twenty-four state legislatures had memorialized Congress expressing their support, the woman suffrage amendment was again defeated in the Senate, this time by only one vote. In hopes of securing victory during the next session, suffrage workers called on civic, church, labor, education, and farm organizations to send Congress resolutions in support of woman suffrage. The effort produced more than 500 resolutions urging congressmen to grant women the right to vote. Like the abolition petitions of bygone years, the resolutions became so numerous and so irritating that an old ruling was revived prohibiting the printing of such material in the *Congressional Record*.

Nonetheless, the flood of petitions along with other lobbying efforts convinced enough congressmen that public sentiment supported woman suffrage, and in 1920 the Nineteenth Amendment was approved by Congress, ratified by the states, and signed into law. The fact that petitioning played a major role in suffragists' strategy to win the vote confirmed the advice Stanton had given almost forty-five years earlier. Women, she had written, could best secure the ballot by exercising the one right they surely possessed: the right of petition. Although "our petitions . . . by the tens of thousands, are piled up in the national archives, unheeded and ignored," Stanton assured women that "yet it is possible to roll up such a mammoth petition, borne into Congress on the shoulders of stalwart men, that we can no longer be neglected or forgotten."[21]

NOTES

INTRODUCTION

1. Petition of the Men and Women of Ohio; Chapman, *Right and Wrong in Massachusetts,* 11–13.

2. Freehling, *Road to Disunion,* 308. Richard Sewell states that by leading many northerners to see that slavery threatened their own civil rights, the petition controversy "proved a godsend" to the abolitionists; see Sewell, *Ballots for Freedom,* 7–8.

3. As Richard J. Carwardine argues, "For many, petitioning represented a means of operating in an era of mass politics without being compromised by the corruption of new partisanship" (Carwardine, *Evangelicals and Politics,* 32). The fact that William Lloyd Garrison forsook the vote though he did petition Congress is discussed in Mayer, *All on Fire,* xiv.

4. This definition of petitioning is drawn from the *Oxford English Dictionary,* and the discussion of the changing function of petitioning in U.S. politics draws on Morgan, *Inventing the People,* 222–30.

Women had petitioned Congress from 1829 to 1831 to oppose removal of the Cherokees from Georgia, yet while their efforts set an important precedent for women's subsequent involvement in abolitionist petitioning, their campaign was relatively short and involved a smaller number of women compared with the sustained mass petitioning by antislavery women. For further discussion of women's involvement in the Cherokee petition campaign and its impact on women's antislavery petitioning, see Chapter 1.

5. David C. Frederick explains that the substantive meaning of the right of petition was shaped by the twin duties of reception and response. He states further that it is possible to claim with some certainty that by the eighteenth century "the right included the expectation that the government would receive the petition and issue a response whatever the subject matter of the plea. . . . The development of the right to petition in practice, therefore, led to the expectation of a response, favorable or not" (Frederick, "John Quincy Adams," 115).

6. This study builds on scholarship about women and political culture by, among others, Mary Ritter Beard, Nancy F. Cott, Linda K. Kerber, Norma Basch, Paula M. Baker, Nancy A. Hewitt, Ann Boylan, Lori D. Ginzberg, Mary P. Ryan, Jan Lewis, Nancy Isenberg, Elizabeth Varon, and Rosemarie Zagarri, who have exam-

ined the ways in which women were denied full citizenship during the formation of the republic and the means through which they attempted to claim their rights throughout the nineteenth century and beyond. See Beard, "Legislative Influence of Unenfranchised Women"; Cott, *Bonds of Womanhood;* Kerber, *Women of the Republic;* Kerber, *"No Constitutional Right to Be Ladies";* Basch, "Equity vs. Equality"; Baker, "Domestication of American Politics"; Hewitt, *Women's Activism and Social Change;* Hewitt, "Social Origins of Women's Antislavery Politics in Western New York"; Boylan, "Women and Politics"; Ginzberg, *Women and the Work of Benevolence;* Ryan, *Women in Public;* Ryan, "Gender and Public Access"; Lewis, "'Of Every Age Sex & Condition'"; Isenberg, *Sex and Citizenship in Antebellum America;* Varon, *We Mean to Be Counted;* and Zagarri, "Rights of Man and Woman."

This analysis also draws on studies of the political nature of women's antislavery activism and petitioning, in particular the work of scholars such as Gerda Lerner, Judith Wellman, and Deborah Bingham Van Broekhoven. See Lerner, "Political Activities of Antislavery Women"; Wellman, "Women and Radical Reform"; and Van Broekhoven, "'Let Your Names Be Enrolled.'" Barnes, *Antislavery Impulse,* devotes almost one full chapter to a discussion of women's role in the petition campaign and suggests that female antislavery petitioning "opened a way toward citizenship." Other works that discuss women's antislavery petitioning include Dumond, *Antislavery;* Sewell, *Ballots for Freedom;* Hersh, *Slavery of Sex;* Melder, *Beginnings of Sisterhood;* and Jeffrey, *Great Silent Army of Abolitionism.* Pertinent works on women and abolitionism include, among others, Lutz, *Crusade for Freedom;* Sterling, *Ahead of Her Time;* Yellin, *Women and Sisters;* Yee, *Black Women Abolitionists;* and Hansen, *Strained Sisterhood.* Yellin and Horne, *Abolitionist Sisterhood,* proved an invaluable resource.

7. Enstad, *Ladies of Labor, Girls of Adventure,* 3, 121–22, 12; Enstad, "Fashioning Political Identities"; Waugh, *Feminine Fictions,* esp. chap. 1; Butler, *Gender Trouble,* 2, 145.

8. Kenneth Cmiel, for instance, notes that public opinion had become so important that when President Jackson exercised unprecedented authority in 1832 by vetoing the charter for the Second Bank of the United States, he addressed his presidential message not to Congress, as was customary, but directly to the public; see Cmiel, *Democratic Eloquence,* 64. Enstad, *Ladies of Labor,* 86, 227 n. 2, succinctly describes the exclusion of women and people of color from the nineteenth-century middle-class public based on the incommensurability of the category of woman with the category of citizen.

9. Ryan, *Women in Public;* Ryan, "Gender and Public Access," 218, 206.

10. *Our Mothers Before Us: Women's Writings to Congress;* Carolyn Brucken, "A Guide to Researching Women's Petitions at the National Archives," personal correspondence, Apr. 17, 1997.

11. Susan B. Anthony, "Speech to the 1863 Convention of the American Anti-

Slavery Society," in *Proceedings of the American Anti-Slavery Society at Its Third Decade* (1864), 74.

CHAPTER ONE

1. Colton, *Right of Petition*, 2.

2. Ibid., 6.

3. Butt, *History of Parliament*, 51, 61; Smellie, "Right of Petition"; Charles E. Rice, "Freedom of Petition"; A. L. Brown, *Governance of Late Medieval England*, 215-17; Myers, "Parliamentary Petitions in the Fifteenth Century," 387.

4. Smellie, "Right of Petition"; Morgan, *Inventing the People*, 224-25; Leys, "Petitioning in the Nineteenth and Twentieth Centuries," 46.

5. Higgins, "Reactions of Women," 216; *True Copy of the Petition of the Gentlewomen, & Trades-men wives.*

6. Higgins, "Reactions of Women," 200-202, 180, 212-13. Cynthia A. Kierner also recognizes the significance of women's petitioning during the English Civil War in relation to subsequent efforts by women. She writes, "Before 1642, women petitioners always acted alone, but radical sectarians in the Civil War era petitioned in groups, setting an important precedent for women's collective political activism" (Kierner, *Southern Women in Revolution*, xx).

7. Morgan, *Inventing the People*, 226-28; Smellie, "Right of Petition," 99; Leys, "Petitioning in the Nineteenth and Twentieth Centuries," 47. Johnson quoted in Smellie, "Right of Petition," 99.

8. Bailey, *Popular Influence upon Public Policy*, 6; Higginson, "Short History," 144-46, 150-53.

9. Petitioning was, English jurist William Blackstone wrote in 1765, the proper reaction to "such public oppressions as tend to dissolve the constitution and subvert the fundamentals of government" (Wills, *Inventing America*, 54-55, 64-65, 377).

10. The Edenton women's petition is reprinted in Ashe, *History of North Carolina*, 1:427-29n.

11. Arthur Iredell to James Iredell, Jan. 31, 1775, quoted in Kerber, *Women of the Republic*, 41.

12. Cott, "Divorce and the Changing Status of Women in Eighteenth-Century Massachusetts," 594; Kerber, *Women of the Republic*, 184. For further analysis of women's divorce petitions during the Revolutionary period, see Lebsock, *Free Women of Petersburg*; Buckley, "'Placed in the Power of Violence'"; and Meehan, "'Not Made Out of Levity.'"

13. Kierner, *Southern Women in Revolution*, 49, xxiv; Kerber, *Women of the Republic*, 85-87.

14. Abigail Adams to Mercy Otis Warren, Apr. 27, 1776, in Rossi, *Feminist Papers,* 12.

15. Brooke, *Heart of the Commonwealth,* 191, 207–9; Bogin, "Petitioning and the New Moral Economy of Post-Revolutionary America," 419–21; Walsh, "Mechanics and Citizens."

16. Kerber, *Women of the Republic,* 99.

17. Horton, *Free People of Color,* 43; Reed, *Platform for Change,* 64.

18. Viet, Bowling, and Bickford, *Creating the Bill of Rights,* 18, 23, 150–52. See also Morgan, *Inventing the People,* 213, and Don L. Smith, "Right to Petition," 80.

19. Higginson, "Short History," 157–58; Morgan, *Inventing the People,* 229–30; Combs, *Jay Treaty,* 161–63; *Annals of Congress,* 4th Cong., 2d sess., Jan. 30, 1797, 2015–24.

20. This observation echoes Jan Lewis's conclusion that during the first three-quarters of the nineteenth century "women's membership in civil society would be defined in relationship to that of free blacks." She notes in particular that "the understanding of women's civil rights emerged most clearly in discussions about attempts to limit the civil rights of free blacks" (Lewis, "'Of Every Age Sex & Condition,'" 381).

21. Carwardine, *Evangelicals and Politics,* 7; Graebner, Fite, and White, *History of the American People,* 1:432. Circulation figure for *Godey's Lady's Book* is from Flexner, *Century of Struggle,* 65.

22. Carwardine, *Evangelicals and Politics,* xvii, 32.

23. Boylan, "Women and Politics," 364–65, 370–71; Lebsock, *Free Women of Petersburg,* 196, 199–203; Kinney quoted in Ginzberg, *Women and the Work of Benevolence,* 51–53.

24. Boylan, "Women and Politics," 372.

25. Blocker, *American Temperance Movements,* 14, 18–19.

26. Hershberger, "Mobilizing Women," 40.

27. Prucha, "Protest by Petition," 43–46.

28. Ibid., 46–47, 49; Hershberger, "Mobilizing Women," 25.

29. Andrew, *From Revivals to Removal,* 210; Hershberger, "Mobilizing Women," 18, 24–25.

30. "Circular Addressed to the Benevolent Ladies of the United States," *Christian Advocate and Journal,* Dec. 25, 1829; Hershberger, "Mobilizing Women," 25–26.

31. Hershberger, "Mobilizing Women," 27; Petition of the Ladies of Steubenville, Ohio.

32. Hershberger, "Mobilizing Women," 28, 27.

33. *Gales and Seaton's Register of Debates,* 21st Cong., 1st sess., Jan. 11, 1830, 506–11, and Feb. 2, 1830, 109; Hershberger, "Mobilizing Women," 29.

34. Prucha, "Protest by Petition," 52–57. See also Andrew, *From Revivals to Removal,* esp. chaps. 7–8.

35. Karcher, *First Woman in the Republic*, 87–90; Hershberger, "Mobilizing Women," 40, 22, 33–34.

36. Colton, *Right of Petition*, 6.

37. Ibid., 7.

CHAPTER TWO

1. *Liberator*, May 5, 1832.

2. Dillon, *Abolitionists*, 4–7; James Brewer Stewart, *Holy Warriors*, 11; Ohline, "Slavery, Economics, and Congressional Politics," 336.

3. Ohline, "Slavery, Economics, and Congressional Politics," 336–37, 340, 351, 354, 359; diGiacomantonio, "'For the Gratification of a Volunteering Society,'" 173–74, 189–90, 197; Knee, "Quaker Petition of 1790," 157.

4. Drescher, "Public Opinion and the Destruction of British Colonial Slavery," 25, 50; Drescher, *Capitalism and Antislavery*, 80, 84–85.

5. James Brewer Stewart, *Holy Warriors*, 23–24, 27; Dillon, *Abolitionists*, 18.

6. Dumond, *Antislavery*, 112; James Brewer Stewart, *Holy Warriors*, 29; Egerton, *Gabriel's Rebellion*; Sidbury, *Ploughshares into Swords*; Jeffrey, *Great Silent Army of Abolitionism*, 15; Mayer, *All on Fire*, 135–36; Miller, *Arguing about Slavery*, 72–73.

7. James Brewer Stewart, *Holy Warriors*, 31; Aptheker, *Abolitionism*, chap. 1. A copy of the Ohio petition can be found in the *Philanthropist*, Jan. 1, 1820. The petition campaign was also mentioned in the *Philanthropist*, Jan. 22, Feb. 5, 1820, and *Annals of Congress*, 16th Cong., 1st sess., Dec. 28, 1819, 800.

8. *Gales and Seaton's Register of Debates*, 20th Cong., 2d sess., Feb. 12, 1827, 1099–1100; William Lloyd Garrison, "To the Editor of *The Boston Courier*," Aug. 11, 12, 1828, in Garrison, *Letters*, 1:66, 65. Years later Garrison would boast that during the 1828 effort he gathered 2,300 names in three or four weeks on a petition for the abolition of slavery in the District of Columbia; see Garrison to Oliver Johnson, Feb. 10, 1836, in Garrison, *Letters*, 2:37.

9. One thousand citizens of the District of Columbia sent a petition complaining about the scenes of slave trading and kidnapping "continually taking place among us." They urged Congress to pass a law declaring that all children born to slaves in the District after July 4, 1828, be freed at age twenty-five years. The petition from the inhabitants of the District of Columbia was printed in *Freedom's Journal*, Feb. 1, 1828, and, years later, in the *Liberator*, Mar. 14, 1835. In New York the Corresponding Committee of that state's Manumission Society saw to the circulation of petitions to Congress and the state legislature calling for abolition in the District. See *Freedom's Journal*, May 9, 1828. In Ohio the Abolition Society of Stark County, meeting on November 3, 1827, passed a resolution instructing a committee of three to draft a memorial to Congress for abolition in the District and to

circulate it. See *Freedom's Journal,* Dec. 7, 1827; Cornish was quoted in *Freedom's Journal,* Feb. 1, 1828.

10. Bethel, *Roots of African American Identity,* 120–23.

11. Gross, *Clarion Call,* 10, 20, 29; Bell, *Survey of the Negro Convention Movement,* 7; Maria Stewart, "An Address Delivered at the African Masonic Hall," Boston, Feb. 27, 1833, in Maria Stewart, *Maria W. Stewart,* 62.

12. Goodman, *Of One Blood,* 4; Garrison, *Thoughts on African Colonization,* 54, 56–57; Whittier, *Justice and Expediency,* 10; Dillon, *Abolitionists,* 43.

13. *Liberator,* Jan. 1, 1831; Dillon, *Abolitionists,* 49; *Liberator,* Feb. 11, Sept. 8, 1832. In their 1833 constitution the Western Reserve Anti-Slavery Society resolved that "the rights of [man] require every citizen to petition Congress, to abolish slavery in the District of Columbia and all territories under their control." In September 1834 the newly founded Tallmade (Ohio) Anti-Slavery Society instructed its Board of Managers to circulate petitions to Congress and the state legislature. In November 1834 members of the founding convention of the New Hampshire Anti-Slavery Society stated that they regarded it "the solemn duty of all the friends of liberty and religion to exert their utmost influence for the immediate abolition of Slavery" in Washington, D.C., and "that to this end it is highly important to send petitions to Congress this present year" (*Emancipator,* Sept. 21, Oct. 12, 26, 1833, Nov. 25, 1834).

14. *Liberator,* Dec. 21, 1833.

15. Nancy A. Hewitt notes that women generally joined men in signing Quaker testimonies against slavery, but the extant Quaker petitions sent to Congress before the 1830s I found in the National Archives were signed by only the officers of the yearly meeting, who were men. See Hewitt, *Women's Activism and Social Change,* 82.

16. Petition of the Female Citizens of the County of Fluvanna to the General Assembly of the Commonwealth of Virginia, printed in the *Liberator,* Feb. 25, 1832, from the *Richmond Whig.* Similar petitions expressing uneasiness over the potential for slave unrest were sent by men to the Virginia and North Carolina legislatures. See Petition of the Inhabitants of Sampson, Bladen, New Hanover, and Duplin Counties to North Carolina Assembly, ca. 1830, and esp. Petition of A. P. Upshur et al., Northampton County, to Virginia Legislature, 1831, both in Schweninger, *Southern Debate over Slavery,* 117–18, 118n, 128–31.

17. Petition of the Females of the State of Pennsylvania. Interestingly the same form of petition used in the 1831 effort was still in circulation in 1837. For an example of the continued circulation, see Petition of the Female Citizens of Philadelphia.

18. The letter signed by the coordinating committee headed by Mott can be found with the Petition of the Females of the State of Pennsylvania. The petition itself was printed in the *Liberator,* Feb. 18, 1832, and comments about the women's petition were offered in the *Liberator,* Feb. 25, 1832.

19. Browne, "Encountering Angelina Grimké," 55; Lydia Maria Child to Mrs. Ellis Gray Loring, Aug. 15, 1835, quoted in Dillon, *Abolitionists*, 91. A detailed account of the mob attack on the meeting of the Boston Female Anti-Slavery Society can be found in Hansen, *Strained Sisterhood*, 1–5, and Dillon, *Abolitionists*, 64–66, 90.

20. *Liberator*, Mar. 24, 1832; "An Address to the Daughters of New England," *Liberator*, Mar. 3, 1832.

21. *Liberator*, Mar. 12, 1831; *Freedom's Journal*, Apr. 20, 1827, June 20, 1828.

22. *Liberator*, Apr. 23, Jan. 15, 1831.

23. *Freedom's Journal*, May 11, 1827; *Liberator*, Apr. 23, 1831.

24. Bacon, *Mothers of Feminism*, 101; Heyrick called for boycotting the products of slave labor in *Immediate, Not Gradual Abolition*. See Williams, "Female Antislavery Movement," 161, and Bacon, "By Moral Force Alone," 278–79.

25. Hansen, *Strained Sisterhood*, 13–14; Swerdlow, "Abolition's Conservative Sisters," 34, 36; Soderlund, "Priorities and Power," 76.

26. Boylan, "Benevolence and Antislavery Activity among African American Women"; Yee, *Black Women Abolitionists;* Scott, "Most Invisible of All"; Lapsansky, "Feminism, Freedom, and Community"; Scott, "On Seeing and Not Seeing"; Sumler-Lewis, "Forten-Purvis Women of Philadelphia"; Porter, "Organized Educational Activities of Negro Literary Societies"; Winch, "'You Have Talents—Only Cultivate Them.'"

27. Hershberger, "Mobilizing Women," 40; Ginzberg, *Women and the Work of Benevolence*, 11–17.

28. Figures for the number of antislavery petitions sent to Congress by women come from the database of the *Our Mothers Before Us* project at the National Archives. The numbers were confirmed in personal correspondence with Sarah Boyle, National Archives, Nov. 5, 1996.

29. The petitioning of British women was begun after women formed a network of antislavery societies throughout the nation. On April 8, 1825, the first women's antislavery society was formed in the home of Lucy Townsend. This group, the Female Society of Birmingham, sparked the formation of a network of seventy-three women's antislavery associations throughout England between 1825 and 1833. See Midgley, *Women against Slavery*, 43–47, 62–67; Drescher, *Capitalism and Antislavery*, 70, 80, 59. These first antislavery petitioning campaigns were followed in 1837–38 by a final signature-gathering effort against the apprenticeship system. A national women's petition on behalf of apprentices addressed in 1838 to the newly crowned Queen Victoria bore the signatures of 700,000 women, a number described as "unprecedented in the annals of petitioning."

30. Garrison to the *Liberator*, May 24, 1833, in Garrison, *Letters*, 1:233; *Liberator*, Sept. 7, 1833; Child, *Appeal in Favor of That Class of Americans Called Africans*, 232. Child erred in stating that 60,000 petitions had been submitted to Parliament; perhaps this was a typographical error, for 6,000 would have been nearly

accurate. From 1830 to 1831 a total of 5,484 antislavery petitions were presented in Parliament, and about 1 percent of them were signed by women. See Midgley, *Women against Slavery*, 67.

31. Fuller, *Prudence Crandall;* Foner, *Three Women Who Dared.* The call to petition was printed in the *Female Advocate* and reprinted in the *Emancipator,* July 27, 1833.

32. *Emancipator,* Apr. 28, 1835, Dec. 1, 1836. Thompson's conscientious efforts to convince women to become abolitionists made him the target of scathing attacks. He was branded a "meddling foreigner" and "an emasculated messenger" of a bunch of "canting old women." The *New York Courier and Inquirer* recommended that Thompson ought to be "packed up like a quintal of codfish, and sent back to the Caledonian damsels who exported him" (quoted in C. Duncan Rice, "Anti-Slavery Mission of George Thompson to the United States," 28).

33. *New England Spectator* quoted in the *Emancipator,* Mar. 10, 1835; *Emancipator,* Mar. 10, 1835; *Liberator,* Oct. 31, 1835.

34. Putnam, *Address Delivered at Concord,* 12.

CHAPTER THREE

1. Petition of the Ladies of Glastenbury; Petition of the Ladies of Marshfield.

2. *Morning Courier and New York Enquirer,* July 9, 12, 1834. The petition of the ladies of New York was presented on February 2, 1835, by Representative John Dickson of New York, and the text of the petition was published in the *Emancipator,* Feb. 24, 1835.

3. Petition of 2,218 Females of Jamaica and Vicinity; Petition of 120 Ladies of Boston; the Philadelphia women's petitioning effort is mentioned in Soderlund, "Priorities and Power," 77–78; Petition of the Citizens of Ohio; Petition of the Women of Harrisville, Ohio.

4. Martineau, *Martyr Age of the United States,* 28–29. The petition is also printed in *Three Years' Female Anti-Slavery Effort in Britain and America,* 43.

5. Petition from the Female Citizens of the State of Ohio; Ladies Petition of Orange County, New York.

6. See, for example, Petition of the Inhabitants of Livingston County, New York. Deborah Bingham Van Broekhoven also notes that "legislators were not ready to consider the mass petitions of females in the same category as those from voters" and that "some abolitionists preferred male petitioning" because men exerted greater influence on congressmen; see Van Broekhoven, "'Let Your Names Be Enrolled,'" 185, 191.

7. Petition of 800 Ladies of New York, 1835.

8. Ginzberg, *Women and the Work of Benevolence,* 77.

9. Ibid., 33. For a thorough discussion of the different types of female reform efforts during the nineteenth century, see Hewitt, *Women's Activism and Social Change*.

10. Petition of 800 Ladies of New York, 1835.

11. Gilbert H. Barnes and Dwight L. Dumond concluded that the Fathers and Rulers of Our Country form was "by far the most popular form for 'female petitions' until 1840. Tens of thousands are in the files of the House of Representatives (boxes 85–126) in the Library of Congress. Except for the short 'sentence forms' distributed by the American Anti-Slavery Society during the period 1837–1840, it was the commonest form in the campaign." Barnes and Dumond include the text of the Fathers and Rulers petition form, attributing its authorship to Theodore Weld. See Weld, *Letters*, 1:175 n. 1, 175–76. Extant signed Fathers and Rulers petitions sent to Congress include, for example, Petition of 600 Ladies of Utica, Oneida County, New York. The *Address to Females in the State of Ohio*, to which the Fathers and Rulers form was attached, was reprinted in the *Emancipator*, July 21, 1836.

12. "Fathers and Rulers of Our Country Petition Form," in Weld, *Letters*, 1:175–76.

13. Muskingham County, Ohio, Female Anti-Slavery Society, *Address to Females*.

14. Jeffrey, *Great Silent Army of Abolitionism*, 77; Van Broekhoven, "'Let Your Names Be Enrolled,'" 182. During the nineteenth century there was a tendency to view religion as resting on the personal or domestic sphere, which was considered particularly feminine. Consequently the general belief was that religion existed outside the secular realm, which was considered particularly masculine. Beginning in the late eighteenth century this dichotomy was reinforced by prescriptive literature that advised women to be devout and virtuous, while men were excused from such standards due to the fact that their "passions" were constantly "subject to be heated by the ferment of business." Statements that women should be more pious than men reflected the fact that as a group women were indeed more religious than men. More women belonged to and joined churches during most of the colonial period, and they dominated church membership in the early nineteenth century as well. Whatever its origins, belief in women's natural inclination toward religion implied that piety was natural for women and somehow unnatural for men. For discussions of gender and religion during the late eighteenth and early nineteenth centuries, see Ruether and Keller, *Women and Religion in America*; Cott, "Young Women in the Second Great Awakening"; Cott, *Bonds of Womanhood*, chap. 4; and Welter, "The Feminization of American Religion, 1800–1860," in Welter, *Dimity Convictions*, 83–102.

15. Catherine H. Birney, *Grimké Sisters*, 174.

16. For examples of antislavery petitions composed for men's signatures and

signed entirely or predominantly by men, see Petition of the Citizens of the United States and Petition of the Citizens of Philadelphia against the Admission of Arkansas.

17. Petition of the Women of Harrisville, Ohio; Petition of the Females of Winthrop, Maine. The text of the petition describes the signers as "citizens of the republic," which indicates that the form was initially written for men's signatures. However, it was circulated by women in Winthrop, Maine, who crossed out "citizens of the republic" and inserted "Females of Winthrop, Me." Examples of the petition form that circulated throughout Vermont during 1836 include Petition of the Females of Washington County, Vermont, and Petition of the Females of Addison County, Vermont.

18. Examples of this form include Petition of the Ladies of Massachusetts and Petition of the Ladies of Dousa, New Hampshire. The extended quotation is from Petition of the Females of Washington County, Vermont.

19. Yellin, *Women and Sisters*, 3–26.

20. Elizabeth Margaret Chandler, "Mental Metempsychosis," in *Genius of Universal Emancipation*, Feb. 1, 1831, quoted in Yellin, *Women and Sisters*, 13.

21. Petition of the Ladies of Dousa, New Hampshire; Sanchez-Eppler, "Bodily Bonds," 32.

22. Ginzberg, *Women and the Work of Benevolence*, 20–22.

23. Petition of the Women of Harrisville, Ohio; Petition of the Females of Washington County, Vermont; Petition of the Females of Addison County, Vermont; Petition of 359 Ladies of Massachusetts; Yellin, *Women and Sisters*, 24–25.

24. This observation builds on Jean Fagan Yellin's argument in her study of the woman-and-sister theme in the rhetoric of women abolitionists. Yellin states that in emphasizing "the speechless agony of the female slave," white antislavery feminists were "identifying with the female slaves in terms of gender but articulating a feminist consciousness that was race-specific" (Yellin, *Women and Sisters*, 25). Karen Sanchez-Eppler, who has also studied the woman-and-sister theme, notes the "difficulty of preventing moments of identification from becoming acts of appropriation." This, she says, "constitutes the essential dilemma of feminist-abolitionist rhetoric" (Sanchez-Eppler, "Bodily Bonds," 31).

25. McInerney, *Fortunate Heirs of Freedom*; Petition of the Females of Washington County, Vermont; Philadelphia Female Anti-Slavery Society, *Address of the Female Anti-Slavery Society of Philadelphia*, 8; Petition of the Female Inhabitants of South Reading, Massachusetts; Petition of the Ladies of Dousa, New Hampshire; Petition of the Ladies of Massachusetts.

26. Examples of this form are the Petition of the Citizens of the Town of Fayston, Vermont; Ladies Petition of Orange County, New York; Petition of the Female Citizens of Ohio; and Petition of the Citizens of Lockport, New York.

27. Osler, "'That Damned Mob.'"

28. Petition of the Women of Harrisville, Ohio.

29. Cogan and Ginzberg, "1846 Petition for Woman's Suffrage."

30. Petition of the Ladies of Glastenbury; Petition of the Ladies of Marshfield; Calhoun quoted in Miller, *Arguing about Slavery*, 30; Miller, *Arguing about Slavery*, 111. The figures on the increase in women's petitions come from the *Our Mothers Before Us* database and were confirmed in personal correspondence with Sarah Boyle, National Archives, Nov. 5, 1996.

31. Miller, *Arguing about Slavery*, 51.

32. *Gales and Seaton's Register of Debates*, 24th Cong., 1st sess., Dec. 16, 1836, 1961–62; Miller, *Arguing about Slavery*, 27, 31–32.

33. *Gales and Seaton's Register of Debates*, 24th Cong., 1st sess., Dec. 21, 1836, 1994–2000.

34. Ibid., Dec. 21, 1836, 2000–2002.

35. Ibid., May 25, 1836, 4031, and May 26, 1836, 4052–53.

36. James Birney to Lewis Tappan, Aug. 10, 1836, in James G. Birney, *Letters*, 1:351.

CHAPTER FOUR

1. American Anti-Slavery Society, *Appeal to the People of the United States*. The Pinckney report, Garrison's remarks, and the pledge to use the gag rule as a firebrand were printed in the *Liberator*, June 4, 1836.

2. Boston Female Anti-Slavery Society, *Address to the Women of Massachusetts*, was issued as a circular in July 1836. A copy of the handbill form can be found in box 84, Library of Congress, box 17, National Archives, Washington, D.C., Sept. 25, 1837. The address was printed in the *Emancipator*, Aug. 25, 1836, and reprinted in *Three Years' Female Anti-Slavery Effort in Britain and America*, 55–56. Muskingham County, Ohio, Female Anti-Slavery Society, *Address to Females*, was printed from the *Philanthropist* in the *Emancipator*, July 21, 1836. Deborah Bingham Van Broekhoven notes that the Kent County (Rhode Island) Female Anti-Slavery Society acknowledged receipt of the Ohio address in its minutes of May 11, 1836. See Van Broekhoven, "'Let Your Names Be Enrolled,'" 184 n. 14; Angelina Grimké, *Appeal to the Christian Women of the South* (for the sake of accessibility, all quotations are taken from the text reprinted in Grimké and Grimké, *Public Years*, 36–79); Philadelphia Female Anti-Slavery Society, *Address of the Female Anti-Slavery Society of Philadelphia*.

3. Muskingham County, Ohio, Female Anti-Slavery Society, *Address to Females;* Angelina Grimké, *Appeal to the Christian Women of the South*, in Grimké and Grimké, *Public Years*, 59–61, 63.

4. Muskingham County, Ohio, Female Anti-Slavery Society, *Address to Females;*

Boston Female Anti-Slavery Society, *Address to the Women of Massachusetts;* Angelina Grimké, *Appeal to the Christian Women of the South,* in Grimké and Grimké, *Public Years,* 66.

5. Boston Female Anti-Slavery Society, *Address to the Women of Massachusetts;* Muskingham County, Ohio, Female Anti-Slavery Society, *Address to Females;* Nye, *Fettered Freedom,* 282–315. Lincoln echoed the Massachusetts women's address when he stated in his 1858 "Speech at the Republican State Convention" in Springfield, Illinois, "A house divided against itself cannot stand. I believe this government cannot endure permanently half slave and half free."

6. Philadelphia Female Anti-Slavery Society, *Address of the Female Anti-Slavery Society of Philadelphia.*

7. Adams quoted in Miller, *Arguing about Slavery,* 216; *Gales and Seaton's Register of Debates,* 24th Cong., 2d sess., Dec. 26, 1836, 1313–14, and Jan. 18, 1837, 1411–12.

8. *Gales and Seaton's Register of Debates,* 24th Cong., 2d sess., Feb. 6, 1837, 1585–86; *Emancipator,* Jan. 19, 1837.

9. Adams, *Letters to Constituents,* 9, 11, 21, 23, 35.

10. Ibid., 36–37.

11. Ibid., 40; Lewis, "'Of Every Age Sex & Condition,'" 381.

12. Barnes, *Antislavery Impulse,* 132.

13. Mary Grew to Maria Weston Chapman, Sept. 9, 1836, quoted in Ira V. Brown, "'Am I Not a Woman and a Sister?,'" 3; Minutes of the Philadelphia Female Anti-Slavery Society, Feb. 9, Aug. 16, 1836, Mar. 2, 1837, quoted in Williams, "Female Antislavery Movement," 172 n. 43. Brown says it was the Philadelphia women who suggested holding a convention, while Williams credits the Boston group.

14. Sterling, *Turning the World Upside Down,* 3–4.

15. Zagarri, "Rights of Man and Woman," 225–26; Ira V. Brown, "Cradle of Feminism," 145–46.

16. The circular was unsigned and makes no claim to issue from a particular antislavery society or committee. It seems clear, however, that the author was a woman because the circular refers to female slaves as "our sisters." Moreover, there is a reference to a slaveholder visiting a relative in a village of Massachusetts in 1836, so it is likely that the author lived in that state. It is probable that the circular was written by Maria Weston Chapman in her capacity as corresponding secretary of the Boston Female Anti-Slavery Society. In May 1836 Chapman had written the letters that sparked the convention idea, and in July of that year she wrote the *Address to the Women of Massachusetts.* The call to the first female antislavery convention was printed in the *Liberator,* Mar. 4, 1837, and in the *Emancipator,* Mar. 16, 1837.

17. Circular announcing the Female Anti-Slavery Convention, *Liberator,* Mar. 4, 1837; *Emancipator,* Mar. 16, 1837.

18. Circular announcing the Female Anti-Slavery Convention, *Liberator*, Mar. 4, 1837, *Emancipator*, Mar. 16, 1837; Wyatt-Brown, *Southern Honor*, 105.

19. The comments from the *National Enquirer* were reprinted in the *Emancipator*, Mar. 16, 1837.

20. Ruth Bogin and Jean Fagan Yellin, introduction to Yellin and Van Horne, *Abolitionist Sisterhood*, 11; Hansen, "Boston Female Anti-Slavery Society," 51–52; Sterling, *Turning the World Upside Down*, 4.

21. Anti-Slavery Convention of American Women, *Proceedings of the Anti-Slavery Convention of American Women, Held in the City of New York*. In addition to the pamphlet version of the proceedings, I consulted those printed in the *Liberator*, June 16, 1837. The convention's discussion of the petitioning plan is also described in Sterling, *Ahead of Her Time*, 47; Sterling, *Turning the World Upside Down*, 24; and Hewitt, *Women's Activism and Social Change*, 91.

22. Barnes, *Antislavery Impulse*, 133–36, for example, implies that the executive committee of the AASS devised the plan for the national campaign. Stanton was quoted in the *Emancipator*, Nov. 24, 1836. The success of the Boston women is discussed in Hansen, "Boston Female Anti-Slavery Society," 51.

23. Minutes of the Anti-Slavery Convention of American Women, in Sterling, *Turning the World Upside Down*, 13.

24. Anti-Slavery Convention of American Women, *Proceedings of the Anti-Slavery Convention of American Women, Held in the City of New York*, in the *Liberator*, June 16, 1837; Sterling, *Turning the World Upside Down*, 17.

25. Anti-Slavery Convention of American Women, *Proceedings of the Anti-Slavery Convention of American Women, Held in the City of New York*, in the *Liberator*, June 16, 1837; Sterling, *Turning the World Upside Down*, 12.

26. Stone's article in the *New York Commercial Advertiser* was reprinted in the *Liberator*, June 2, 1837.

27. Bacon, "By Moral Force Alone," 280; Winch, "'You Have Talents—Only Cultivate Them,'" 116. Nonetheless, most of the work was done by Grimké, and when she reissued the pamphlet later in the year, she considered affixing her name as author; see Lerner, *Grimké Sisters*, 214–15. The idea of including Grimké's name on the second edition of the *Appeal* was discussed in a letter to her from Theodore Weld; see Theodore Weld to Angelina Grimké, Dec. 15, 1837, in Weld, *Letters*, 1:494–95.

28. Anti-Slavery Convention of American Women, *Appeal to the Women of the Nominally Free States*.

29. Ibid.

30. Ibid. Jean Fagan Yellin agrees that this passage from *An Appeal to the Women of the Nominally Free States* was "crucial to the development of nineteenth-century American feminism." The concept Angelina Grimké articulated, Yellin explains, is that freedom means the ability to engage in significant action, which Grimké

defined as public speech. Grimké's ultimate conclusion, Yellin notes, was that free women should speak out in public. See Yellin, *Women and Sisters,* 34–36.

31. Dillon, *Benjamin Lundy and the Quest for Negro Freedom,* 221–27.

32. Boston Female Anti-Slavery Society, *Address to the Women of New England.*

33. Ibid.

34. Barnes, *Antislavery Impulse,* 262 n. 15.

35. The petition was printed in the *Friend of Man,* Aug. 2, 1837.

36. The circular was published in the *Liberator,* June 23, 1837, and in the *Friend of Man,* Aug. 2, 1837.

37. Petition of the Citizens of Philadelphia for Repeal of the Gag Rule. Another strong statement against the gag rule was signed by Abby Kelley and 1,026 women of Lynn, Massachusetts, and yet another by 191 ladies of Oberlin, Ohio. See Petition of Eliza C. Stiles and Petition of Mrs. Levi Burnell.

38. Petition of Elizabeth Wilson.

39. Ibid.

40. Petition circular in the *Liberator,* June 23, 1837.

41. Ibid.

42. Ibid.

43. Letter from a member of the Philadelphia Female Anti-Slavery Society written on the back of a petition from Women of Bedford County, Pennsylvania, January 15, 1838, box 94, Library of Congress, box 22, National Archives, Washington, D.C.

44. Henrietta Sargent to Abby Kelley, July 16, 1841, Foster Papers; Mary G. Chapman to John O. Burleigh, Sept. 10, 1838, box 133, Library of Congress, box 38, National Archives, Washington, D.C.

45. *Liberator,* July 14, 1837.

46. *Emancipator,* Aug. 17, 24, Sept. 17, 1837.

47. Report of the Dorcester [Massachusetts] Female Anti-Slavery Society, in the *Liberator,* Mar. 23, 1838; Melder, "Abby Kelley and the Process of Liberation," 246.

48. Chapman quoted in Williams, "Female Antislavery Movement," 171–72; Stanton, Anthony, and Gage, *History of Woman Suffrage,* 1:342. Yellin also emphasizes the important role female antislavery conventions played in the emergence of the women's rights movement: "*The Anti-Slavery Conventions of American Women,* held in New York in 1837 and in Philadelphia in 1838 and 1839, were signal events in American history. They opened a new path for women's political concerns, offering an organized expression of those concerns a decade before the first women's rights convention at Seneca Falls, New York, in 1848. They were racially integrated, with black women and white women working together in a common cause. They drew their strength from women all across the region. And the principal participants went on to shape other nineteenth-century reform movements" (Yellin and Van Horne, *Abolitionist Sisterhood,* ix).

CHAPTER FIVE

1. *Liberator,* Aug. 4, 1837.

2. Cott, *Bonds of Womanhood,* 101, 103. Cott drew these statistics of signature rates from Kenneth A. Lockridge, *Literacy in Colonial New England* (New York: Norton, 1974), 38–42, 57–78. The statistic on female academies comes from Kelley, "Reading Women/Women Reading," 407. The link between sign literacy and the reading of novels is made by Davidson, "Female Education, Literacy, and the Politics of Sentimental Fiction."

3. Davidson, "Female Education, Literacy, and the Politics of Sentimental Fiction," 311; Kelley, "Reading Women/Women Reading," 410, 403.

4. Van Broekhoven, "'Let Your Names Be Enrolled,'" 182.

5. *Liberator,* Aug. 4, 1837.

6. Juliana A. Tappan to Anne Weston, July 21, 1837, quoted in Ginzberg, *Women and the Work of Benevolence,* 273.

7. Maria Weston Chapman, *Right and Wrong in Massachusetts,* 27; *Liberator,* Sept. 3, Aug. 4, 1837; Peck quoted in Van Broekhoven, "'Let Your Names Be Enrolled,'" 188.

8. Stanton quoted in Kraditor, *Up from the Pedestal,* 114; Kerber, *Women of the Republic,* 9, 119–20.

9. Sarah Grimké, *Letters on the Equality of the Sexes* (1837), in Grimké and Grimké, *Public Years,* 239; Hanna H. Smith to Abby Kelley, July 25, 1839, Foster Papers; *Friend of Man,* July 12, 1837.

10. Petition of the Females of Winthrop, Maine.

11. Frances E. Willard, "A White Life for Two" (1890), in Campbell, *Man Cannot Speak for Her,* 2:335–36. I wish to thank Campbell for bringing Willard's appeal for name reform to my attention.

12. Hansen, *Strained Sisterhood,* 55–56, 101.

13. Lerner, "Political Activities of Antislavery Women," 120–21; Barnes, *Antislavery Impulse,* 136–37.

14. *Liberator,* Aug. 4, 1837. Judith Wellman also notes that circulating petitions "forced abolitionists to confront their own neighbors with carefully constructed antislavery arguments" (Wellman, "Women and Radical Reform," 117).

15. Lerner, "Political Activities of Antislavery Women," 125; Chapman quoted in Ginzberg, *Women and the Work of Benevolence,* 81–82; *Emancipator,* Dec. 1, 1836; Lydia Maria Child to Ellis and Louisa Loring, July 10, 1838, and Child to Henrietta Sargent, Nov. 18, 1838, in Child, *Selected Letters,* 77, 93.

16. *Emancipator,* Aug. 17, 1837.

17. "A Lecture, Delivered Sunday Evening, by Albert A. Folsom, Pastor of the Universal Church, Hingham, Massachusetts," extracted in *Liberator,* Sept. 22, 1837.

18. Quoted in Boston Female Anti-Slavery Society, *Right and Wrong in Boston,* 53; Winslow, *"Appropriate Sphere of Woman,"* 16.

19. The Massachusetts lecture tour was the Grimkés' second oratorical venture. They had been trained as abolition lecturers by Theodore Weld at the convention of antislavery agents held in New York City, November 8–27, 1836. After their training the sisters stayed in New York to give parlor talks to women about the evils of slavery. See Lerner, *Grimké Sisters*, 113–19, and Grimké and Grimké, *Public Years*, 23, 85.

20. Lerner, *Grimké Sisters*, 127.

21. *Liberator*, June 23, 1837.

22. *Liberator*, June 9, 1837.

23. "The Pastoral Letter of the General Association of Congregational Clergy," *Liberator*, Aug. 11, 1837; "Appeal of Abolitionists, of the Theological Seminary, Andover, Mass.," *Liberator*, Aug. 25, 1837.

24. Matthews, *Rise of Public Woman*, 70, 106; Angelina E. Grimké to Theodore Weld and John Greenleaf Whittier, Aug. 20, 1837, in Grimké and Grimké, *Public Years*, 281.

25. *Emancipator*, Oct. 5, 1837.

26. Beecher, *Essay on Slavery and Abolitionism*, 3–6, 97, 101. Beecher, founder of the Hartford Female Academy, had met Angelina Grimké in 1832 when the young Quaker woman, who was considering enrolling in her school, traveled from Philadelphia to Connecticut to pay a visit. Though Grimké was dissuaded from attending by her orthodox Quaker associates, she continued to admire Beecher and in 1837 employed the celebrated educator's words as the epitaph of her *Appeal to the Women of the Nominally Free States*. See Lerner, *Grimké Sisters*, 74–77.

27. Beecher, *Essay on Slavery and Abolitionism*, 103–4.

28. Grimké's *Letters to Catherine* [sic] *E. Beecher* were printed in the form of thirteen letters in the *Liberator* between June 23 and November 3, 1837. The letters were printed in the *Emancipator* between July and November 1837 and in the *Friend of Man* between July and December 1837. They were published by Isaac Knaap in book form in 1838. See Grimké and Grimké, *Public Years*, 146 n. The quotation is from Angelina Grimké, *Letters to Beecher*, in Grimké and Grimké, *Public Years*, 193.

29. Angelina Grimké, *Letters to Beecher*, in Grimké and Grimké, *Public Years*, 193–94.

30. Sarah Grimké, *Letters on the Equality of the Sexes*, in Grimké and Grimké, *Public Years*, 262–63.

31. John Greenleaf Whittier to Sarah and Angelina Grimké, Aug. 14, 1837, in Grimké and Grimké, *Public Years*, 280; Lerner, *Grimké Sisters*, 199; Angelina E. Grimké to Weld and Whittier, Aug. 20, 1837, in Grimké and Grimké, *Public Years*, 281–85. For an excellent analysis of the debate among Whittier, Weld, and Grimké, see Browne, *Angelina Grimké*, chap. 5.

32. Lerner, *Grimké Sisters*, 154; Lerner, "Political Activities of Antislavery Women," 123; Grimké and Grimké, *Public Years*, 141, 352–53.

33. Miller, *Arguing about Slavery*, 277–79.

34. American Anti-Slavery Society, *Correspondence between Elmore and Birney*, 65; Barnes, *Antislavery Impulse*, 266 n. 39, 131; Nye, *Fettered Freedom*, 37.

35. Miller, *Arguing about Slavery*, 279–82.

36. Angelina E. Grimké to Jane Smith, Feb. 7, 1838, in Grimké and Grimké, *Public Years*, 306; Lerner, *Grimké Sisters*, 167.

37. Maria Weston Chapman to William Lloyd Garrison, *Liberator*, Mar. 2, 1838; Japp, "Esther or Isaiah?," 340.

38. A text of the exordium of Grimké's speech was printed in the *Liberator*, Mar. 2, 1838. I wish to thank Phyllis M. Japp for alerting me that the text printed in the *Liberator* is more complete than the one printed in Grimké and Grimké, *Public Years*, 310–12. Despite the fact that the original and complete manuscript of the speech has not been found, it is clear that Grimké said much more than has been anthologized. Evidence that the speech was much longer includes the editor's note at the bottom of the text of the exordium printed in the *Liberator* that states, "The orator then proceeded to discuss the merits of the petitions." Moreover, in a letter to Garrison reporting on the event, Maria Weston Chapman provided a transcription of another part of the speech in which Grimké discussed the war in Florida. See *Liberator*, Mar. 2, 1838.

39. Ladies' New York City Anti-Slavery Society, *Third Annual Report*, 10; Anti-Slavery Convention of American Women, *Proceedings of the Anti-Slavery Convention of American Women Held In Philadelphia*, 5, 7. In addition to being published in pamphlet form, the proceedings of the second convention were printed in the *Liberator*, July 27, 1838. Tappan referred to the murder of Elijah Lovejoy, an antislavery newspaper editor in Alton, Illinois. On November 8, 1837, Lovejoy's press was destroyed by protesters, and he was killed during the altercation. Abolitionists depicted Lovejoy as a martyr for civil rights who was slain by the conspiring slaveocracy while protecting the right of freedom of expression. Abolitionists linked Lovejoy's murder with the gag on antislavery petitions because both exemplified ways in which the slave power denied the rights of northerners.

40. Angelina Grimké, "Speech at Pennsylvania Hall," in Grimké and Grimké, *Public Years*, 319–21.

41. Ibid., 322, 323.

42. Ira V. Brown, "'Am I Not a Woman and a Sister?,'" 11–12.

43. *Emancipator*, May 24, 1838.

44. Anti-Slavery Convention of American Women, *Address to the Senators and Representatives of the Free States*.

45. Ibid.

CHAPTER SIX

1. Adams, *Speech on the Right of the People to Petition*, 76–77.

2. *Gales and Seaton's Register of Debates*, 24th Cong., 1st sess., Dec. 22, 1835, 2032–33, and 2d sess., Jan. 9, 1837, 1325.

3. Ibid., 2d sess., Jan. 9, 1837, 1337, and 1st sess., Dec. 22, 23, 1835, Jan. 12, 1836, 2032, 2064, 2170–71; *Congressional Globe*, 26th Cong., 1st sess., Jan. 28, 1840, 450.

4. *Gales and Seaton's Register of Debates*, 24th Cong., 2d sess., Jan. 9, 1837, 1337, and 1st sess., Dec. 22, 1835, Jan. 12, 1836, 2032, 2170–71.

5. Ibid., 2d sess., Feb. 7, 1837, 1616. When in 1816 Samuel Kercheval wrote to Jefferson that citizens in some sections of Virginia were attempting to claim a right of representation for their slaves, Jefferson responded,

> Were our state a pure democracy, in which all its inhabitants should meet together to transact all their business, there would yet be excluded from their deliberation, 1. Infants, until arrived at years of discretion. 2. Women, who, to prevent depravation of morals and ambiguity of issue could not mix promiscuously in the public meetings of men. 3. Slaves, from whom the unfortunate state of things with us takes away the right of will and property. Those then who had no will could be permitted to exercise none in the popular assembly; and of course, could delegate none to an agent in a representative assembly.

See Thomas Jefferson to Samuel Kercheval, Sept. 5, 1816, in Jefferson, *Writings*, 10:45n–46n; *Gales and Seaton's Register of Debates*, 24th Cong., 2d sess., Jan. 9, 1837, 1329–30.

6. *Gales and Seaton's Register of Debates*, 24th Cong., 1st sess., Dec. 23, 1835, 2070; 2d sess., Jan. 9, 1837, 1338, 1333, and Jan. 8, 1837, 1338–39; 1st sess., Dec. 22, 1835, 2032–33.

7. Ibid., 1st sess., Dec. 23, 1835, 2064, and 2d sess., Jan. 9, 1837, 1329, 1337; Kerber, "Meanings of Citizenship," 835–36; Kerber, *"No Constitutional Right to Be Ladies."*

8. *Gales and Seaton's Register of Debates*, 24th Cong., 1st sess., Dec. 22, 1835, 2032–33.

9. Ibid., 1st sess., Feb. 2, 1835, 1131–32.

10. Ibid., 2d sess., Jan. 9, Feb. 7, 1837, 1315, 1624.

11. Adams, *Speech on the Right of the People to Petition*, 77–78, 74.

12. *Gales and Seaton's Register of Debates*, 24th Cong., 2d sess., Feb. 6, 1837, 1589.

13. Ibid., 2d sess., Feb. 6, 1837, 1589, 1596.

14. Ibid., 2d sess., Feb. 9, 1837, 1675, and Jan. 9, 1837, 1315.

15. Adams, *Speech on the Right of the People to Petition*, 69, 65–66; *Gales and Seaton's Register of Debates*, 24th Cong., 2d sess., Feb. 7, 1837, 1645.

16. Adams, *Speech on the Right of the People to Petition*, 70–75.

17. Ibid., 75–76.

18. Ibid., 81, 68.

19. Ibid., 65, 77. Abigail Adams had written to her statesman husband, John Adams, on March 31, 1776: "In the new code of laws which I suppose it will be necessary for you to make I desire you would remember the ladies, and be more generous and favorable to them than your ancestors. Do not put such unlimited power into the hands of the husbands. Remember all men would be tyrants if they could. If particular care and attention is not paid to the ladies we are determined to foment a rebellion, and will not hold ourselves bound by any laws in which we have no voice, or representation" (Abigail Adams to John Adams, Mar. 31, 1776, in Rossi, *Feminist Papers*, 10–11). On the petitions for suffrage directed at the New York legislature, see Cogan and Ginzberg, "1846 Petition for Woman's Suffrage," 427–39.

20. Adams, *Memoirs*, 10:35–36.

21. Ibid., 36–37.

22. The importance of *Martin v. Commonwealth* in emerging constructions of female citizenship is examined in Kerber, *Women of the Republic*, 132–36, and Kerber, "Meanings of Citizenship." Among the state constitutional conventions that considered the prospect of granting women the rights of suffrage and office holding was that held in New York in 1821. See Zagarri, "Rights of Man and Woman," 227–28. While congressmen had chastised the propriety of women petitioning against removal of the Cherokee from Georgia, there occurred no sustained debate about women's right to petition or their status as citizens. See Hershberger, "Mobilizing Women," 29.

23. Zagarri, "Rights of Man and Woman," 203–30.

24. Adams, *Speech on the Right of the People to Petition*, 69, 65–66.

25. Zagarri, "Rights of Man and Woman," 230.

CHAPTER SEVEN

1. Report of the Fifth Annual Meeting of the New England Anti-Slavery Convention, *Liberator*, June 8, 1838.

2. For other discussions of the decline in women's organized petitioning activities, see Wellman, "Women and Radical Reform," 121–24; Lerner, "Political Activities of Antislavery Women," 125–26; and Van Broekhoven, "'Let Your Names Be Enrolled,'" 190–99.

3. *Liberator*, Oct. 26, 1838, May 3, 1839.

4. *Liberator*, July 20, Aug. 3, 1838.

5. Grimké biographers and historians of abolitionism have never mentioned this document likely because it has remained buried in the records of Congress for more than a century and a half. See Angelina Grimké, *Appeal to the Women of the United States*, Feb. 10, 1839, box 133, Library of Congress, box 38, National Ar-

chives, Washington, D.C. The petition to which the *Appeal* is attached was dated September 10, 1838.

6. Angelina Grimké, *Appeal to the Women of the United States* (1838).

7. Lerner, *Grimké Sisters*, 209.

8. Anti-Slavery Convention of American Women, *Circular of the Anti-Slavery Convention of American Women*, 25–28. Gilbert Barnes argued that the convention's address merely "paid lip-service to the circulation of petitions; but all of its time was taken up with" other subjects. Yet in addition to passing resolutions about the importance of continuing to petition, delegates devoted the entire address to expounding on the reasons why women had the right to and should petition. See Barnes, *Antislavery Impulse*, 273–74 n. 20.

9. Quoted in Miller, *Arguing about Slavery*, 344–45.

10. Barnes, *Antislavery Impulse*, 167–70.

11. Ibid., 176.

12. Ibid., 159; Hansen, *Strained Sisterhood*, 25–28.

13. Stewart quoted in Barnes, *Antislavery Impulse*, 149.

14. Miller, *Arguing about Slavery*, 360–71.

15. Barnes, *Antislavery Impulse*, 165–67, 277–78 n. 12.

16. Ibid., 177–79; Miller, *Arguing about Slavery*, 404–8.

17. Wellman, "Women and Radical Reform," 121; Soderlund, "Priorities and Power," 78–79; Petition of the Philadelphia Female Anti-Slavery Society. Despite its placement in the 1843 folder at the National Archives, the petition was dated by the authors as June 2, 1841.

18. Petition of 678 Women of Pennsylvania; Petition of 42 Citizens of Philadelphia; Petition of 37 Legal Voters and 40 Women of Columbia County; Petition of Louisa Bedford and 48 Other Ladies of Pennsylvania; Petition of Louisa Bedford and 59 Other Ladies of Philadelphia; Petition of M. S. Thorn and 77 Others; Petition of Ann W. Paxson and 37 Women of Pennsylvania; Memorial of 208 Women of Pennsylvania.

19. Petition of Charlotte Hartford and 178 Other Women of Boston; Petition of Sarah B. Litch and 100 others; Petition of Sarah Chapman and 721 Other Women of Boston; Petition of C. Swan and 80 Others; Petition of Hosea Trumball and 137 of Upton, Mass.; Petition of Caroline Wilkie with 110 Others; Petition of 61 Females of Braintree, Mass.; Petition of Sophia Foss and 71 Other Women of Southboro, Mass.; Petition of Hannah Faxon and 241 Others; Petition of Louisa Loring and 635 Other Women of Boston, Mass.; Great Petition to Congress from Citizens of Massachusetts, December 13, 1841–March 3, 1842. A similar request was made by another form of petition circulated widely in Massachusetts, signed by members of both sexes. See, for example, Petition of Charlotte Hartford and 178 Other Women of Boston, Jan. 14, 1842. *Congressional Globe* quoted in Miller, *Arguing about Slavery*, 468.

20. For example, the Petition of 585 Inhabitants of the State of New York; Peti-

tion of 857 Citizens of Cortlandville, Cortland County, NY; Petition of 1,111 Citizens of Oneida County, NY; Petition of Sarah H. Wicks and 85 Other Women of Oneida County, NY; Petition of 298 Female Inhabitants of the County of Lewis; Petition of 197 Ladies of the Town of Norway, New York. See also Petition of the Citizens of the 17th Congressional District in the State of New York.

21. Petition of 59 Females of the State of Indiana; Petition of 69 Females of the State of Indiana; Petition of 127 Females of the State of Indiana; Petition of 75 Females of the State of Indiana; Petition of 37 Inhabitants of Madison County, Indiana; Petition of the Citizens of Randolph County, Illinois (signed by 104 females and 167 males); Petition of Amy Newburn and 180 Other Women of Putnam County, Ill.; Petition of Lydia R. Finney and 254 Others; Petition from Mrs. M. P. Dascomb and 175 Other Ladies of Oberlin, Ohio; Petition from Mount Pleasant, Jefferson County, Ohio, for the Abolition of Slavery (signed by 73 men and 83 women); Petition from Mount Pleasant, Jefferson County, Ohio, against the Annexation of Texas; Petition of Phoebe B. Wood and 119 Others.

22. Petition of the Citizens of Pennsylvania Protesting against Rule 21; Great Petition to Congress from Citizens of Massachusetts, February 14, 1842–March 3, 1843; Petition from the Inhabitants of the Town of Nantucket; Petition from the Citizens of Ashtabula, Ohio.

23. Gunderson, *Log-Cabin Campaign*, 4, 7–8, 135–39; Holt, *Rise and Fall of the American Whig Party*, 106–7; Daniel Webster, "Remarks to the Ladies of Richmond," in Webster, *Works*, 2:105–8; Varon, *We Mean to be Counted*, 71–72, 78–79; Zboray and Zboray, "Whig Women, Politics, and Culture in the Campaign of 1840."

24. Petition of Rebecca Buffum and 27 Female Citizens.

25. Judith Wellman argues that development of the national state, which supplanted local and religious definitions of community and citizenship, relegated women to the status not only of nonvoters but also nonentities. While I agree that the increasing importance of the vote made lack of the franchise a more acute problem for women, I do not agree that women were nonentities. Given that hundreds of thousands of enfranchised men continued to petition congressmen against slavery, the right of petition continued to exert some degree of political power, and women had established their right to petition Congress. See Wellman, "Women and Radical Reform," 124.

26. Examples of the Women of America form include Petition of Alma Lyman and 52 Others; Petition of Sarah W. Wainright and 411 Women; Petition of Phoebe Knife and 804 Other Ladies; Petition of Sarah Forbes and 187 Other Ladies of Ashtabula, Co., OH; and Petition of E. A. Wetmore and 779 Others. Women of America petitions from Ohio, Illinois, New York, Pennsylvania, Connecticut, and other states can also be found among the extant documents in the records of Congress. Van Broekhoven, *Devotion of These Women*, chap. 6, notes the impact of European revolutions on the rhetoric of this form of petition.

27. The inability of Congress to establish civil government in states created by the Mexican Cessation is detailed in Potter, *Impending Crisis*, chap. 4. Leonard Richards argues that the major reason for the repeal of the gag rule was that northern Democrats finally broke from the grip of their southern colleagues to vote against the gag. Northern Democrats jumped ship in December 1844, Richards explains, because they felt betrayed by the party. Northern congressmen expected that Martin Van Buren would be chosen as the Democratic candidate by the presidential nominating convention held in Baltimore. But southern members passed a rule requiring not a majority but a two-thirds vote to secure the nomination. This move effectively gave southerners a veto over the ticket, and the result was that James Polk, who served as Speaker of the House when the first gag was instituted and was a slaveholder, won the nomination. Their candidate defeated by dirty politics, northern Democrats, particularly those from Van Buren's home state of New York, felt little loyalty to the party. They voted with northern Whigs to abolish the gag rule. See Richards, *Congressman John Quincy Adams*, 178. This analysis is repeated in Miller, *Arguing about Slavery*, 480–82.

28. Potter, *Impending Crisis*, 96.

29. Ibid., 99.

30. Circular of the American and Foreign Anti-Slavery Society attached to Petitions from Citizens of Ohio; circular of the American and Foreign Anti-Slavery Society attached to Petitions of 288 Citizens of Union County, Indiana.

31. Other petitions against the Fugitive Slave Law signed by women include, for example, Petition of the Ladies of Mercer County; Petition of the Inhabitants of Pennsylvania; Memorial of the Citizens of Potter County; Petition of the Citizens of Pennsylvania for Alteration of the Law; Petition of T. R. Townsend and Others; Petition of Mrs. Elizabeth Rodman and 1,728 Ladies; and Petition of 1,193 Citizens of Abington, Mass. Other petitions against the Fugitive Slave Law signed by Massachusetts women include Seven Petitions of Citizens of the State of Mass (from Needham, Raynham, Sherburne, Lancaster, Princeton, Norton, and Natick); Petition of Lydia Winslow and 172 Other Females; Petition of 448 Citizens of Canton, Mass. (signed by 227 men and 221 women); Petition of the Citizens of West Bridgewater, Mass. (signed by 131 men and 161 women); Petition of 293 Citizens of Georgetown, Mass. (signed by 178 men and 115 women); Petition of 392 Citizens of Hingston, Mass. (signed by 183 men and 209 women); and Petition of 2,833 Citizens of Portage County, OH. Other petitions from Ohio on the same topic include, for example, the Petition of the Citizens of Cuyahoga County, Ohio, and Memorial of Robert Willes and 92 Other Citizens of Ohio.

32. Petition of Citizens of Pennsylvania Praying for Alteration of the Law of 1793 (signed by 400 men and women, "colored people," of Allegheny County).

33. Potter, *Impending Crisis*, 163–65.

34. Petition of M. Truesdall and 103 women of Elgin, Ill.

35. Resolutions from Public Meeting; Petition of the Women of Greece County,

Ohio; Remonstrance of 78 Ladies of Oberlin; Petition of 414 Ladies of Oberlin; Remonstrance of 643 Women of Ohio City; Petition of the Ladies of Troy, Michigan; Petition from the Citizens of Wisconsin.

36. Remonstrance of Lucia W. G. Merrill and 136 Other Women; Petition of the Women of Andover, Mass. The first signer of this petition was Harriet Beecher Stowe, author of *Uncle Tom's Cabin* and sister of Catharine E. Beecher. The signers dated the petition February 10, 1854.

37. Petition of the Women of Iowa; Petition of Citizens of New York for Reconciliation.

38. Petition of James Hutchinson and 162 Others; Petition of the Citizens of Walworth, Wisconsin.

39. Memorial from Citizens of Skullyhill County, Pennsylvania. This petition was signed by 127 women of the Welsh Congregational Church of Mineisville. Likewise, Celia Manger and 153 women of Wisconsin entreated Congress, "by our love for our country, by our love for those who go forth to fight its battles, by the sacred names of those who have fallen on the field, as well as by our love of liberty for ourselves and for all," to enact a law proclaiming the slaves free. See Memorial of Celia Manger and 153 women of Wisconsin.

40. Hamand, "Woman's National Loyal League," 40; Hamand Venet, *Neither Ballots nor Bullets*, 103–4.

41. For a description of Angelina Grimké Weld's return to the platform, see Lerner, *Grimké Sisters*, 263–64. Julie Roy Jeffrey notes, "Given the goals of the [National Loyal League], its founders' failure to make it biracial was an ironic commentary on the limitations of white abolitionism and perhaps on the focus of black women's past efforts on elevating free blacks in the North. Although black women certainly favored the emancipation of slaves and the attainment of black legal and civil rights, and although black and white women did cooperate during the war, black and white abolitionist women continued to pursue many of their objectives, whether shared or not, independently of one another" (Jeffrey, *Great Silent Army of Abolitionism*, 217).

42. The text of this petition is taken from the Petition of the Women of the United States. It was also printed in the *Liberator*, Oct. 2, 1863.

43. Hamand Venet, *Neither Ballots nor Bullets*, 146.

44. Hamand, "Woman's National Loyal League," 44.

45. Hamand Venet, *Neither Ballots nor Bullets*, 109.

46. Angelina Grimké, "Address to the Soldiers of Our Second Revolution." Lerner, *Grimké Sisters*, 264–65, discusses the address.

47. Stanton, *Appeal to the Women of the Republic*.

48. Quoted in Hamand, "Woman's National Loyal League," 50.

49. Ibid., 49–52; Flexner, *Century of Struggle*, 111–12; Sumner's speech is reprinted in the *Liberator*, Apr. 1, 1864, and Stanton, Anthony, and Gage, *History of Woman Suffrage*, 2:78–80.

50. Hamand Venet, *Neither Ballots nor Bullets*, 146; Flexner, *Century of Struggle*, 111, 365 n. 13; Hamand, "Woman's National Loyal League," 53–54. These and other massive Loyal League petitions sent to the 38th Congress (Dec. 7, 1863–Mar. 3, 1865), which are so fragile that they cannot be unrolled to be read, can be found in oversized document drawer 16, National Archives, Washington, D.C.

AFTERWORD

1. Barnes, *Antislavery Impulse*, 266 n. 35; Hamand Venet, *Neither Ballots nor Bullets*, 14.

2. Barnes, *Antislavery Impulse*, 266 n. 40; note from the clerk, 1864, SEN 38A-H20, Kansas Box 97, 38th Cong., Records of the U.S. Senate, Record Group 46, National Archives, Washington, D.C.

3. Sewell, *Ballots for Freedom*, 7–8.

4. Miller, *Arguing about Slavery*, 24; Barnes, *Antislavery Impulse*, 110; report of the Starksborough, Vermont, Anti-Slavery Society, *Emancipator*, May 26, 1836.

5. Dumond, *Antislavery*, 246; Sterling, *Ahead of Her Time*, 35. Explicit statements about the importance of petitioning to the success of the antislavery movement can be found in a variety of primary sources. "Nothing can be made a substitute" for the "*neighborhood influence*" petitioners brought to bear as they agitated house-to-house, proclaimed the *Friend of Man*. The petition volunteers, declared the *National Enquirer*, rendered a vital service to the cause because they carried information "where our editors and lecturers are unable to penetrate." See *Friend of Man*, Sept. 27, 1837; *National Enquirer* (n.d.); and Report of the Starksborough, Vermont, Anti-Slavery Society, *Emancipator*, May 26, 1836, all quoted in Barnes, *Antislavery Impulse*, 143–45.

6. Lerner, "Political Activities of Antislavery Women," 125–26.

7. Frederick, "John Quincy Adams," 119.

8. Hardy, *Solemn Covenant*, 248; Petition and Resolutions in Favor of Constitutional Amendment; Petition of Mrs. C. W. Bickley and Others.

9. *New York Times*, Jan. 27, 1900, and *New York Evening Journal*, Jan. 26, 1900, quoted in Hardy, *Solemn Covenant*, 250. After the success of the petition campaign to deny Roberts his congressional seat, petitioners continued to push for a constitutional amendment prohibiting polygamy. In 1904 the Democratic Party formally endorsed such an amendment in their national platform, and throughout the first two decades of the twentieth century petitioners to Congress continued to denounce Mormons and call for an antipolygamy amendment. Nonetheless, a half-century after it had begun, the campaign for an antipolygamy amendment died in the 1920s as anti-Mormon sentiment decreased appreciably after World War I. See Hardy, *Solemn Covenant*, 261, 300.

10. *Our Mothers Before Us: Women and Democracy*, 5:16; Grant, *Anti-Lynching*

Movement, 31, 33, 65, 66; Memorial of Citizens of the United States (I wish to thank Alysha Black, Center for Legislative Archives, for giving me the opportunity to view this petition in the "treasure vault" of the National Archives); Petition of 2,413 Citizens of Massachusetts (the Massachusetts petition was followed a month later by, among others, an identical one signed by some 390 women and men from Englewood, New Jersey: Petition from the Citizens of New Jersey); Ragsdale and Treese, *Black Americans in Congress,* 160. Another example of petitions sent during the national drive for this legislation is the Petition of 114 Citizens Protesting against the Crime of Lynching. This petition, signed by women and men of Pennsylvania, stated simply that the signers endorsed the antilynching bill introduced by Representative White.

11. Petition of the Young Ladies Protective League of Washington, D.C. In 1918, for example, Katherine Beard, Susie Marse, John W. Thompson, and other members of the Colored Voters' Republican Council of the State of New York petitioned the committee in charge of considering the bill to request that it be passed. The petition exposed the hypocrisy of white racism, stating that the horrible crimes of lynch mobs were "staring our men in the face [while] they are still marching onward with breasts to the front facing shot and shell to establish the democracy of the world" (Petition of the Colored Voters' Republican Council of the State of New York). See also Grant, *Anti-Lynching Movement,* 168; Fascell, "Ten Historic Congressional Decisions," 11; Schamel et al., *Guide to the Records,* 214.

12. "The Declaration of Sentiments and Resolutions" (1848), in Campbell, *Man Cannot Speak for Her,* 2:36; Cogan and Ginzberg, "1846 Petition for Woman's Suffrage," 427–39; DuBois, *Elizabeth Cady Stanton, Susan B. Anthony,* 14, 18–19; Kerr, *Lucy Stone,* 60; Deckard, *Women's Movement,* 256.

13. DuBois, *Feminism and Suffrage,* 53–55, 59–61; Flexner, *Century of Struggle,* 145–47. My interpretation of the meaning of the Fourteenth Amendment and the rhetorical barriers it created differs from that of Flexner, who writes that it "raised the issue of whether women were actually citizens of the United States." On the contrary, the issue it raised was not whether women were citizens but whether there was a difference between male citizenship and female citizenship. The amendment begins with the definition "All persons born or naturalized in the United States and subject to the jurisdiction thereof, are citizens of the United States and of the State wherein they reside," yet it penalizes states that deny suffrage to "male citizens" while establishing no consequences for the denial of suffrage to females who meet the definition of "citizen."

14. Petition for Universal Suffrage.

15. Hamand Venet, *Neither Ballots nor Bullets,* 152–53; Stanton, *National Anti-Slavery Standard,* Jan. 6, 1866, quoted in Hamand Venet, *Neither Ballots nor Bullets,* 152; Hamand, "Woman's National Loyal League," 55; DuBois, *Feminism and Suffrage,* 61–62.

16. Petition for a Constitutional Amendment; DuBois, *Feminism and Suffrage,*

63–66, 71–77. Circulation of the various petitions is discussed in Stone, *Appeal to the Men and Women of America*. The *Appeal* and petition were also published in the *National Anti-Slavery Standard*. See Hamand, "Woman's National Loyal League," 55.

17. Believing that male leadership in the American Equal Rights Association was ignoring the needs of women, in May 1869 Stanton and Anthony formed the National Woman Suffrage Association for women only. This group sought immediate enfranchisement of women and felt no need to use Republican Party channels to achieve their goals. Moderates such as Stone and her husband, Henry Blackwell, held a competing convention in November 1869 to form the American Woman Suffrage Association. This organization concentrated on passage of the Fifteenth Amendment, which further guaranteed adult male suffrage, and announced itself willing to postpone attainment of woman suffrage until the freedmen's right to vote had been secured. See Flexner, *Century of Struggle*, 154–55; DuBois, *Feminism and Suffrage*, 189–202; Hamand, "Woman's National Loyal League," 55–56.

18. Text taken from Petition for Woman Suffrage from the Residents of the State of Colorado.

19. These figures were publicized by the National Woman Suffrage Association in its 1877 letter "To the Friends of Woman Suffrage." The letter was attached to Petition for Woman Suffrage, 1877, HR45A-H11.7. From her 1848 address to the first women's rights convention to her 1861 speech to the New York Judiciary Committee, Stanton had based her case for universal suffrage on the principle that all Americans possessed natural rights—blacks and women are no exception and should be granted the vote. But by 1869, likely out of frustration for having been betrayed by former abolition allies, Stanton no longer depicted white women and black men as partners in suffering. She found it rhetorically beneficial to contrast the two in order to demonstrate the superiority of white middle-class women, who, she believed, deserved the vote. Stanton scolded Gerrit Smith for considering "it important, for the best interests of the nation . . . that every type and shade of degraded, ignorant manhood should be enfranchised, before even the higher classes of womanhood should be admitted to the polls." That same year Stanton declared in her "Address to the National Woman Suffrage Convention," "If American women find it hard to bear the oppressions of their own Saxon fathers, the best orders of manhood, what may they not be called to endure when all the lower orders of foreigners now crowding our shores legislate for them and their daughters. Think of Patrick and Sambo and Hans and Yung Tung, who do not know the difference between a monarchy and a republic, who can not read the Declaration of Independence or Webster's spelling book, making laws for Lucretia Mott, Ernestine L. Rose, and Anna E. Dickinson" (DuBois, *Elizabeth Cady Stanton, Susan B. Anthony*, 120). See also Stanton, "Address to the National Woman Suffrage Convention, Washington, D.C., January 19, 1869," in Stanton, Anthony, and Gage, *History of Woman Suffrage*, 2:353. According to DuBois, *Elizabeth Cady*

Stanton, Susan B. Anthony, 119, similar racist statements recur in Stanton's rhetoric from 1868 to 1869. See also Petition for Woman Suffrage from the Colored Citizens of the District of Columbia; Terborg-Penn, *African American Women in the Struggle for the Vote,* 46–47; National Woman Suffrage Association, *To the Friends of Woman Suffrage;* American Woman Suffrage Association, "Response to NWSA's Petition for a Sixteenth Amendment," Feb. 4, 1878, in Stanton, Anthony, and Gage, *History of Woman Suffrage,* 3:104.

20. Flexner, *Century of Struggle,* 226, 257, 274, 278.

21. Ibid., 299–300, 319–27, 337; National Woman Suffrage Association, *Appeal to the Women of the United States for a Sixteenth Amendment.*

BIBLIOGRAPHY

CONGRESSIONAL RECORDS AND PETITIONS

Annals of Congress. 1789–1824.

Catalog of Women's Signatures on Petitions Sent to the House of Representatives, 1789–1816. Center for Legislative Archives, National Archives, Washington, D.C. Unpublished, 1994.

Congressional Globe. 1833–73.

Force, Peter. *American Archives: Consisting of a collection of authentick records, state papers, debates, and letters and other notices of publick affairs, the whole forming a documentary history of the origin and progress of the North American colonies; of the causes and accomplishment of the American revolution; and of the Constitution of government for the United States, to the final ratification thereof.* 9 vols. Washington, D.C.: U.S. Congress, 1837–53.

Gales and Seaton's Register of Debates in Congress. 1824–37.

Great Petition to Congress from Citizens of Massachusetts, Asking Congress to Forever Separate Them from All Connections with Slavery, December 13, 1841–March 3, 1842. HR27A-H1.6, Record Group 233, National Archives, Washington, D.C.

Great Petition to Congress from Citizens of Massachusetts, Asking Congress to Forever Separate Them from All Connections with Slavery, February 14, 1842–March 3, 1843. HR27A-H1.7, Record Group 233, National Archives, Washington, D.C.

Ladies Petition of Orange County, New York, for Abolition of Slavery in the District of Columbia, 1836. HR24A-G22.4, Library of Congress box 47, National Archives box 3, Record Group 233, National Archives, Washington, D.C.

Memorial from Citizens of Skullyhill County, Pennsylvania, Asking Congress to Pass an Act for Emancipation of Slaves, December 11, 1861. HR37A-G7.2, Record Group 233, National Archives, Washington, D.C.

Memorial of 208 Women of Pennsylvania Asking That Everything May Be Abolished in the Constitution and Laws of the United States Which in Any Manner Sanctions or Sustains Slavery, February 20, 1847. HR29A-G24.1, Record Group 233, National Archives, Washington, D.C.

Memorial of Celia Manger and 153 Women of Wisconsin for the Abolition of

Slavery in the U.S. as the Most Speedy Method of Weeding out the Rebellion, January 16, 1862. HR37A-G7.2, Record Group 233, National Archives, Washington, D.C.

Memorial of Citizens of the United States Praying a Hearing before the Judiciary Committee in Respect to the Lawless Outrages Committed in Some of the Southern States upon Persons Accused of Crime, February 3, 1893. SEN 52A-J14.4, Record Group 46, National Archives, Washington, D.C.

Memorial of Robert Willes and 92 Other Citizens of Ohio for the Repeal of the Fugitive Slave Law, 1854. HR33A-G26.4, Record Group 233, National Archives, Washington, D.C.

Memorial of the Citizens of Potter County, Pennsylvania, Praying for a Repeal of the Fugitive Slave Law, December 13, 1850. HR31A-G9.5, Record Group 233, National Archives, Washington, D.C.

Memorial of the Mormon Women of Utah to the President and the Congress of the United States, April 6, 1886. Washington, D.C.: n.p., 1886.

Our Mothers Before Us: Women and Democracy, 1789–1920. Washington, D.C.: Foundation for the National Archives, 1998.

Our Mothers Before Us: Women's Writings to Congress, 1789–1920. Database and collection. Center for Legislative Archives, National Archives, Washington, D.C.

Petition and Resolutions in Favor of Constitutional Amendment for Polygamy from the Woman's Missionary Society, Central Presbyterian Church, December 4, 1900. HR56A-H13.4, Record Group 233, National Archives, Washington, D.C.

Petition for a Constitutional Amendment Prohibiting All Political Distinction on Account of Sex, January 12, 1869–January 15, 1869. SEN 40A-H10.3, Record Group 46, National Archives, Washington, D.C.

Petition for Universal Suffrage, 1866. HR39A-H14.9, Record Group 233, National Archives, Washington, D.C.

Petition for Woman Suffrage, 1877, HR45A-H11.7, Record Group 233, National Archives, Washington, D.C.

Petition for Woman Suffrage from the Colored Citizens of the District of Columbia, 1877. HR45A-H11.7, Record Group 233, National Archives, Washington, D.C.

Petition for Woman Suffrage from the Residents of the State of Colorado, January 19, 1877. HR44A-H8.4, Record Group 233, National Archives, Washington, D.C.

Petition from Mount Pleasant, Jefferson County, Ohio, against the Annexation of Texas and the Admission of a New Slave State and Any Abridgment of the Right of Petition Signed by Joseph L. Righter and 80 Other Men and by Jane Robinson and 97 Other Women, January 10, 1843. HR27A-H1.1, Record Group 233, National Archives, Washington, D.C.

Petition from Mount Pleasant, Jefferson County, Ohio, for the Abolition of Slavery in the District of Columbia and the Territories of the US and the Domestic Slave Trade, also against Any More of the Public Revenue Paid by the Free States Being Expended in Carrying on the War in Florida or in the Settlement of Florida, January 10, 1843. HR27A-H1.1, Record Group 233, National Archives, Washington, D.C.

Petition from Mrs. M. P. Dascomb and 175 Other Ladies of Oberlin, Ohio, Praying Congress to Abolish Slavery in the District of Columbia, March 3, 1843. HR27A-H1.7, Record Group 233, National Archives, Washington, D.C.

Petition from the Citizens of Ashtabula, Ohio, for Immediate Abolition in the District of Columbia, 1840. HR26A-H1.2, Record Group 233, National Archives, Washington, D.C.

Petition from the Citizens of New Jersey Praying for Congress to Make the Act of Lynching a Crime against the United States, February 21, 1900. Judiciary, HR56A-H13.3, Record Group 233, National Archives, Washington, D.C.

Petition from the Citizens of Wisconsin against Accession of Slave Territory, 1854. HR33A-G26.4, Record Group 233, National Archives, Washington, D.C.

Petition from the Female Citizens of the State of Ohio for Abolition of Slavery in the District of Columbia, 1836. HR24A-G22.4, Library of Congress box 71, National Archives box 12, Record Group 233, National Archives, Washington, D.C.

Petition from the Inhabitants of the Town of Nantucket to End the Slave Trade in the District of Columbia, January 31, 1843. HR27A-H1.6, Record Group 233, National Archives, Washington, D.C.

Petition of 37 Inhabitants of Madison County, Indiana, against Annexation of Texas, February 7, 1842. HR27A-H1.7, Record Group 233, National Archives, Washington, D.C.

Petition of 37 Legal Voters and 40 Women of Columbia County for the Release of the People of the Free States from All Obligations Supporting Slavery, February 8, 1843. HR27A-H1.7, Record Group 233, National Archives, Washington, D.C.

Petition of 42 Citizens of Philadelphia for Repeal of the Fugitive Slave Law, March 29, 1842. HR27A-H1.7, Record Group 233, National Archives, Washington, D.C.

Petition of 61 Females of Braintree, Mass., against Any New State into the Union Which Tolerates Slavery, March 29, 1842. HR27A-H1.7, Record Group 233, National Archives, Washington, D.C.

Petition of 59 Females of the State of Indiana Praying Congress to Reject All Proposals Looking in Any Way towards the Annexation of Texas, August 25, 1842. HR27A-H1.1, Record Group 233, National Archives, Washington, D.C.

Petition of 69 Females of the State of Indiana Praying Congress to Reject All

Proposals Looking in Any Way towards the Annexation of Texas, August 25, 1842. HR27A-H1.1, Record Group 233, National Archives, Washington, D.C.

Petition of 75 Females of the State of Indiana Praying Congress to Reject All Proposals Looking in Any Way towards the Annexation of Texas, August 25, 1842. HR27A-H1.1, Record Group 233, National Archives, Washington, D.C.

Petition of 114 Citizens Protesting against the Crime of Lynching, February 6, 1900. HR 56A-H13.3, Record Group 233, National Archives, Washington, D.C.

Petition of 120 Ladies of Boston, Massachusetts, against Slavery and the Slave Trade in the District of Columbia, February 23, 1835. HR23A-H1.2, Library of Congress box 49, National Archives box 4, Record Group 233, National Archives, Washington, D.C.

Petition of 127 Females of the State of Indiana Praying Congress to Reject All Proposals Looking in Any Way towards the Annexation of Texas, August 25, 1842, HR27A-H1.1, Record Group 233, National Archives, Washington, D.C.

Petition of 197 Ladies of the Town of Norway, New York, Remonstrating against the Annexation of Texas, December 9, 1845. HR29A-G21.1, Record Group 233, National Archives, Washington, D.C.

Petition of 218 Females of Jamaica and Vicinity on Slavery and the Slave Trade in the District of Columbia, March 5, 1834. HR 23A-G4.3, Record Group 233, National Archives, Washington, D.C.

Petition of 293 Citizens of Georgetown, Mass., for Repeal of the Fugitive Slave Law, February 5, 1851. HR31A-G9.5, Record Group 233, National Archives, Washington, D.C.

Petition of 298 Female Inhabitants of the County of Lewis, State of New York, Remonstrating against the Annexation of Texas, December 9, 1845. HR29A-G21.1, Record Group 233, National Archives, Washington, D.C.

Petition of 359 Ladies of Massachusetts for Abolition of Slavery in the District of Columbia, January 18, 1836. HR24A-H1.3, Record Group 233, National Archives, Washington, D.C.

Petition of 392 Citizens of Hingston, Mass., for Repeal of the Fugitive Slave Law, February 6, 1851. HR31A-G9.5, Record Group 233, National Archives, Washington, D.C.

Petition of 414 Ladies of Oberlin, Loraine County, OH, against Repeal of the Missouri Compromise, 1854. HR33A-G26.5, Record Group 233, National Archives, Washington, D.C.

Petition of 448 Citizens of Canton, Mass., for Repeal of the Fugitive Slave Law, February 5, 1851. HR31A-G9.5, Record Group 233, National Archives, Washington, D.C.

Petition of 585 Inhabitants of the State of New York to Separate NY from Slavery, December 16, 1844. HR28A-H1.1, Record Group 233, National Archives, Washington, D.C.

Petition of 600 Ladies of Utica, Oneida County, New York, for Abolition of

Slavery and the Slave Trade in the District of Columbia, March 21, 1836.
Library of Congress box 47, National Archives box 3, Record Group 233,
National Archives, Washington, D.C.

Petition of 678 Women of Pennsylvania to Alter Laws to Relieve the State of Any
Cost for Sustaining Slavery, January 10, 1842. HR27A-H1.7, Record Group 233,
National Archives, Washington, D.C.

Petition of 800 Ladies of New York, *Emancipator*, February 24, 1835.

Petition of 857 Citizens of Cortlandville, Cortland County, NY, for the Abolition
of Slavery in the District, December 16, 1844. HR28A-G5.1, Record Group 233,
National Archives, Washington, D.C.

Petition of 1,111 Citizens of Oneida County, NY, to Abolish Slavery in the
District of Columbia and Territories, December 20, 1844. HR28A-G5.1,
Record Group 233, National Archives, Washington, D.C.

Petition of 1,193 Citizens of Abington, Mass., for Repeal of the Fugitive Slave
Law, February 5, 1851. HR31A-G9.5, Record Group 233, National Archives,
Washington, D.C.

Petition of 2,413 Citizens of Massachusetts Arguing for National Legislation
against the Crime of Lynching and Mob Violence, January 20, 1900. HR
56A-H13.3, Record Group 233, National Archives, Washington, D.C.

Petition of 2,833 Citizens of Portage County, OH, Praying for the Repeal of the
Fugitive Slave Law, December 30, 1850. HR31A-G9.5, Record Group 233,
National Archives, Washington, D.C.

Petition of Alma Lyman and 52 Others, against Extension of Slavery and
Continuation of the Slave Trade, January 19, 1849. HR30A-G9.2, Record
Group 233, National Archives, Washington, D.C.

Petition of Amy Newburn and 180 Other Women of Putnam County, Ill., for
Abolition of Slavery in the District of Columbia, March 4, 1846. HR29A-G3.2,
Record Group 233, National Archives, Washington, D.C.

Petition of Ann W. Paxson and 37 Women of Pennsylvania for Removing
Involuntary Servitude, January 18, 1847, HR29A-G21.2, Record Group 233,
National Archives, Washington, D.C.

Petition of Caroline Wilkie with 110 Others, Inhabitants of South Willbraham,
Mass., That Neither Florida or Any Other New State May Be Admitted into
the Union Whose Constitution of Government Shall Tolerate Domestic
Slavery, March 29, 1842. HR27A-H1.7, Record Group 233, National Archives,
Washington, D.C.

Petition of Charlotte Hartford and 178 Other Women of Boston, Protesting
against Rule 21, June 12, 1841–January 14, 1842. HR27A-H1.7, Record Group
233, National Archives, Washington, D.C.

Petition of Citizens of New York for Reconciliation. SEN36A-J3, Record Group
46, oversized document drawer 15, National Archives, Washington, D.C.

Petition of Citizens of Pennsylvania Praying for Alteration of the Law of 1793

Relative to Fugitive Slaves, May 22, 1850–July 15, 1850. HR31A-G9.5, Record Group 233, National Archives, Washington, D.C.

Petition of C. Swan and 80 Others of Hubbardston, Mass., against Admission of Slave States, January 24, 1842. HR27A-H1.7, Record Group 233, National Archives, Washington, D.C.

Petition of E. A. Wetmore and 779 Others (women), of Utica, NY, Praying Congress to Prevent the Expansion of Slavery, to Withdraw the Protection of Government from the American Slave Trade and to Suppress Slavery Wherever Congress Has Jurisdiction, 1849. HR30A-G5.1, Record Group 233, National Archives, Washington, D.C.

Petition of Elizabeth Wilson and 106 Women of the State of Ohio Remonstrating against the Annexation of Texas to This Union, January 7, 1839. Library of Congress box 126, National Archives box 35, Record Group 233, National Archives, Washington, D.C.

Petition of Eliza C. Stiles and 1,026 Women of Lynn, Mass., Remonstrating against the Resolution of December 21, 1837, March 12, 1838, to Lie. Library of Congress box 110, National Archives box 29, Record Group 233, National Archives, Washington, D.C.

Petition of Hannah Faxon and 241 Others, Women of Abington, Mass., Praying That Neither Florida or Any Other New State May Be Admitted into the Union Whose Constitution of Government Shall Tolerate Domestic Slavery, February 21–March 3, 1843. HR27A-H1.7, Record Group 233, National Archives, Washington, D.C.

Petition of Hosea Trumball and 137 of Upton, Mass., of Whom 52 Are Legal Voters against Admission of Texas to the Union as a Slave State, March 29, 1842. HR27A-H1.1, Record Group 233, National Archives, Washington, D.C.

Petition of James Hutchinson and 162 Others, Praying for the Abolition of Slavery, December 16, 1861. HR37A-G7.2, Record Group 233, National Archives, Washington, D.C.

Petition of Louisa Bedford and 48 Other Ladies of Pennsylvania Praying That No Slave Be Returned to a State Where He Is Not Allowed to Read the Bible, December 31, 1844. HR28-G10.2, Record Group 233, National Archives, Washington, D.C.

Petition of Louisa Bedford and 59 Other Ladies of Philadelphia Praying Congress to Alter the Laws to Relieve the Citizens of the State from Supporting Slavery, December 31, 1844. HR28-G10.2, Record Group 233, National Archives, Washington, D.C.

Petition of Louisa Loring and 635 Other Women of Boston, Mass., That Congress Should Reject Proposals for Allowing Florida into the Union as a Slave State, January 21, 1842. HR27A-H1.6, Record Group 233, National Archives, Washington, D.C.

Petition of Lydia R. Finney and 254 Others, Ladies of Oberlin, OH, for Repeal of the 21st Rule of the House of Representatives, August 25, 1842, HR27A-H1.7, Record Group 233, National Archives, Washington, D.C.

Petition of Lydia Winslow and 172 Other Females Residing in the Town of Westport, Mass., Praying for the Repeal of the Fugitive Slave Law, December 23, 1850. HR31A-G9.5, Record Group 233, National Archives, Washington, D.C.

Petition of Mrs. C. W. Bickley and Others Favoring Anti-polygamy Amendments to the Constitution, February 2, 1901. HR56A-H13.4, Record Group 233, National Archives, Washington, D.C.

Petition of Mrs. Elizabeth Rodman and 1,728 Ladies of New Bedford in the State of Mass., Praying that the Fugitive Slave Law, So Called, May be Appealed, December 30, 1850. HR31A-G9.5, Record Group 233, National Archives, Washington, D.C.

Petition of Mrs. Levi Burnell and 190 Ladies of Oberlin, Ohio, Praying that Mr. Patton's Resolution be Rescinded, June 4, 1838. Library of Congress box 110, National Archives box 29, Record Group 233, National Archives, Washington, D.C.

Petition of M. S. Thorn and 77 Others—E. L. Paxson and 55 Others—Women of Pa. Praying Congress to Abolish Everything in the Constitution or Laws of the U.S. Which in Any Manner Sanction or Sustain Slavery, February 26, 1847. HR29A-G8.9, Record Group 233, National Archives, Washington, D.C.

Petition of M. Truesdall and 103 Women of Elgin, Ill., Opposing the Kansas-Nebraska Bill, March 11, 1854. Library of Congress box 153, National Archives box 45, Record Group 233, National Archives, Washington, D.C.

Petition of Phoebe Knife and 804 Other Ladies of New York City, 1849. HR30A-G9.2, Record Group 233, National Archives, Washington, D.C.

Petition of Phoebe B. Wood and 119 Others, Ladies of Marion County, OH, Praying Abolition of Slavery in the District of Columbia and Against the Admission of Texas, December 12, 1844, HR28A-H1.1, Record Group 233, National Archives, Washington, D.C.

Petition of Rebecca Buffum and 27 Female Citizens of Ohio, December 22, 1842. HR27A-H1.7, Record Group 233, National Archives, Washington, D.C.

Petition of Sarah B. Litch and 100 Others, Women of Boston, Protesting against Rule 21, June 12, 1841–January 14, 1842. HR27A-H1.7, Record Group 233, National Archives, Washington, D.C.

Petition of Sarah Chapman and 721 Other Women of Boston, Massachusetts, That This House Would Rescind the Standing Rule of the House, No. 21, on the Subject of Petitions Touching Slavery, January 21, 1842. HR27A-H1.6, Record Group 233, National Archives, Washington, D.C.

Petition of Sarah Forbes and 187 Other Ladies of Ashtabula, Co., OH, 1849. HR30A-G5.1, Record Group 233, National Archives, Washington, D.C.

Petition of Sarah H. Wicks and 85 Other Women of Oneida County, NY, Praying for Abolition of Slavery in the District of Columbia and the Territories, February 18, 1845. HR28A-G5.1, Record Group 233, National Archives, Washington, D.C.

Petition of Sarah W. Wainright and 411 Women for the Abolition of Slavery and the Slave Trade in the District of Columbia, February 6, 1849. HR30A-G5.1, Record Group 233, National Archives, Washington, D.C.

Petition of Sophia Foss and 71 Other Women of Southboro, Mass., That No New State Be Admitted to the Union Whose Constitution Tolerates Slavery, April 4, 1842. HR27A-H1.7, Record Group 233, National Archives, Washington, D.C.

Petition of the Citizens of Cuyahoga County, Ohio, Asking for Repeal of the Fugitive Slave Law, October 1850. HR31A-G9.5, Record Group 233, National Archives, Washington, D.C.

Petition of the Citizens of Lockport, New York, for the Abolition of Slavery and the Slave Trade in the District of Columbia and the Territories, January 18– June 6, 1836. HR 24A-H1.3, Tabled, Library of Congress box 47, National Archives box 3, Record Group 233, National Archives, Washington, D.C.

Petition of the Citizens of Ohio for Abolition of Slavery in the District of Columbia and the Territories, February 18, 1834. HR 23A-G 4.3, Library of Congress box 48, National Archives box 3, Record Group 233, National Archives, Washington, D.C.

Petition of the Citizens of Pennsylvania for Alteration of the Law of 1793 Relative to Fugitive Slaves, May 22–July 15, 1850. HR31A-G9.5, Record Group 233, National Archives, Washington, D.C.

Petition of the Citizens of Pennsylvania Protesting against Rule 21, December 15, 1841. HR27A-H1.6, Record Group 233, National Archives, Washington, D.C.

Petition of the Citizens of Philadelphia against the Admission of Arkansas as a Slave State, June 6, 1836. HR24A-H1.4, Library of Congress box 46, National Archives box 3, Record Group 233, National Archives, Washington, D.C.

Petition of the Citizens of Philadelphia for Repeal of the Gag Rule, February 14, 1838. Library of Congress box 110, National Archives box 29, Record Group 233, National Archives, Washington, D.C.

Petition of the Citizens of Randolph County, Illinois, Praying Congress to Recommend Amendments to the Constitution That Will Provide for the Abolition of Slavery, December 16, 1844. HR28A-G10.2, Record Group 233, National Archives, Washington, D.C.

Petition of the Citizens of the 17th Congressional District in the State of New York, Protesting against the Admission of Texas to the Union, December 1, 1845. HR29A-G21.1, Record Group 233, National Archives, Washington, D.C.

Petition of the Citizens of the Town of Fayston, Vermont, for the Abolition of Slavery in the District of Columbia, February 29, 1836. HR24-G22.4, Library of Congress box 75, National Archives box 14, Record Group 233, National Archives, Washington, D.C.

Petition of the Citizens of the United States on Slavery and the Slave Trade in the District of Columbia, January 27, 1834. HR23A-G4.3, Library of Congress box 48, National Archives box 3, Record Group 233, National Archives, Washington, D.C.

Petition of the Citizens of Walworth, Wisconsin, Praying Congress to Enact the War Power to Abolish Slavery, January 29, 1861. HR37A-G7.2, Record Group 233, National Archives, Washington, D.C.

Petition of the Citizens of West Bridgewater, Mass., for Repeal of the Fugitive Slave Law, February 5, 1851. HR31A-G9.5, Record Group 233, National Archives, Washington, D.C.

Petition of the Colored Voters' Republican Council of the State of New York Praying Congress to Pass the Dyer Bill, June 14, 1918. HR65A-H8.2, Record Group 233, National Archives, Washington, D.C.

Petition of the Female Citizens of Ohio for the Abolition of Slavery in the District of Columbia, 1836. HR24A-G22.4, Library of Congress box 71, National Archives box 12, Record Group 233, National Archives, Washington, D.C.

Petition of the Female Citizens of Philadelphia for the Abolition of the Slave Trade in the District of Columbia, 1838. HR25th, Library of Congress box 117, National Archives box 31, Record Group 233, National Archives, Washington, D.C.

Petition of the Female Inhabitants of South Reading, Massachusetts, against the Admission of the Territory of Arkansas to the Union as a Slaveholding State, June 6, 1836. HR24A-H1.4, Library of Congress box 46, National Archives box 3, Record Group 233, National Archives, Washington, D.C.

Petition of the Females of Addison County, Vermont, for the Abolition of Slavery in the District of Columbia and Various States, April 18, 1836. HR24-G22.4, Library of Congress box 47, National Archives box 3, Record Group 233, National Archives, Washington, D.C.

Petition of the Females of the State of Pennsylvania, December 29, 1831. HR22A-H1.25, Tabled, Library of Congress box 58, National Archives box 6, Record Group 233, National Archives, Washington, D.C.

Petition of the Females of Washington County, Vermont, for the Abolition of Slavery in the District of Columbia and Various States, 1836. HR24-G22.4, Library of Congress box 75, National Archives box 14, Record Group 233, National Archives, Washington, D.C.

Petition of the Females of Winthrop, Maine, for the Abolition of Slavery in the District of Columbia, March 21, 1836. HR24-G22.4, Library of Congress box 75, National Archives box 14, Record Group 233, National Archives, Washington, D.C.

Petition of the Inhabitants of Livingston County, New York, against the
Admission of Florida and Texas, n.d. [ca. 1843]. HR27A-H1.1, Record Group
233, National Archives, Washington, D.C.

Petition of the Inhabitants of Pennsylvania for Repeal of the Fugitive Slave Law,
December 11, 1850. HR31A-G9.5, Record Group 233, National Archives,
Washington, D.C.

Petition of the Ladies of Dousa, New Hampshire, for Abolition of Slavery in the
District of Columbia, 1836. HR24-G22.4, Library of Congress box 75, National
Archives box 14, Record Group 233, National Archives, Washington, D.C.

Petition of the Ladies of Glastenbury for Abolition of Slavery in the District of
Columbia, 1836. HR24A-H1.3, Library of Congress box 47, National Archives
box 3, Record Group 233, National Archives, Washington, D.C.

Petition of the Ladies of Marshfield for Abolition of Slavery in the District of
Columbia, December 18, 1835, to June 6, 1836. HR24A-H1.3, Record Group 233,
National Archives, Washington, D.C.

Petition of the Ladies of Massachusetts for Abolition of Slavery in the District of
Columbia, December 18, 1835, to June 6, 1836. HR24A-H1.3, Record Group 233,
National Archives, Washington, D.C.

Petition of the Ladies of Mercer County, PA, for Repeal of the Fugitive Slave
Law, January 10–March 13, 1850. HR31A-G9.5, Record Group 233, National
Archives, Washington, D.C.

Petition of the Ladies of Steubenville, Ohio, protesting Indian Removal,
February 15, 1830. HR21A-H1.1, Record Group 233, National Archives,
Washington, D.C.

Petition of the Ladies of Troy, Michigan, against the Nebraska Bill, March 6–
May 19, 1854. HR33A-G26.2, Record Group 233, National Archives,
Washington, D.C.

Petition of the Men and Women of Ohio Praying Congress to Abolish Slavery in
the District of Columbia, February 18, 1834. HR23A-G4.3, Library of Congress
box 48, National Archives box 3, Record Group 233, National Archives,
Washington, D.C.

Petition of the Philadelphia Female Anti-Slavery Society Praying Congress to
Alter the Laws to Relieve the Citizens of the State from Supporting Slavery,
February 21, 1843–March 3, 1843. HR27A-H1.7, Record Group 233, National
Archives, Washington, D.C.

Petition of the Women of Andover, Mass., Remonstrating against the Repeal of
the Missouri Compromise, February 10, 1854. SEN33A-J6, Record Group 46,
National Archives, Washington, D.C.

Petition of the Women of Greece County, Ohio, against Admission of Nebraska
as a Slave State, 1854. HR33A-G26.2, Record Group 233, National Archives,
Washington, D.C.

Petition of the Women of Harrisville, Ohio, for Abolition of Slavery in the

District of Columbia and Immediate Enfranchisement, June 13, 1834.
HR23A-HRG4.3, Record Group 233, National Archives, Washington, D.C.
Petition of the Women of Iowa for Cessation of Hostilities, 1861–62.
HR37A-G7.12, Record Group 233, National Archives, Washington, D.C.
Petition of the Women of the United States Praying for Emancipation of All
Persons of African Descent. SEN 38A-H20, Kansas box 97, Record Group 233,
National Archives, Washington, D.C.
Petition of the Young Ladies Protective League of Washington, D.C., Praying
Congress to Make the Act of Lynching a Crime against the United States, 1917.
HR65A-H8.2, Record Group 233, National Archives, Washington, D.C.
Petition of T. R. Townsend and Others, Citizens of Oswego, County, New York,
to Secure Alleged Fugitives the Right of Trial by Jury, April 18, 1850–April 23,
1850. HR31A-G9.5, Record Group 233, National Archives, Washington, D.C.
"Petitions and Memorials, Resolutions of State Legislatures, and Related
Documents Which Were Tabled." Record Groups 233 and 46. Records of
Congress, National Archives, Washington, D.C.
Petitions from Citizens of Ohio, March 27, 1850. HR31A-G9.5, Record Group 233,
National Archives, Washington, D.C.
Petitions of 288 Citizens of Union County, Indiana, May 3, 1850. HR31A-G23.1,
Record Group 233, National Archives, Washington, D.C.
Remonstrance of 78 Ladies of Oberlin, Loraine County, OH, against Repeal of
the Missouri Compromise, March 23, 1854. HR33A-G26.5, Record Group 233,
National Archives, Washington, D.C.
Remonstrance of 643 Women of Ohio City, Cuyahoga County, Ohio, against
Repeal of the Missouri Compromise, March 6–May 19, 1854. HR33A-G26.5,
Record Group 233, National Archives, Washington, D.C.
Remonstrance of Lucia W. G. Merrill and 136 Other Women of Montague,
Mass., against Opening the Territories of the United States to Slavery,
March 10, 1854. HR33A-G10.1, Record Group 233, National Archives,
Washington, D.C.
Resolutions from Public Meeting Opposing Repeal of the Missouri Compromise
Held in Youngstown, Ohio, 1854. HR33A-G26.5, Record Group 233, National
Archives, Washington, D.C.
Schamel, Charles E., Mary Rephlo, Rodney Ross, David Kepley, Robert W.
Coren, and James Gregory Bradsher. *Guide to the Records of the United States
House of Representatives at the National Archives, 1789–1989.* Bicentennial ed.
100th Cong., 2d sess., January 1989, Doc. No. 100-245.
Seven Petitions of Citizens of the State of Mass Praying for the Repeal of the
Fugitive Slave Law, February 19, 1850. HR31A-G9.5, Record Group 233,
National Archives, Washington, D.C.
*True Copy of the Petition of the Gentle-women, & Trades-men wives, in and about the
City of London. Delivered to the Honorable, the Knights, Citizens, and Burgesses of*

the House of Commons, assembled in Parliament, Feb. 4, 1641. Together with their several reasons, why their Sex ought thus to Petition as well as the Men, and the manner how both their Petitions and reasons were delivered. Likewise the Answer which the Honorable Assembly sent to them by Mr. Pym, as they stood at the House door. London: J. Wright, 1642. Microfilm, Early English Books, 1641–1700, 1296:57.

JOURNALS AND NEWSPAPERS

Antislavery Examiner (New York, N.Y.)
Emancipator (New York, N.Y.)
Freedom's Journal (New York, N.Y.)
Friend of Man (Utica, N.Y.)
Liberator (Boston, Mass.)
Morning Courier and New York Enquirer
National Anti-Slavery Standard (New York, N.Y.)
Philanthropist (Mt. Pleasant, Ohio)

ADDRESSES, ANTHOLOGIES, COLLECTIONS, MEMOIRS, AND SPEECHES

Adams, John Quincy. *Letters of John Quincy Adams to his Constituents of the Twelfth Congressional District of Massachusetts. To which is added his Speech in Congress, delivered February 9, 1837.* Boston: Isaac Knapp, 1837.
———. *Speech on the right of the People, Men and Women, to Petition; on the Freedom of Speech and Debate in the House of Representatives of the United States; on the Resolutions of Seven State Legislatures and the Petitions of More than One Hundred Thousand Petitioners, Relating to the Annexation of Texas to this Union. Delivered in the House of Representatives of the United States, in fragments in the morning hour, from the 16th of June to the 7th of July, 1838, inclusive.* Washington, D.C.: Gales and Seaton, 1838.
———. *Memoirs of John Quincy Adams, Comprising Portions of His Diary from 1795 to 1848.* Edited by Charles Francis Adams. 12 vols. Philadelphia: J. B. Lippincott, 1874–77.
American Anti-Slavery Society. *An Appeal to the People of the United States. Liberator,* July 9, 1836.
———. *Correspondence between the Hon. F. H. Elmore, One of the South Carolina Delegation to Congress, and James G. Birney, One of the Secretaries of the American Anti-Slavery Society. Antislavery Examiner 8.* New York: AASS, 1838.
Anti-Slavery Convention of American Women. *An Appeal to the Women of the*

Nominally Free States, Issued by an Anti-Slavery Convention of American Women, Held in Adjournment from the 9th to the 12th of May, 1837. New York: William S. Dorr, 1837.

———. *An Address to the Free Colored People of the United States, Published by an Anti-Slavery Convention of American Women. Held in Adjournments from the 9th to the 12th of May, 1837.* Philadelphia: Merrihew and Gunn, 1838.

———. *An Address to the Senators and Representatives of the Free States, in the Congress of the United States.* Philadelphia: Merrihew and Gunn, 1838.

———. *Circular of the Anti-Slavery Convention of American Women.* In *Proceedings of the Third Anti-Slavery Convention of American Women, Held in the City of Philadelphia, May 1st, 2d and 3d, 1839.* Philadelphia: Merrihew and Thompson, 1839.

Aptheker, Herbert, ed. *A Documentary History of the Negro People in the United States.* New York: International Publishers, 1951.

Barnard, Henry, ed. *Slavery: A Bibliography and Union List of the Microfilm Collection.* Sanford, N.C.: Microfilming Corp. of America, 1980.

Beecher, Catharine E. *An Essay on Slavery and Abolitionism with Reference to the Duty of American Females.* Philadelphia: Henry Perkins, 1837.

Birney, James G. *A Letter on the Political Obligations of Abolitionists.* 1839. Reprint, New York: Arno Press, 1969.

———. *Letters of James Gillespie Birney, 1831–1857.* Edited by Dwight L. Dumond. 2 vols. New York: D. Appleton-Century, 1938.

Boston Female Anti-Slavery Society. "Address of the Boston Female Anti-slavery Society to the Women of England." In *Right and Wrong in Boston, Number Three: Annual Report of the Boston Female Antislavery Society.* Boston: The Society, 1837.

———. *Address of the Boston Female Anti-Slavery Society to the Women of Massachusetts.* In *Three Years' Anti-Slavery Effort in Britain and America.* Glasgow: Aird and Russell, 1837.

———. *An Address of the Boston Female Anti-Slavery Society to the Women of New England. Liberator,* June 16, 1837.

———. *Right and Wrong in Boston, Number Three: Annual Report of the Boston Female Anti-Slavery Society.* Boston: The Society, 1837.

Bourne, George. *Slavery Illustrated in Its Effects upon Woman and Domestic Society.* Boston: Isaac Knapp, 1837.

Calhoun, John C. *The Works of John C. Calhoun.* Edited by Richard Cralle. 6 vols. New York: D. Appleton, 1853–57.

Campbell, Karlyn Kohrs, ed. *Man Cannot Speak for Her: Key Texts of the Early Feminists.* 2 vols. New York: Praeger, 1989.

Chandler, Elizabeth Margaret. *Essays, Philanthropic and Moral.* Edited by Benjamin Lundy. Philadelphia: Lemuel Howell, 1836.

———. *The Poetical Works of Elizabeth Margaret Chandler: With a Memoir of Her*

Life and Character, by Benjamin Lundy. Philadelphia: Lemuel Howell, 1836. Reprint, Miami: Mnemosyne, 1969.

Channing, William Ellery. *Tribute of William Ellery Channing to the American Abolitionists, for their Vindication of Freedom of Speech.* New York: American Antislavery Society, 1861.

Chapman, Maria Weston. *Right and Wrong in Massachusetts.* Boston: Henry L. Deveraux, 1840.

Child, Lydia Maria. *An Appeal in Favor of That Class of Americans Called Africans.* Boston: Allen and Ticknor, 1833.

———. *Anti-Slavery Catechism.* Newburyport, Mass.: Charles Whipple, 1836.

———. *The Evils of Slavery, and the Cure.* Newburyport, Mass.: Charles Whipple, 1836.

———. *Letters from New York, First Series.* New York: Charles S. Francis, 1843.

———. *The Collected Correspondence of Lydia Maria Child, 1817–1880.* Edited by Patricia G. Holland and Milton Meltzer. Millwood, N.Y.: Kraus Microform, 1980.

———. *Lydia Maria Child: Selected Letters, 1817–1880.* Edited by Milton Meltzer and Patricia G. Holland. Amherst: University of Massachusetts Press, 1982.

Colton, Calvin. *Abolition a Sedition* [*sic*]. Philadelphia: G. W. Donohue, 1839.

———. *The Right of Petition.* N.p., 1840.

Concord, New Hampshire, Female Anti-Slavery Society. *An Address Delivered Before the Concord Female Anti-Slavery Society at Its Annual Meeting, 25 December 1837. To Which is Added, Their Third Annual Report of Said Society.* Concord, N.H.: William, White, 1838.

Foster, Abby Kelley, Papers. American Antiquarian Society, Worcester, Mass.

Garrison, William Lloyd. *Thoughts on African Colonization.* Boston: Garrison and Knapp, 1832.

———. *The Letters of William Lloyd Garrison.* Edited by Walter M. Merrill and Louis Ruchames. 2 vols. Cambridge: Harvard University Press, Belknap Press, 1971.

Grimké, Angelina. *An Appeal to the Christian Women of the South.* New York: n.p., 1836.

———. *An Appeal to the Women of the United States.* N.p., 1838.

———. *Letters to Catherine* [*sic*] *E. Beecher, in Reply to an Essay on Slavery and Abolitionism, addressed to A. E. Grimké.* Boston: Isaac Knapp, 1838.

———. "Speech before the Legislative Committee of the Massachusetts Legislature, Feb. 21, 1838." *Liberator,* May 2, 1838.

———. "Speech in Pennsylvania Hall, May 16, 1838." In *History of Woman Suffrage,* edited by Elizabeth Cady Stanton, Susan B. Anthony, and Matilda J. Gage, 1:334–36. New York: Fowler and Wells, 1881.

———. "Address to the Soldiers of Our Second Revolution." *Liberator,* October 2, 1863.

Grimké, Sarah. *An Epistle to the Clergy of the Southern States.* New York: n.p., 1836.

———. *Letters on the Equality of the Sexes and the Condition of Woman, Addressed to Mary Parker, President of the Boston Female Anti-Slavery Society.* Boston: Isaac Knapp, 1838.

Grimké, Sarah M., and Angelina E. Grimké. "Letter to Clarkson." *Friend of Man,* April 5, 1837.

———. *The Public Years of Sarah and Angelina Grimké: Selected Writings, 1835–1839.* Edited by Larry Ceplair. New York: Columbia University Press, 1989.

Heyrick, Elizabeth. *Immediate, Not Gradual Abolition; Or, An Inquiry into the Shortest, Safest, and Most Effectual Means of Getting Rid of West Indian Slavery.* London: Knight and Bagster, 1824.

Hooper, William Henry. *The Utah Bill. A Plea for Religious Liberty. Speech of Hon. W. H. Hooper, of Utah, Delivered in the House of Representatives, March 23, 1870, Together With the Remonstrance of the Citizens of Salt Lake City, in Mass Meeting, held March 31, 1870, to the Senate of the United States.* Washington, D.C.: Gibson Brothers, 1870.

Jefferson, Thomas. *The Writings of Thomas Jefferson.* Edited by Paul Leicester Ford. 10 vols. New York: G. P. Putnam's Sons, 1892–99.

Martineau, Harriet. *The Martyr Age of the United States.* Boston: Weeks, Jordan, 1839.

Mott, James, and Lucretia Mott. *James and Lucretia Mott: Life and Letters.* Edited by Anna Davis Hallowell. Boston: Houghton, Mifflin, 1884.

Muskingham County, Ohio, Female Anti-Slavery Society. *An Address to Females in the State of Ohio. Emancipator,* July 21, 1836.

National Woman Suffrage Association. *An Appeal to the Women of the United States for a Sixteenth Amendment.* N.p., November 10, 1876. HR44A-H8.4, National Archives, Washington, D.C.

———. *To the Friends of Woman Suffrage.* N.p., 1877. HR45A-H11.7, National Archives, Washington, D.C.

Philadelphia Female Anti-Slavery Society. *An Address of the Female Anti-Slavery Society of Philadelphia to the Women of Pennsylvania with the Form of a Petition to the Congress of the U. States.* Philadelphia: Merrihew and Gunn, 1836.

Putnam, John Milton. *An Address Delivered at Concord, New Hampshire, December 25, 1835, Before the Female Anti-Slavery Society of that Place. By John M. Putnam, Pastor of the Congregational Church in Dumbarton. Published at the request of the Society.* Concord, N.H.: Elbridge G. Chase, 1836.

Rossi, Alice S., ed. *The Feminist Papers: From Adams to de Beauvoir.* Boston: Northeastern University Press, 1973.

The Sentiments of an American Woman. Philadelphia: n.p., 1780.

Stanton, Elizabeth Cady. *An Appeal to the Women of the Republic.* Woman's National Loyal League, January 25, 1864. SEN 38A-H2o, National Archives, Washington, D.C.

Stewart, Maria. *Maria W. Stewart, America's First Black Woman Political Writer: Essays and Speeches.* Edited by Marilyn Richardson. Bloomington: Indiana University Press, 1987.

Stone, Lucy. *An Appeal to the Men and Women of America.* January 29, 1869. Petitions and Memorials, SEN 40A-H10.3, 40th Congress, Records of the U.S. Senate, Record Group 46, National Archives, Washington, D.C.

Sunderland, Rev. La Roy. *The Testimony of God Against Slavery, or a Collection of Passages from the Bible, Which Show the Sin of Holding Property in Man. With Notes.* Boston: Webster and Southard, 1835.

Walker, David. *Walker's Appeal, In Four Articles; Together With A Preamble, To The Coloured Citizens of the World, But In Particular, And Very Expressly, To Those Of The United States of America.* 2d ed. with corrections. Boston: David Walker, 1830.

Washington, George. *The Writings of George Washington.* Edited by Worthington Chauncey Ford. 14 vols. New York: G. P. Putnam's Sons, 1889–93.

Webster, Daniel. *The Works of Daniel Webster, 1782-1852.* 6 vols. Boston: Little, Brown, 1854.

Weld, Theodore Dwight. *Letters of Theodore Dwight Weld, Angelina Grimké Weld, and Sarah Grimké, 1822-1844.* Edited by Gilbert H. Barnes and Dwight W. Dumond. 2 vols. New York: D. Appleton-Century, 1934.

Whittier, John G. *Justice and Expediency; Slavery Considered with a View to Its Rightful and Effectual Remedy, Abolition.* Haverhill, Mass.: C. P. Thayer, 1833. Reprinted in *Essays and Pamphlets on Antislavery.* Westport, Conn.: Negro Universities Press, 1970.

———. *The Letters of John Greenleaf Whittier, 1828-1845.* Edited by John B. Pickard. 3 vols. Cambridge: Harvard University Press, Belknap Press, 1975.

Winslow, Hubbard. *"The Appropriate Sphere of Woman": A Discourse Delivered in the Bowdoin Street Church, July 9, 1837.* Boston: n.p., 1837.

MINUTES, PROCEEDINGS, RECORDS, AND REPORTS

American Anti-Slavery Society. *Annual Report of the American Antislavery Society.* New York: Dorr and Butterfield, 1834–37.

———. *Proceedings of the American Anti-Slavery Society at Its Third Decade.* New York, 1864. Reprint, New York: Arno Press, 1969.

Anti-Slavery Convention of American Women. *Proceedings of the Anti-Slavery Convention of American Women, Held in the City of New York, May 9th, 10th, 11th, and 12th, 1837.* New York: William S. Dorr, 1837.

———. *Proceedings of the Anti-Slavery Convention of American Women, Held in the City of Philadelphia, May 15th, 16th, 17th and 18th, 1838.* Philadelphia: Merrihew and Gunn, 1838.

—————. *Proceedings of the Third Anti-Slavery Convention of American Women, Held in the City of Philadelphia, May 1st, 2d and 3d, 1839.* Philadelphia: Merrihew and Thompson, 1839.

Boston Female Anti-Slavery Society. *Annual Report of the Boston Female Anti-Slavery Society.* Boston: The Society, 1834–44.

—————. *Report of the Boston Female Anti-Slavery Society, with a Concise Statement of Events Previous and Subsequent to the Annual Meeting of 1835.* Boston: Boston Female Anti-Slavery Society, 1836.

Glasgow Ladies Auxiliary Emancipation Society. *Three Year's Female Anti-Slavery Effort, in Britain and America: Being a Report of the Proceedings of the Glasgow Ladies Auxiliary Emancipation Society, Since Its Formation in January 1834.* Glasgow: Aird and Russell, 1837.

Ladies' New York City Anti-Slavery Society. *Third Annual Report of the Ladies' New-York City Anti-Slavery Society.* New York: William S. Dorr, 1838.

Lynn (Mass.) Female Anti-Slavery Society. Records of the Lynn, Massachusetts, Female Anti-Slavery Society. Lynn Historical Society, Anti-Slavery Collection, Boston Public Library, Boston, Mass.

Massachusetts Anti-Slavery Society. *Annual Report Presented to the Massachusetts Anti-Slavery Society by Its Board of Managers.* Westport, Conn.: Negro Universities Press, 1833–53.

Massachusetts General Court Joint Special Committee. *Report and Resolves on the Right of Petition.* N.p., 1838.

National Negro Conventions. *Minutes of the Proceedings of the National Negro Conventions, 1830–1864.* Edited by Howard Holman Bell. 1913. Reprint, New York: Arno Press, 1969.

Philadelphia Female Anti-Slavery Society. *Annual Report of the Philadelphia Female Anti-Slavery Society.* Philadelphia: The Society, 1834–69.

ARTICLES, BOOKS, AND DISSERTATIONS

Abzug, Robert H. *Cosmos Crumbling: American Reform and the Religious Imagination.* New York: Oxford University Press, 1994.

Andrew, John A. *Abolitionism: A Revolutionary Movement.* Boston: Twayne, 1989.

—————. *From Revivals to Removal: Jeremiah Evarts, the Cherokee Nation, and the Search for the Soul of America.* Athens: University of Georgia Press, 1992.

Aptheker, Herbert. *Abolitionism: A Revolutionary Movement.* Boston: Twayne, 1989.

Ashe, Samuel A'Court. *History of North Carolina.* 8 vols. Greensboro, N.C.: Charles L. Van Noppen, 1908.

Auer, Jeffery J., ed. *Antislavery and Disunion, 1858–1861: Studies in the Rhetoric of Compromise and Conflict.* New York: Harper and Row, 1963.

Bacon, Margaret Hope. *Valiant Friend: The Life of Lucretia Mott.* New York: Walker, 1980.

———. *Mothers of Feminism: The Story of Quaker Women in America.* San Francisco: Harper and Row, 1986.

———. "'One Great Bundle of Humanity': Frances Ellen Watkins Harper, 1825–1911." *Pennsylvania Magazine of History and Biography* 113 (January 1989): 21–43.

———. "By Moral Force Alone: The Antislavery Women and Nonresistance." In *The Abolitionist Sisterhood: Women's Political Culture in Antebellum America,* edited by Jean Fagan Yellin and John C. Van Horne, 275–97. Ithaca: Cornell University Press, 1994.

Bailey, Raymond C. *Popular Influence upon Public Policy: Petitioning in Eighteenth-Century Virginia.* Westport, Conn.: Greenwood Press, 1979.

Baker, Paula. "The Domestication of American Politics: Women and American Political Society, 1780–1920." *American Historical Review* 89 (June 1984): 620–47.

Barnes, Gilbert H. *The Antislavery Impulse, 1830-1844.* New York: Harcourt, Brace and World, 1933.

Basch, Norma. "Equity vs. Equality: Emerging Concepts of Women's Political Status in the Age of Jackson." *Journal of the Early Republic* 3 (Fall 1983): 297–318.

Beard, Mary Ritter. "The Legislative Influence of Unenfranchised Women." In *Mary Ritter Beard: A Sourcebook,* edited by Ann J. Lane, 89–94. New York: Schocken Books, 1977.

Bell, Howard Holman. *A Survey of the Negro Convention Movement, 1830-1861.* New York: Arno Press, 1969.

Bemis, Samuel Flagg. *John Quincy Adams and the Union.* New York: Knopf, 1956.

Bender, Thomas. *The Antislavery Debate: Capitalism and Abolitionism as a Problem in Historical Interpretation.* Berkeley: University of California Press, 1992.

Bethel, Elizabeth Rauh. *The Roots of African American Identity: Memory and History in Free Antebellum Communities.* New York: St. Martin's Press, 1997.

Birney, Catherine H. *The Grimké Sisters: Sarah and Angelina Grimké, the First American Women Advocates of Abolition and Woman's Rights.* Boston: Lee and Shepard, 1885.

Blackwell, Alice Stone. *Lucy Stone: Pioneer of Woman's Rights.* Boston: Little, Brown, 1930.

Blauvelt, Martha Tomhave. "Women and Revivalism." In *Women and Religion in America,* edited by Rosemary Radford Ruether and Mary Skinner Keller. Vol. 1, *The Nineteenth Century,* 1–45. San Francisco: Harper and Row, 1981.

Blocker, Jack S., Jr. *American Temperance Movements: Cycles of Reform.* Boston: Twayne, 1989.

Bogin, Ruth. "Petitioning and the New Moral Economy of Post-Revolutionary America." *William and Mary Quarterly* 3 (July 1988): 391–425.

Bordin, Ruth. *Women and Temperance: The Quest for Power and Liberty, 1873–1900.* Philadelphia: Temple University Press, 1990.

Bowers, John W., and Donovan Ochs. *The Rhetoric of Agitation and Control.* Reading, Mass.: Addison-Wesley, 1971.

Boydston, Jeanne, Mary Kelley, and Anne Margolis, eds. *The Limits of Sisterhood: The Beecher Sisters on Women's Rights and Woman's Sphere.* Chapel Hill: University of North Carolina Press, 1988.

Boylan, Ann M. "Women and Politics in the Era before Seneca Falls." *Journal of the Early Republic* 10 (Fall 1990): 363–82.

———. "Benevolence and Antislavery Activity among African American Women in New York and Boston, 1820–1840." In *The Abolitionist Sisterhood: Women's Political Culture in Antebellum America,* edited by Jean Fagan Yellin and John C. Van Horne, 119–37. Ithaca: Cornell University Press, 1994.

Bronner, Edwin B. "An Early Example of Political Action by Women." *Bulletin of the Friends Historical Association* 43 (1954): 29–32.

Brooke, John L. *The Heart of the Commonwealth: Society and Political Culture in Worcester County, Massachusetts, 1713–1861.* Cambridge: Cambridge University Press, 1989.

Brown, A. L. *The Governance of Late Medieval England, 1272–1461.* London: Edward Arnold, 1989.

Brown, Amy Benson. "'A System of Complicated Crimes': The (Con)Fusion of Subjects in Angelina Grimké's Public Speeches." *Women's Studies* 27 (December 1997): 31–59.

Brown, Elisabeth Potts, and Susan Mosher Stuard, eds. *Witness for Change: Quaker Women over Three Centuries.* New Brunswick: Rutgers University Press, 1989.

Brown, Ira V. "The Cradle of Feminism: The Philadelphia Female Anti-Slavery Society, 1833–1840." *Pennsylvania Magazine of History and Biography* 102 (April 1978): 143–66.

———. "'Am I Not a Woman and a Sister?': The Anti-Slavery Convention of American Women, 1837–1839." *Pennsylvania History* 50 (January 1983): 1–19.

Browne, Stephen H. "'Like Gory Spectres': Representing Evil in Theodore Weld's *American Slavery As It Is.*" *Quarterly Journal of Speech* 80 (August 1994): 277–92.

———. "Encountering Angelina Grimké: Violence, Identity, and the Creation of Radical Community." *Quarterly Journal of Speech* 82 (February 1996): 55–73.

———. *Angelina Grimké: Rhetoric, Identity, and the Radical Imagination.* East Lansing: Michigan State University Press, 1999.

Buckley, Thomas E. "'Placed in the Power of Violence': The Divorce Petition of

Evelina Gregory Roane, 1824." *Virginia Magazine of History and Biography* 100 (January 1992): 29–78.

Burgess, John W. *The Middle Period, 1817–1858.* New York: Charles Scribner's Sons, 1897.

Butler, Judith. *Gender Trouble: Feminism and the Subversion of Identity.* New York: Routledge, 1990.

Butt, Ronald. *A History of Parliament: The Middle Ages.* London: Constable, 1989.

Carwardine, Richard J. *Evangelicals and Politics in Antebellum America.* Knoxville: University of Tennessee Press, 1997.

Chace, Elizabeth Buffum. *Anti-Slavery Reminiscences.* Central Falls, R.I.: n.p., 1891.

Cmiel, Kenneth. *Democratic Eloquence: The Fight over Popular Speech in Nineteenth-Century America.* New York: William Morrow, 1990.

Cogan, Jacob Katz, and Lori D. Ginzberg. "The 1846 Petition for Woman's Suffrage, New York State Constitutional Convention." *Signs* 22 (Winter 1997): 424–39.

Combs, Jerald A. *The Jay Treaty: Political Battleground of the Founding Fathers.* Berkeley: University of California Press, 1970.

Cott, Nancy F. "Young Women in the Second Great Awakening." *Feminist Studies* 3 (Fall 1975): 15–29.

————. "Divorce and the Changing Status of Women in Eighteenth-Century Massachusetts." *William and Mary Quarterly,* 3d ser., 33 (October 1976): 586–614.

————. *The Bonds of Womanhood: Woman's Sphere in New England, 1780–1835.* New Haven: Yale University Press, 1977.

Cromwell, John Wesley. *The Early Negro Convention Movement.* 1904. Reprint, Arno Press, 1969.

Cromwell, Otelia. *Lucretia Mott.* 1958. Reprint, New York: Russell and Russell, 1971.

Dannenbaum, Jed. *Drink and Disorder: Temperance Reform in Cincinnati from the Washingtonian Revival to the WCTU.* Urbana: University of Illinois Press, 1984.

Daughton, Suzanne M. "The Fine Texture of Enactment: Iconicity as Empowerment in Angelina Grimké's Pennsylvania Hall Address." *Women's Studies in Communication* 18 (Spring 1995): 19–43.

Davidson, Cathy N. "Female Education, Literacy, and the Politics of Sentimental Fiction." *Women's Studies International Forum* 9 (1986): 309–12.

Davis, David Brion. *The Problem of Slavery in the Age of Revolution, 1770–1823.* Ithaca: Cornell University Press, 1975.

Davis, Thomas J. "Emancipation Rhetoric, Natural Rights, and Revolutionary New England: A Note on Four Black Petitions in Massachusetts, 1773–1777." *New England Quarterly* 62 (June 1989): 248–63.

Deckard, Barbara. *The Women's Movement.* New York: Harper and Row, 1975.

Dick, Robert C. *Black Protest: Issues and Tactics*. Westport, Conn.: Greenwood
    Press, 1974.
diGiacomantonio, William C. "'For the Gratification of a Volunteering Society':
    Antislavery and Pressure Group Politics in the First Federal Congress."
    Journal of the Early Republic 15 (Summer 1995): 169–97.
Dillon, Merton L. *Benjamin Lundy and the Quest for Negro Freedom*. Urbana:
    University of Illinois Press, 1966.
———. *The Abolitionists: The Growth of a Dissenting Minority*. DeKalb: Northern
    Illinois University Press, 1974.
Douglas, Ann. *The Feminization of American Culture*. New York: Knopf, 1977.
Drescher, Seymour. "Public Opinion and the Destruction of British Colonial
    Slavery." In *Slavery and British Society, 1776–1846*, edited by James Walvin,
    22–48. Baton Rouge: Louisiana State University Press, 1982.
———. *Capitalism and Antislavery: British Mobilization in Comparative Perspective*.
    New York: Oxford University Press, 1987.
———. "British Way, French Way: Opinion Building and Revolution in the
    Second French Slave Emancipation." *American Historical Review* 96 (June
    1991): 709–34.
DuBois, Ellen Carol. *Feminism and Suffrage: The Emergence of an Independent
    Women's Movement in America, 1848–1869*. Ithaca: Cornell University Press,
    1978.
———, ed. *Elizabeth Cady Stanton, Susan B. Anthony: Correspondence, Writings,
    Speeches*. New York: Schocken Books, 1981.
Dumond, Dwight L. *Antislavery: The Crusade for Freedom in America*. New York:
    Norton, 1961.
Egerton, Douglas R. *Gabriel's Rebellion: The Virginia Slave Conspiracies of 1800 and
    1802*. Chapel Hill: University of North Carolina Press, 1993.
Eltis, David. *Economic Growth and the Ending of the Transatlantic Slave Trade*. New
    York: Oxford University Press, 1987.
Enstad, Nan. "Fashioning Political Identities: Cultural Studies and the Historical
    Construction of Political Subjects." *American Quarterly* 50 (December 1998):
    745–82.
———. *Ladies of Labor, Girls of Adventure: Working Women, Popular Culture, and
    Labor Politics at the Turn of the Twentieth Century*. New York: Columbia
    University Press, 1999.
Epstein, Barbara Leslie. *The Politics of Domesticity: Women, Evangelism, and
    Temperance in Nineteenth-Century America*. Middletown, Conn.: Wesleyan
    University Press, 1981.
Fascell, Dante B. "Ten Historic Congressional Decisions." *Congressional Record:
    Extension of Remarks*. 100th Cong., 1st sess., June 18, 1987, 11.
Flexner, Eleanor. *Century of Struggle: The Woman's Rights Movement in the United
    States*. Cambridge: Harvard University, Belknap Press, 1975.

Foner, Philip S. *Three Women Who Dared: Prudence Crandall, Margaret Douglass, Myrtilla Miner, Champions of Antebellum Black Education.* Westport, Conn.: Greenwood Press, 1984.

Formisano, Robert P. *The Transformation of Political Culture: Massachusetts Parties, 1790s–1840s.* New York: Oxford University Press, 1983.

Foster, Elizabeth Read. "Petitions and the Petition of Right." *Journal of British Studies* 14 (November 1974): 22–45.

Fraser, Peter. "Public Petitioning and Parliament before 1832." *History* 46 (October 1961): 195–211.

Frederick, David C. "John Quincy Adams, Slavery, and the Disappearance of the Right to Petition." *Law and History Review* 9 (Spring 1991): 113–55.

Freehling, William W. *Prelude to Civil War: The Nullification Controversy in South Carolina.* New York: Harper and Row, 1965.

———. *The Road to Disunion: Secessionists at Bay, 1776–1854.* New York: Oxford University Press, 1991.

Friedman, Jean E. *The Enclosed Garden: Women and Community in the Evangelical South, 1830–1900.* Chapel Hill: University of North Carolina Press, 1985.

Fuller, Edmund. *Prudence Crandall: An Incident of Racism in Nineteenth-Century Connecticut.* Middletown, Conn.: Wesleyan University Press, 1971.

Giddings, Paula. *When and Where I Enter: The Impact of Black Women on Race and Sex in America.* New York: Bantam Books, 1984.

Gillespie, Joanna Bowen. "'The Clear Leadings of Providence': Pious Memoirs and the Problems of Self-Realization for Women in the Early Nineteenth Century." *Journal of the Early Republic* 5 (Summer 1985): 197–221.

Ginzberg, Lori D. *Women and the Work of Benevolence: Morality, Politics, and Class in the Nineteenth-Century United States.* New Haven: Yale University Press, 1990.

Glickstein, Jonathan A. *Concepts of Free Labor in Antebellum America.* New Haven: Yale University Press, 1991.

Goodman, Paul. *Of One Blood: Abolitionism and the Origins of Racial Equality.* Berkeley: University of California Press, 1998.

Gordon, Sarah Barringer. *The Mormon Question: Polygamy and Constitutional Conflict in Nineteenth-Century America.* Chapel Hill: University of North Carolina Press, 2002.

Graebner, Norman A., Gilbert C. Fite, and Philip L. White. *A History of the American People.* New York: McGraw Hill, 1971.

Grant, Donald L. *The Anti-Lynching Movement, 1883–1932.* San Francisco: R and E Research Associates, 1975.

Gross, Bella. *Clarion Call: The History and Development of the Negro People's Convention Movement in the United States from 1817 to 1840.* New York: n.p., 1947.

Gunderson, Robert Gray. *The Log-Cabin Campaign.* Lexington: University Press of Kentucky, 1957.

Guy, J. A. "The Origins of the Petition of Right Reconsidered." *Historical Journal* 25 (1982): 289–312.

Halbersleben, Karen. "'She Hath Done What She Could': Women's Participation in the British Antislavery Movement, 1825–1870." Ph.D. diss., State University of New York, Buffalo, 1987.

Hamand, Wendy F. "The Woman's National Loyal League: Feminist Abolitionists and the Civil War." *Civil War History* 35 (1989): 39–58.

Hamand Venet, Wendy. *Neither Ballots nor Bullets: Women Abolitionists and the Civil War.* Charlottesville: University Press of Virginia, 1991.

Hansen, Debra Gold. *Strained Sisterhood: Gender and Class in the Boston Female Anti-Slavery Society.* Amherst: University of Massachusetts Press, 1993.

———. "The Boston Female Anti-Slavery Society and the Limits of Gender Politics." In *The Abolitionist Sisterhood: Women's Political Culture in Antebellum America,* edited by Jean Fagan Yellin and John C. Van Horne, 45–65. Ithaca: Cornell University Press, 1994.

Hardy, B. Carmon. *Solemn Covenant: The Mormon Polygamous Passage.* Urbana: University of Illinois Press, 1992.

Harper, Ida Husted. *The Life and Work of Susan B. Anthony.* Indianapolis: Bowen-Merrill, 1899.

Haskins, George L. "The Petitions of Representatives in the Parliaments of Edward I." *English Historical Review* 53 (January 1938): 1–20.

Henry, Katherine. "Angelina Grimké's Rhetoric of Exposure." *American Quarterly* 49 (June 1997): 328–55.

Hersh, Blanche Glassman. *The Slavery of Sex: Feminist Abolitionists in America.* Chicago: University of Illinois Press, 1978.

Hershberger, Mary. "Mobilizing Women, Anticipating Abolition: The Struggle against Indian Removal in the 1830s." *Journal of American History* 86 (June 1999): 15–40.

Hewitt, Nancy A. "The Social Origins of Women's Antislavery Politics in Western New York." In *Crusaders and Compromisers: Essays on the Relationship of the Antislavery Struggle to the Antebellum Party System,* edited by Alan M. Kraut, 205–34. Westport, Conn.: Greenwood Press, 1983.

———. *Women's Activism and Social Change: Rochester, New York, 1822–1872.* Ithaca: Cornell University Press, 1984.

———. "Yankee Evangelicals and Agrarian Quakers: Gender, Religion, and Class in the Formation of Feminist Consciousness in Nineteenth-Century Rochester, New York." *Radical History Review* 28–30 (1984): 327–42.

———. "Feminist Friends: Agrarian Quakers and the Emergence of Woman's Rights in America." *Feminist Studies* 12 (Spring 1986): 27–49.

Higgins, Patricia. "The Reactions of Women, with Special Reference to Women

Petitioners." In *Politics, Religion, and the English Civil War,* edited by Brian
Manning, 177–222. London: Edward Arnold, 1973.

Higginson, Stephen A. "A Short History of the Right to Petition Government for
the Redress of Grievances." *Yale Law Review Journal* 96 (1986): 142–66.

Hoganson, Kristin. "Garrisonian Abolitionists and the Rhetoric of Gender,
1850–1860." *American Quarterly* 45 (December 1993): 558–95.

Holdsworth, William Searle. *A History of English Law.* Boston: Little, Brown,
1923, 1938.

Holt, Michael F. *The Rise and Fall of the American Whig Party: Jacksonian Politics
and the Onset of the Civil War.* New York: Oxford University Press, 1999.

Horton, James Oliver. "Freedom's Yoke: Gender Conventions among
Antebellum Free Blacks." *Feminist Studies* 12 (Spring 1986): 51–76.

———. *Free People of Color: Inside the African American Community.* Washington,
D.C.: Smithsonian Institution Press, 1993.

Howard, Warren S. *American Slavers and the Federal Law, 1837–1862.* Berkeley:
University of California Press, 1963.

Hudson, Winthrop S. "Early Nineteenth-Century Evangelical Religion and
Women's Liberation." *Foundations* 23 (April–June 1980): 181–85.

Hutson, James H. *A Decent Respect to the Opinions of Mankind.* Washington, D.C.:
Library of Congress, 1975.

Isaac, Rhys. *The Transformation of Virginia, 1740–1790.* Chapel Hill: University of
North Carolina Press, 1982.

Isenberg, Nancy. *Sex and Citizenship in Antebellum America.* Chapel Hill:
University of North Carolina Press, 1998.

James, Janet Wilson. *Women in American Religion.* Philadelphia: University of
Pennsylvania Press, 1980.

Jameson, John Alexander. *A Treatise on Constitutional Conventions: Their History,
Powers, and Modes of Proceeding.* 4th ed. Chicago: Callaghan, 1887.

Jameson, J. Franklin. "The Early Political Uses of the Word *Convention.*" *American
Historical Review* 3 (April 1898): 477–87.

Japp, Phyllis M. "Esther or Isaiah?: The Abolitionist-Feminist Rhetoric of
Angelina Grimké." *Quarterly Journal of Speech* 71 (August 1985): 335–48.

Jeffrey, Julie Roy. *The Great Silent Army of Abolitionism: Ordinary Women in the
Antislavery Movement.* Chapel Hill: University of North Carolina Press, 1998.

Jolliffe, John Edward Austin. *The Constitutional History of Medieval England.*
London: Adam and Charles Black, 1937.

Karcher, Carolyn L. *The First Woman in the Republic: A Cultural Biography of Lydia
Maria Child.* Durham, N.C.: Duke University Press, 1994.

Kelley, Mary. "Reading Women/Women Reading: The Making of Learned
Women in Antebellum America." *Journal of American History* 83 (September
1996): 401–24.

Kennedy, George. "The Rhetoric of the Early Christian Liturgy." In *Language and*

Worship of the Church, edited by David Jasper and R. C. D. Jasper, 26–43. New York: St. Martin's Press, 1990.

Kerber, Linda K. *Women of the Republic: Intellect and Ideology in Revolutionary America.* New York: Norton, 1980.

——. "Separate Spheres, Female Worlds, Woman's Place: The Rhetoric of Women's History." *Journal of American History* 75 (June 1988): 9–39.

——. "The Meanings of Citizenship." *Journal of American History* 84 (December 1997): 833–54.

——. *"No Constitutional Right to Be Ladies": Women and the Obligations of Citizenship.* New York: Hill and Wang, 1998.

Kerr, Andrea Moore. *Lucy Stone: Speaking Out for Equality.* New Brunswick, N.J.: Rutgers University Press, 1995.

Kierner, Cynthia A. *Southern Women in Revolution, 1776-1800: Personal and Political Narratives.* Columbia: University of South Carolina Press, 1998.

Knee, Stuart E. "The Quaker Petition of 1790: A Challenge to Democracy in Early America." *Slavery and Abolition* 6 (September 1985): 151–59.

Knights, Mark. "Petitioning and the Political Theorists: John Locke, Algernon Sidney, and London's 'Monster' Petition of 1680." *Past and Present* 138 (February 1993): 94–111.

Kraditor, Aileen A. *Means and Ends in American Abolitionism: Garrison and His Critics on Strategy and Tactics, 1834-1850.* Chicago: Ivan R. Dee, 1967.

——. *Up from the Pedestal: Selected Writings in the History of American Feminism.* Chicago: Quadrangle, 1968.

Kraut, Alan. "The Forgotten Reformers: A Profile of Third Party Abolitionists in Antebellum New York." In *Antislavery Reconsidered: New Perspectives on the Abolitionists,* edited by Lewis Perry and Michael Fellman, 119–48. Baton Rouge: Louisiana State University Press, 1979.

Lapsansky, Emma Jones. "Feminism, Freedom, and Community: Charlotte Forten and Women Activists in Nineteenth-Century Philadelphia." *Pennsylvania Magazine of History and Biography* 113 (January 1989): 3–19.

Laurence, Anne. "Women's Work and the English Civil War." *History Today* 42 (June 1992): 20–25.

Lebsock, Suzanne. *The Free Women of Petersburg: Status and Culture in a Southern Town, 1784-1860.* New York: Norton, 1984.

Lerner, Gerda. "The Lady and the Mill Girl: Changes in the Status of Women in the Age of Jackson." *Mid-Continent American Studies Journal* 10 (Spring 1969): 5–15.

——. "The Political Activities of Antislavery Women." In *The Majority Finds Its Past: Placing Women in History,* edited by Gerda Lerner, 112–28. New York: Oxford University Press, 1979.

——. *The Feminist Thought of Sarah Grimké.* New York: Oxford University Press, 1998.

————. *The Grimké Sisters from South Carolina: Pioneers for Woman's Rights and Abolition*. 2d ed. New York: Oxford University Press, 1998.

Lewis, Jan. "'Of Every Age Sex & Condition': The Representation of Women in the Constitution." *Journal of the Early Republic* 15 (Fall 1995): 359–87.

Leys, Colin. "Petitioning in the Nineteenth and Twentieth Centuries." *Political Studies* 31 (1955): 45–64.

Ludlum, Robert P. "The Antislavery 'Gag Rule': History and Argument." *Journal of Negro History* 26 (April 1941): 202–43.

Lutz, Alma. *Crusade for Freedom: Women in the Antislavery Movement*. Boston: Beacon Press, 1968.

Mack, Peter. "Rhetoric and Liturgy." In *Language and Worship of the Church*, edited by David Jasper and R. C. D. Jasper, 82–109. New York: St. Martin's Press, 1990.

Magdol, Edward. "A Window on the Abolitionist Constituency: Antislavery Petitions, 1836–1839." In *Crusaders and Compromisers: Essays on the Relationship of the Antislavery Struggle to the Antebellum Party System*, edited by Alan M. Kraut, 45–70. Westport, Conn.: Greenwood Press, 1983.

————. *The Antislavery Rank and File: A Social Profile of the Abolitionists' Constituency*. Westport, Conn.: Greenwood Press, 1986.

Mandel, Bernard. *Labor: Free and Slave*. New York: Associated Authors, 1955.

M'Arthur, Ellen A. "Women Petitioners and the Long Parliament." *English Historical Review* 24 (October 1909): 698–709.

Matthews, Glenna. *The Rise of Public Woman: Women's Power and Woman's Place in the United States, 1630–1970*. New York: Oxford University Press, 1992.

May, Robert E. "Southern Elite Women, Sectional Extremism, and the Male Political Sphere: The Case of John A. Quitman's Wife and Female Descendants, 1847–1931." *Journal of Mississippi History* 50 (November 1988): 251–85.

Mayer, Henry. *All on Fire: William Lloyd Garrison and the Abolition of Slavery*. New York: St. Martin's Press, 1998.

McBride, David. "Black Protest against Racial Politics: Gardner, Hinton, and Their Memorial of 1838." *Pennsylvania History* 66 (April 1979): 149–62.

McFaul, John M. "Expediency vs. Morality: Jacksonian Politics and Slavery." *Journal of American History* 62 (June 1975): 24–39.

McInerney, Daniel J. *The Fortunate Heirs of Freedom: Abolition and Republican Thought*. Lincoln: University of Nebraska Press, 1994.

McKivigan, John R. *The War against Proslavery Religion: Abolition and the Northern Churches, 1830–1865*. Ithaca: Cornell University Press, 1984.

McMurry, Linda O. *To Keep the Waters Troubled: The Life of Ida B. Wells*. New York: Oxford University Press, 1998.

Meehan, Thomas R. "'Not Made Out of Levity': Evolution of Divorce in Early

Pennsylvania." *Pennsylvania Magazine of History and Biography* 92 (October 1968): 441-64.

Melder, Keith E. *Beginnings of Sisterhood: The American Woman's Rights Movement, 1800-1850.* New York: Schocken Books, 1977.

———. "Abby Kelley and the Process of Liberation." In *The Abolitionist Sisterhood: Women's Political Culture in Antebellum America,* edited by Jean Fagan Yellin and John C. Van Horne, 231-48. Ithaca: Cornell University Press, 1994.

Midgley, Clare. *Women against Slavery: The British Campaigns, 1780-1870.* London: Routledge, 1992.

Miller, William Lee. *Arguing about Slavery: The Great Battle in the United States Congress.* New York: Knopf, 1996.

Morgan, Edmund S. *Inventing the People: The Rise of Popular Sovereignty in England and America.* New York: Norton, 1988.

Morgan, Edmund S., and Helen M. Morgan. *The Stamp Act Crisis: Prologue to Revolution.* Chapel Hill: University of North Carolina Press, 1953.

Myers, Alec Reginald. "Parliamentary Petitions in the Fifteenth Century." *English Historical Review* 52 (July 1937): 385-404.

Nicholls, David. "Addressing God as Ruler: Prayer and Petition." *British Journal of Sociology* 44 (March 1993): 125-41.

Nye, Russel B. *Fettered Freedom: Civil Liberties and the Slavery Controversy, 1830-1860.* East Lansing: Michigan State University Press, 1949.

Oates, Stephen B. *The Fires of Jubilee: Nat Turner's Fierce Rebellion.* New York: Harper and Row, 1975.

Ohline, Howard A. "Slavery, Economics, and Congressional Politics, 1790." *Journal of Southern History* 46 (August 1980): 335-60.

"On Letting the Laity Litigate: The Petition Clause and Unauthorized Practice Rules." *University of Pennsylvania Law Review* 132 (July 1984): 1515-45.

Osler, Anne Lewis. "'That Damned Mob': Northern and Southern Women Writers and the Coming of the American Civil War." Ph.D. diss., University of Wisconsin, Madison, 1995.

Parsons, Lynn H. "Censuring Old Man Eloquent: Foreign Policy and Disunion, 1842." *Capitol Studies* 3 (Fall 1975): 89-106.

Pease, Jane E., and William H. Pease. *They Who Would Be Free: Blacks' Search for Freedom, 1830-1861.* New York: Anteneum, 1974.

Pease, William Henry, ed. *The Antislavery Argument.* Indianapolis: Bobbs-Merrill, 1965.

Perry, Lewis, and Michael Fellman, eds. *Antislavery Reconsidered.* Baton Rouge: Louisiana State University Press, 1979.

Porter, Dorothy B. "The Organized Educational Activities of Negro Literary Societies, 1828-1846." *Journal of Negro Education* 5 (October 1936): 555-76.

Potter, David M. *The Impending Crisis, 1848-1861.* New York: Harper and Row, 1976.

Prucha, Francis Paul. "Protest by Petition: Jeremiah Evarts and the Cherokee Indians." *Proceedings of the Massachusetts Historical Society* 97 (1985): 43–58.

Quarles, Benjamin. *Black Abolitionists.* New York: Oxford University Press, 1969.

Rable, George G. "Slavery, Politics, and the South: The Gag Rule as a Case Study." *Capitol Studies* 3 (Fall 1975): 69–87.

Ragsdale, Bruce A., and Joel D. Treese. *Black Americans in Congress, 1870-1989.* Washington, D.C.: U.S. Government Printing Office, 1990.

Ramsay, David. *Ramsay's History of South Carolina.* Newberry, S.C.: W. J. Duffie; Charleston: Walker, Evans, 1858.

Rayner, Doris. "The Forms and Machinery of the 'Commune Petition' in the Fourteenth Century." *English Historical Review* 56 (October 1941): 549–70.

Reed, Harry. *Platform for Change: The Foundations of the Northern Free Black Community, 1775-1865.* East Lansing: Michigan State University Press, 1994.

Rice, C. Duncan. "The Anti-Slavery Mission of George Thompson to the United States, 1834–1835." *Journal of American Studies* 2 (April 1968): 13–31.

Rice, Charles E. "Freedom of Petition." In *Encyclopedia of the American Constitution,* edited by Leonard W. Levy, Kenneth L. Karst, and Dennis J. Mahoney, 2:789–90. New York: Macmillan, 1986.

Richards, Leonard L. *The Life and Times of Congressman John Quincy Adams.* New York: Oxford University Press, 1986.

Ruether, Rosemary Radford, and Rosemary Skinner Keller, eds. *Women and Religion in America.* Vol. 1, *The Nineteenth Century.* San Francisco: Harper and Row, 1981.

Ryan, Mary P. "A Woman's Awakening: Evangelical Religion and the Families of Utica, New York, 1800–1840." In *Women in American Religion,* edited by Janet Wilson James, 89–110. Philadelphia: University of Pennsylvania Press, 1980.

———. *Cradle of the Middle Class: The Family in Oneida County, New York, 1790-1865.* New York: Cambridge University Press, 1981.

———. *Women in Public: Between Banners and Ballots, 1825-1880.* Baltimore: Johns Hopkins University Press, 1990.

———. "Gender and Public Access: Women's Politics in Nineteenth-Century America." In *Feminism, the Public and Private,* edited by Joan B. Landes, 195–222. Oxford: Oxford University Press, 1998.

Samuels, Shirley. *The Culture of Sentiment: Race, Gender, and Sentimentality in Nineteenth-Century America.* New York: Oxford University Press, 1992.

Sanchez-Eppler, Karen. "Bodily Bonds: The Intersecting Rhetorics of Feminism and Abolitionism." *Representations* 24 (Fall 1988): 28–59.

Schweninger, Loren, ed. *The Southern Debate over Slavery: Petitions to Southern Legislatures, 1778-1864.* Urbana: University of Illinois Press, 2001.

Scott, Anne Firor. "On Seeing and Not Seeing: A Case of Historical Invisibility." *Journal of American History* 71 (June–September 1984): 7–21.

———. "Most Invisible of All: Black Women's Voluntary Associations." *Journal of Southern History* 56 (February 1990): 3–22.

———. *The Southern Lady: From Pedestal to Politics, 1830–1930.* Charlottesville: University Press of Virginia, 1995.

Sewell, Richard H. *Ballots for Freedom: Antislavery Politics in the United States, 1837–1860.* New York: Oxford University Press, 1976.

Sidbury, James. *Ploughshares into Swords: Race, Rebellion, and Identity in Gabriel's Virginia, 1730–1810.* New York: Cambridge University Press, 1997.

Sklar, Kathryn Kish. *Catharine Beecher: A Study in American Domesticity.* New York: Norton, 1976.

———. "'Women Who Speak for an Entire Nation': American and British Women at the World Anti-Slavery Convention, London, 1840." In *The Abolitionist Sisterhood: Women's Political Culture in Antebellum America,* edited by Jean Fagan Yellin and John C. Van Horne, 301–33. Ithaca: Cornell University Press, 1994.

Smellie, Kingsley Bryce. "Right of Petition." In *Encyclopedia of the Social Sciences,* edited by Edwin R. A. Seligman and Alvin Johnson, 98–101. New York: Macmillan, 1937.

Smith, Don L. "The Right to Petition for Redress of Grievances: Constitutional Development and Interpretations." Ph.D. diss., Texas Tech University, 1971.

Smith, Kimberly K. *The Dominion of Voice: Riot, Reason, and Romance in Antebellum Politics.* Lawrence: University Press of Kansas, 1999.

Smith, Robert G. "The Arguments over Abolition Petitions in the House of Representatives in December, 1835: A Toulmin Analysis." Ph.D. diss., University of Minnesota, 1962.

Smith-Rosenberg, Carroll. "Beauty, the Beast, and the Militant Women: A Case Study in Sex Roles and Social Stress in Jacksonian America." *American Quarterly* 23 (October 1971): 562–84.

Soderlund, Jean. "Women's Authority in Pennsylvania and New Jersey Meetings, 1680–1760." *William and Mary Quarterly,* 3d ser., 44 (October 1987): 722–49.

———. "Priorities and Power: The Philadelphia Female Anti-Slavery Society." In *The Abolitionist Sisterhood: Women's Political Culture in Antebellum America,* edited by Jean Fagan Yellin and John C. Van Horne, 67–88. Ithaca: Cornell University Press, 1994.

Stansell, Christine. *City of Women: Sex and Class in New York, 1789–1860.* New York: Knopf, 1986.

Stanton, Elizabeth Cady. *Eighty Years and More: Reminiscences, 1815–1897.* 1898. Reprint, New York: Schocken Books, 1971.

Stanton, Elizabeth Cady, Susan B. Anthony, and Matilda J. Gage, eds. *History of Woman Suffrage.* 6 vols. New York: Fowler and Wells, 1919–22.

Sterling, Dorothy, ed. *Turning the World Upside Down: The Anti-Slavery Convention of American Women, Held in New York City, May 9-12, 1837*. New York: Feminist Press at the University of New York, 1987.

———. *Ahead of Her Time: Abby Kelley and the Politics of Antislavery*. New York: Norton, 1991.

Stewart, James Brewer. *Holy Warriors: The Abolitionists in American Society*. New York: Hill and Wang, 1976.

Stoneburner, Carol, and John Stoneburner. *The Influence of Quaker Women on American History*. Lewiston, N.Y.: Edwin Mellon Press, 1986.

Sumler-Lewis, Janice. "The Forten-Purvis Women of Philadelphia and the American Anti-Slavery Crusade." *Journal of Negro History* 66 (Winter 1981-82): 281-88.

Swerdlow, Amy. "Abolition's Conservative Sisters: The Ladies' New York City Anti-Slavery Societies, 1834-1840." In *The Abolitionist Sisterhood: Women's Political Culture in Antebellum America*, edited by Jean Fagan Yellin and John C. Van Horne, 31-44. Ithaca: Cornell University Press, 1994.

Terborg-Penn, Rosalyn. *African American Women in the Struggle for the Vote, 1850-1920*. Bloomington: Indiana University Press, 1998.

Turley, David. *The Culture of English Antislavery, 1780-1860*. London: Routledge, 1991.

Tyrrell, Ian R. *Sobering Up: From Temperance to Prohibition in Antebellum America, 1800-1860*. Westport, Conn.: Greenwood Press, 1979.

Van Broekhoven, Deborah Bingham. "'Let Your Names Be Enrolled': Method and Ideology in Women's Antislavery Petitioning." In *The Abolitionist Sisterhood: Women's Political Culture in Antebellum America*, edited by Jean Fagan Yellin and John C. Van Horne, 179-99. Ithaca: Cornell University Press, 1994.

———. *The Devotion of These Women: Rhode Island in the Antislavery Network*. Amherst: University of Massachusetts Press, 2002.

Van Wagoner, Richard S. *Mormon Polygamy: A History*. 2d ed. Salt Lake City: Signature Books, 1989.

Varon, Elizabeth. "'The Ladies Are Whigs': Lucy Barbour, Henry Clay, and Nineteenth-Century Virginia Politics." *Virginia Cavalcade* 41 (Autumn 1992): 72-83.

———. "Tippecanoe and the Ladies, Too: White Women and Party Politics in Antebellum Virginia." *Journal of American History* 82 (September 1995): 494-521.

———. *We Mean to Be Counted: White Women and Politics in Antebellum Virginia*. Chapel Hill: University of North Carolina Press, 1998.

Viet, Helen E., Kenneth R. Bowling, and Charlene Bangs Bickford, eds. *Creating the Bill of Rights: The Documentary Record from the First Federal Congress*. Baltimore: Johns Hopkins University Press, 1991.

von Holst, H. *The Constitutional and Political History of the United States*. Chicago: Callaghan, 1887.

Walsh, James P. "Mechanics and Citizens: The Connecticut Artisan Protest of 1792." *William and Mary Quarterly* 42 (January 1985): 66–89.

Walters, Ronald G. *The Antislavery Appeal*. Baltimore: Johns Hopkins University Press, 1976.

Walvin, James, ed. *Slavery and British Society, 1776-1846*. Baton Rouge: Louisiana State University Press, 1982.

Ward, John William. *Andrew Jackson, Symbol for an Age*. New York: Oxford University Press, 1955.

Waugh, Patricia. *Feminine Fictions: Revisiting the Postmodern*. London: Routledge, 1989.

Wellman, Judith. "Women and Radical Reform in Antebellum Upstate New York: A Profile of Grassroots Female Abolitionists." In *Clio Was a Woman: Studies in the History of American Women*, edited by Mabel E. Deutrich and Virginia C. Purdy, 113-27. Washington, D.C.: Howard University Press, 1980.

Wells, Ida B. *Crusade for Justice: The Autobiography of Ida B. Wells*, edited by Alfreda M. Duster. Chicago: University of Chicago Press, 1970.

Welter, Barbara. *Dimity Convictions*. Athens: Ohio University Press, 1976.

Wiecek, William. *The Sources of Antislavery Constitutionalism in America, 1760-1848*. Ithaca: Cornell University Press, 1977.

Williams, Carolyn L. "Religion, Race, and Gender in Antebellum American Radicalism: The Philadelphia Female Anti-Slavery Society, 1833-1870." Ph.D. diss., University of California, Los Angeles, 1991.

———. "The Female Antislavery Movement: Fighting against Racial Prejudice and Promoting Women's Rights in Antebellum America." In *The Abolitionist Sisterhood: Women's Political Culture in Antebellum America*, edited by Jean Fagan Yellin and John C. Van Horne, 159-77. Ithaca: Cornell University Press, 1994.

Wills, Garry. *Inventing America: Jefferson's Declaration of Independence*. New York: Vintage Books, 1978.

Winch, Julie. "'You Have Talents—Only Cultivate Them': Philadelphia's Black Female Literary Societies and the Abolitionist Crusade." In *The Abolitionist Sisterhood: Women's Political Culture in Antebellum America*, edited by Jean Fagan Yellin and John C. Van Horne, 101-18. Ithaca: Cornell University Press, 1994.

Wood, Betty. "White Women, Black Slaves, and the Law in Early National Georgia: The Sunburg Petition of 1791." *Historical Journal* 35 (September 1992): 611-22.

Wood, Gordon. *The Creation of the American Republic, 1776-1787*. New York: Norton, 1969.

Wright, John. *Early Prayer Books of America; Being a Descriptive Account of Prayer*

Books Published in the United States, Mexico and Canada. St. Paul, Minn.: privately printed, 1896.

Wyatt-Brown, Bertram. *Southern Honor: Ethics and Behavior in the Old South.* New York: Oxford University Press, 1982.

Yee, Shirley J. *Black Women Abolitionists: A Study in Activism, 1828–1860.* Knoxville: University of Tennessee Press, 1992.

Yellin, Jean Fagan. *Women and Sisters: The Antislavery Feminists in American Culture.* New Haven: Yale University Press, 1989.

Yellin, Jean Fagan, and John C. Van Horne, eds. *The Abolitionist Sisterhood: Women's Political Culture in Antebellum America.* Ithaca: Cornell University Press, 1994.

Zaeske, Susan. "The 'Promiscuous Audience' Controversy and the Emergence of the Early Woman's Rights Movement." *Quarterly Journal of Speech* 81 (May 1995): 191–207.

Zagarri, Rosemarie. "The Rights of Man and Woman in Post-Revolutionary America." *William and Mary Quarterly,* 3d ser., 55 (April 1998): 203–30.

Zboray, Ronald J., and Mary Saracino Zboray. "Whig Women, Politics, and Culture in the Campaign of 1840: Three Perspectives from Massachusetts." *Journal of the Early Republic* 17 (Summer 1997): 277–315.

INDEX

Lewis, Sarah, 149
Lincoln, Abraham, 77, 164, 167, 168, 196 (n. 5)
Literacy, political, 8, 106-7, 110, 199 (n. 14)
Literary societies, female, 42
Lockean philosophy, 143
Lovejoy, Elijah, 201 (n. 39)
Lucas, Stephen E., xi, xii
Lundy, Benjamin, 33, 90
Lynching, 2, 6, 13, 176, 177-78, 209 (n. 11)

Madison, James, 32
Magna Carta, 13
Marital titles, 109
Martin v. Commonwealth, 142
Massachusetts: antislavery women and state legislature, 120-21, 122-23; Great Petition to Congress, 155, 156, 165; petition of the women of Andover, 164, 166
Massachusetts Anti-Slavery Society, 147
McInerney, Daniel J., 66
Methodists, 82, 87
Ministers. *See* Clergy
Missouri Compromise, 32-33, 163
Monroe, James, 24
Moral duty, women's: used to justify petitioning, 7, 43, 47-48, 59, 61, 105, 148; replaced by right of citizenship, 8, 74, 77, 99, 103-4; and abolitionism, 29, 43; as rhetorical strategy, 59-60; challenged as justification, 127-28, 142. *See also* Citizenship; Moral superiority, women's; Political identity, women's: transformation of
Moral suasion, 2-3, 34-35, 43, 46, 145, 146, 151
Moral superiority, women's: used to

justify petitioning, 3, 65-68, 76, 124; and Revolutionary War ideals, 67; and political motivations, 74. *See also* Moral duty, women's
Motherhood, appeals to, 83, 87, 124, 136
Mott, Lucretia, 36, 82-83, 85, 86, 98, 123, 168

Names. *See* Labeling; Signatures
National Archives, xi, 173
National character, 66-68
National Negro Conventions, 33-34
Natural rights, 3, 12, 14, 80, 87-90, 116, 123, 124. *See also* Petition, right of
New England Anti-Slavery Society, 35, 145
Newspapers, antislavery, 101-3, 116
New York, N.Y., female antislavery convention in, 82, 84-85
New York State Anti-Slavery Society, 152
Nineteenth Amendment, 183-84. *See also* Woman suffrage
Novels: and free labor argument, 67; and women's signatures, 106
Nye, Russell, 77

Osborn, Charles, 32
Our Mothers Before Us project, xi-xii, 6

Parker, Mary, 85, 91, 149
Parliament, 11, 13-15, 30, 43-44
Pastoral letters, 113, 118
Patton, John, 79, 120, 128, 133
Petition, right of: nature and custom of, 1, 3, 16; as women's sole means of political influence, 1, 3, 116, 122, 145, 149, 159, 170, 180; subversive potential of, 1, 7, 12-13, 15, 18; history of, in America, 3, 11-13, 15-16, 18-21; and ruler's obligation to re-

ply, 3, 12, 13, 15; and slaves, 4, 20, 78–81; history of, in England, 11, 12, 13, 15; First Amendment and, 12, 19–20, 80; as method of bypassing suffrage, 13, 28; and American Revolution, 15–17; limits to, 20–21; and right of reception, 21; women's claims to, 74, 76, 87–88, 116–17, 170, 204 (n. 8); women's, debated by Congress, 126–43; and character of petitioners, 128–29, 132–36, 137–38

Petitioning, antislavery men's: history of, 14–36 passim; and public opinion, 20; national abolitionist leaders and, 35; moral suasion and, 35, 46, 145, 146, 151; published forms and, 50–51; labeling and citizenship in, 51; rhetoric of, 55, 60–61; signature gathering and, 110; politicization of, 146–47, 154

Petitioning, antislavery women's: acceptance of, 1, 9, 147, 164, 172, 176, 185 (n. 4); first collective, 1, 37; impact of, 2, 171–72, 174–84; gag rules and, 8, 72–74, 75–77, 78, 81, 92, 103, 160; history of, 14–46 passim; Cherokee removal campaign and, 27; immediate abolitionism and, 34; deterrences from, 38–41, 49, 53–54 (*see also* Appropriate behavior, women's); boycotting and, 41–42; reasons for increase in, 42–43; British women's effect on, 7, 43–46; phases of, 48–69, 74–125, 145–64, 167–72; published forms and, 50–51; audiences for, 52–53; and Thirteenth Amendment, 167–72; number of signatures, 173–74

—1831–36, 48–69; long petition forms, 48, 51; tone of, 48, 54–59; prayer and moral duty in, 48, 59–60; labeling and citizenship in, 51, 57; politi-

cal identity and, 51–52, 54, 61, 66; pattern of signatures in, 52, 58; "Fathers and Rulers of Our Country" form, 55, 56, 58, 59, 193 (n. 11); woman-and-sister appeal, 62–66; and national character, 66–69. *See also* Moral duty, women's; Moral superiority, women's; Prayer

—1837–40, 74–125; citizenship as justification for, 74, 77, 89, 91, 103, 116–17, 121; conventions and calls to petition, 74, 81–92, 121–25; centralization of, 81–86, 99–103; and appeals to motherhood, 83, 87; short petition forms, 92, 95, 96, 97–98; tone of, 97–99; transformation of political identity in, 105–11, 125; signatures and, 106–9; signature gathering and, 109–10; political experience and, 109–11; criticism of female petitioners, 111–18, 125; and female moral superiority, 124, 125

—1840–54, 145–64; decline in, 146, 154; overt political activity in, 146, 160; politicization of abolitionism and, 146–48, 151, 154; pattern of signatures in, 147, 156–57; acceptance of, 147, 164; decentralization of, 151–52, 154–55; local petition drives, 154; Great Petition to Congress, 155, 156, 165; and electoral politics, 157; language of, 157–60, 163; Women of America petitions, 158–60, 205 (n. 26); identity of national citizenship in, 159–60

—1861–65, 167–72; number of signatures, 146; Woman's National Loyal League and, 168–71; convincing women to petition, 170; and passage of Thirteenth Amendment, 171–72

Petitioning, collective, 3, 9, 12–13, 16, 23, 28, 37

Republican Party, 146, 164, 167, 179–80, 210 (n. 17)
Ryan, Mary, 5

Scottish Enlightenment philosophy, 143
Seneca Falls convention, 68–69, 160, 178
Separate spheres: petitioning and, 1, 86, 114–15, 118, 126, 128; women's rejection of, 69; Catharine E. Beecher on, 115–16; politics and religion and, 193 (n. 14). *See also* Appropriate behavior, women's
Shays's Rebellion, 18
Signatures: patterns of, 52, 58, 147, 156–57, 162; gathering of, 53, 81, 99, 101–2, 105, 109–11; forgery of, 81, 100; and political literacy, 106–7; and identity, 106–8; marital titles and, 109
Slade, William, 119, 152
Slave power conspiracy theme, 77, 124, 158
Slavery: and northern civil rights, 7–8, 67, 77, 124, 158, 185 (n. 2); and slave trade, 19, 30, 31; images of, in antislavery rhetoric, 63–64, 66
Slaves: and right of petition, 4, 20, 78–81; petitioning of, 30; revolts of, 32, 34
Smith, William, 20
Social networks: and signature gathering, 2, 101, 110; organized petitioning and, 103
Society of Friends. *See* Quakers
Soderlund, Jean R., 154
Stanton, Elizabeth Cady, 103, 108, 168, 170, 179–81, 184, 210 (nn. 17, 19)
Stanton, Henry B., 86, 120
State legislatures: antislavery women

and, 6, 120–21, 122–23; Quakers and, 30
Stewart, Maria, 34
Stone, Lucy, 179, 210 (n. 17)
Stowe, Harriet Beecher, 27, 207 (n. 36)
Suffrage: free black, 4; white male, 21; 1834 petition for universal, 68. *See also* Woman suffrage
Sumner, Charles, 170–71
Swanwick, John, 20

Tappan, Arthur, 27, 38, 49, 69, 146, 149
Tappan, Juliana, 107, 121, 201 (n. 39)
Taylor, Zachary, 158, 161
Temperance, 2, 9, 13, 23, 43, 107
Territories, U.S., 20, 48, 50, 124, 155, 156, 158–61
Texas, annexation of, 48, 119, 126, 145; abolitionism and, 90; Boston Female Anti-Slavery Society address on, 90–92; women's petitions against, 97, 99, 156
Thirteenth Amendment, 9, 48, 146, 147, 167–72
Thompson, George, 45, 88, 192 (n. 32)
Three-fifths clause, 31, 80, 92
Turner, Nat, 34, 36, 69

Ultraism, 38, 53–54, 66
Unitarianism, 43, 87
Universalism, 43

Van Broekhoven, Deborah, 60, 108, 160, 192 (n. 6)
Van Buren, Martin, 69–70, 119
Venet, Wendy Hamand, 171
Violence: against free blacks, 34, 49, 178; against abolitionists, 38, 201 (n. 39); against Philadelphia antislavery convention, 123. *See also* Lynching

Virtue: and Revolutionary War principles, 67; and right of petition, 128–29, 131, 132–36, 137–38; of slaveholders, 136
Voting. *See* Suffrage; Woman Suffrage

Webster, Daniel, 157
Weld, Theodore, 107, 116, 149, 154; and "Fathers and Rulers of Our Country" petition form, 55; and female antislavery convention, 85; and organized petitioning, 86; on abolitionism and women's rights, 118; advocates politicization and gradual emancipation, 146; role in abolition lobby, 154
Wellman, Judith, 154
Whig Party, 152, 153–54, 157
Whiskey Rebellion, 18
Whittier, John Greenleaf: on immediate abolition, 34; and organized petitioning, 86; on abolitionism and women's rights, 117–18
Wills, Garry, 16
Wilmot Proviso, 161
Wise, Henry A., 152
Woman-and-sister appeal, 62–66
"Woman question," 144, 145–48, 150–51

Woman's National Loyal League, 48, 168–72, 207 (n. 41)
Woman's sphere. *See* Separate spheres
Woman suffrage: linked to right of petition, 8, 106, 117, 125, 140; petition campaign for, 13, 178–84; earliest appeal for, 68–69; conventions for, 68–69, 178, 183; female antislavery conventions and, 103; John Quincy Adams and, 140; associations for, 180, 183, 210 (n. 17)
Women of America petitions, 158–60, 205 (n. 26)
Women's rights: of citizenship, 4, 8, 9, 74–76, 77, 127–31, 132; first national debate concerning, 8, 142; linked to black's rights, 81, 88; abolitionism and, 117–18, 147–48, 149–50; ideology of feminism and, 176; petitioning Congress for, 179; effect of antislavery conventions on, 198 (n. 48). *See also* Citizenship; Petition, right of; Woman suffrage

Yellin, Jean Fagan, 63, 194 (n. 24)

Zagarri, Rosemary, 82, 142–43

GENDER & AMERICAN CULTURE